Maintenance of Buildings

AND THEIR INTERNAL ENVIRONMENT

B. D. HUTCHINSON B.Sc., M.Inst.P.
Principal Lecturer, Hong Kong Polytechnic

J. BARTON
Principal Lecturer, Manchester College of Building

N. ELLIS A.I.O.B., A.R.S.H.
Formerly Lecturer, School of Building,
City of Leicester Polytechnic

BUTTERWORTHS

London–Boston–Sydney–Wellington–Durban–Toronto

The Butterworth Group

United Kingdom **Butterworth & Co (Publishers) Ltd**
London: 88 Kingsway, WC2B 6AB

Australia **Butterworths Pty Ltd**
Sydney: 586 Pacific Highway, Chatswood, NSW 2067
Also at Melbourne, Brisbane, Adelaide and Perth

Canada **Butterworth & Co (Canada) Ltd**
Toronto: 2265 Midland Avenue Scarborough, Ontario, M1P 4S1

New Zealand **Butterworths of New Zealand Ltd**
Wellington: 33–35 Cumberland Place, CPO Box 472

South Africa **Butterworth & Co (South Africa) (Pty) Ltd**
Durban: 152–154 Gale Street

USA **Butterworth (Publishers) Inc**
Boston: 10 Tower Office Park, Woburn, Massachusetts 01801

First published 1975
Reprinted 1978, 1981

© Butterworth & Co (Publishers Ltd, 1975

ISBN 0 408 00372 3

Printed in England by The Pitman Press, Bath

PREFACE

The aim of this book is to provide a foundation for the study of maintenance and repair of buildings with regard to both the fabric of the building and its internal environment. It has been written in such a manner that it requires the reader to have very little background knowledge to obtain a great deal of benefit, and it should be of assistance to the layman who is simply interested in taking good care of his own house. Its main interest, however, will be to students who are preparing for building examinations, including, in the UK :

Royal Institution of Chartered Surveyors (all sections)
The Incorporated Society of Valuers and Auctioneers
The Institute of Building
H.N.C. and H.N.D. examinations in Building
Public Health Inspectors Diploma.

In addition, practical surveyors, estate agents and managers and maintenance contractors and their operatives will all find something of interest in this book.

It has been split into three sections. Section 1 deals with the traditional type of maintenance and repair met with in more established syllabi, Section 2 deals with the internal environment of buildings and Section 3 with the management and organizational aspect of the work.

The authors are extremely grateful to the widow of Mr N. Ellis who has allowed them free access to her husband's unfinished manuscript on the subject, which he was preparing for Newnes—Butterworths at the time of his death, and also to Mr P. K. Barton, B.Sc., M.I.O.B., for his valuable help with Section 3.

1975   B.D.H., J.B.

iii

CONTENTS

Preface

SECTION 1 GENERAL STRUCTURE

SECTION 2 INTERNAL ENVIRONMENT

SECTION 3 ADMINISTRATIVE ASPECTS

Section 1
General Structure

CHAPTER 1

GENERAL PRINCIPLES

'That which is taken from the ground tends to return to the ground.' This is a well known statement of fact and it explains clearly why some form of maintenance is required. This basically sums up the problems of deterioration and the care entailed in its prevention, which are the subject of this book.

Buildings in their many shapes and forms provide us with the built-up areas of cities, towns and villages in which we live. These areas are composed of buildings of various types and age intended for a large number of different purposes. They are valuable assets for individuals, groups and companies. These assets represented by the buildings have, over the years and when they have been preserved, increased in value. This preservation of buildings constitutes the maintenance programme described in this book, and during recent years this aspect has grown in importance and is now considered to be as important as construction.

A review of the stock of buildings in the UK a few years ago revealed that of some 16 000 000 houses approximately one-half were built before 1914, and about a quarter of these were even built before 1850. This shows the age and type range of properties which one may expect to meet.

They may be roughly classified as shown below.

Ancient buildings. Ancient buildings are those which were built before the nineteenth century and conform to no particular building standards.

Nineteenth-century buildings. Nineteenth-century buildings were built during the Regency and Victorian periods when the expansion caused by the industrial revolution caused the indiscriminate growth of industrial towns and cities. They were generally of a poor or low technical standard of construction and a vast amount of terraced development meant very poor quality buildings and conditions of overcrowding.

Twentieth-century buildings. Twentieth-century buildings are usually divided into two groups: those built before 1945 to a minimum standard governed by building bylaws, and those built after 1945 using more modern techniques and materials, with the minimum standards being governed by modern building regulations.

Usage. The type of building may also be considered according to its use, and may be classified as domestic, commercial, industrial or public property. It is apparent that each type may need individual consideration and it will be necessary to use slightly different approaches for their individual requirements.

Many of the ancient buildings have stood the test of time but have weathered with age, although they may remain stable by virtue of their weight and the size of their members. Often when remedial work is considered in order to preserve their form and appearance, special care and treatment will be required depending on their method and form of construction. The buildings constructed during the nineteenth century, which still form large areas of our towns and cities, are now substandard and have been neglected and allowed to decay in many ways. Many of these properties now form part of the slum clearance programmes while others with adequate preservation will serve their purpose for many years to come.

Modern buildings built to better standards with present day materials and techniques are expected to give better service. They can be subdivided into modern traditional buildings and industrialized buildings, which also have their own individual problems. Industrialized buildings, especially high rise systems, have yet to prove themselves. These taller buildings or tower blocks, built to a height never before thought possible, pose new problems because of their height, atmosphere conditions, high winds and the greater loads on the structure. However, time alone will be the test.

BUILDING STANDARDS

The building standards followed are mainly concerned with the stability of the building, the weather tightness of the structure, the temperature level, the optimum use of the building and of course its lasting qualities. In order to preserve these standards it is necessary for regular maintenance to be carried out on the structure.

Broadly speaking, maintenance commences immediately the building has been constructed, when we immediately become concerned with the performance of the materials and the standard of workmanship. If and when these fail, deterioration begins and defects will become apparent requiring remedial work to be carried out, and even when this is completed it will still require regular maintenance to preserve it.

Materials and structures differ in durability and life, and each has a certain maximum life, therefore the choice of materials is a matter either of policy or of economics. It depends on the proposed life span of a building as to whether the choice will be to either repair or replace at the end of the useful period. The decision, which has to be made by the building owner, designer or maintenance supervisor, is a matter of balancing the initial construction cost against the ensuing maintenance costs. The remainder of this chapter surveys briefly the main points, most of which will be considered in greater depth in the relevant chapters that follow.

General principles of building

This section considers the various basic principles of structures and materials, with special reference to the subject of maintenance and repair. These principles of building technology are the basic considerations when discussing conditions, defects and failures in building structures, and they will now be considered briefly, together with the subject of maintenance and repair, which requires a clear understanding of how these individual subjects interweave and overlap to produce satisfactory structures and conditions.

Loading, strength and stability

Buildings are a series of platforms or floors which carry various loads and are supported by load-bearing walls or framed structures. The structural requirements are that all units of the structure shall be of sufficient strength and be capable of supporting the loads that they must carry. They must also be of adequate stiffness and stability so that they are able to support themselves against possible distortion. If these conditions are adequately met then the building structure will remain sound; otherwise a failure may occur. The various factors that affect the requirements are considered below.

Types of load   Types of load include dead loads (i.e. the actual weight of the structure), and imposed loads (i.e. the weight of the furniture and fittings, storage, persons and movable weights, the effect of the wind causing pressure, snow causing weight, and shock vibrations, etc.) as shown in *Figure 1.1*.

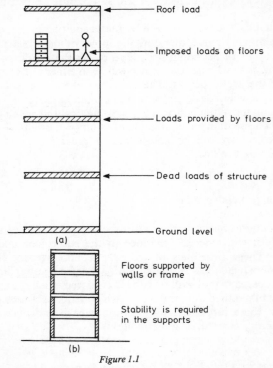

Roof load

Imposed loads on floors

Loads provided by floors

Dead loads of structure

Ground level

(a)

Floors supported by walls or frame

Stability is required in the supports

(b)

Figure 1.1

These loads will vary according to the usage of the building and will have to be considered when diagnosing a failure. A building is designed for a particular use and, of course, with adequate strength. In time, however, both the use of the building and the strength of its component materials may change.

Material strength Materials of adequate strength are obviously required to support the main loads and other units. The choice will either be between the different types of material available or between different grades of the same material. Strength is the first consideration and economics the second. As a guide to the choice of materials, resort can be made to published data, the results of tests, etc., and of course general experience.

6

Imposed stresses   The loading of structures causes reactions upon the material units in the form of compression, tension or shear stresses, the actual effect depending on the load and how it is applied (i.e. vertically, horizontally, or otherwise) (*Figure 1.2*).

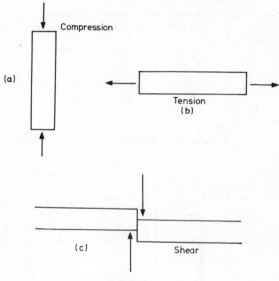

Figure 1.2

The materials chosen must be capable of supporting these imposed stresses. Tests can be performed that will reveal the failing strength under certain conditions and a factor of safety may be used in order to give the working strength of a material.

$$\text{Factor of safety} = \frac{\text{Failing strength}}{\text{Working strength}}$$

$$\text{Working strength} = \frac{\text{Failing strength}}{\text{Factor of safety}}$$

The factor of safety chosen will differ according to the type of material used and the conditions under which it has to be used.

Wind pressure   Wind pressure varies according to the direction and intensity of the wind and affects the vertical, inclined and horizontal surfaces according to their situations (*Figure 1.3*). This causes areas of compression and rarefaction (suction) which will result in the loading or lifting of the structure. A careful study of the effects of wind on buildings is necessary, and of the effect of adjacent buildings which may cause deviations of the air currents. These changes of wind pressure become more important with increasing height and exposure. Experiments with wind tunnels can be carried out in an attempt to predict the effects of the surrounding environment and differing wind speeds.

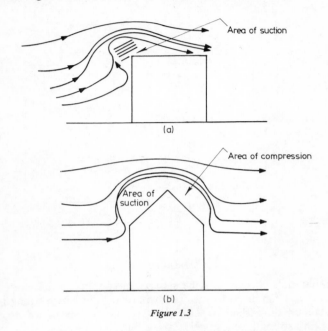

Figure 1.3

Impact and fatigue   Normal impact and vibrations may be absorbed by the materials themselves due to their natural strength and resilience. Sudden impact or explosions may cause great stress, resulting in the possible fracture of the structure. High rise, prefabricated buildings of certain types may be more susceptible to this type of explosion (e.g. Ronan Point, the whole of one side of which collapsed when an explosion occurred in one storey). Vibrations from machinery or traffic should be absorbed easily by the structural materials, but if excessive, continuous or unexpected they may cause movement within the structure or general fatigue which may affect the life of the material.

Superstructure and foundations   The design and success of a building

8

depends ultimately upon the foundations. Building loads can now be calculated and they need to be adequately supported by the ground soils, as shown in *Figure 1.4*.

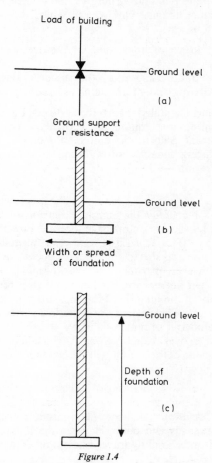

Figure 1.4

Foundations are designed according to the load and bearing capacity of the soil. The load can either be spread over sufficient ground area or taken lower down to a layer of ground with a better bearing capacity. Conditions may change and affect the support, causing settlement and soil movements. Uneven settlement can be extremely serious as the increased stresses applied to certain parts of a building may cause cracking of the materials.

9

Dimensional stability of materials

Another factor to be considered is that of the dimensional changes that may occur in materials and structural units when the physical conditions of exposure change. One way in which these changes may be classified is as follows:

Deformation due to loadings, affecting the elastic or non-elastic state of the material.

Expansion and contraction of the material due to temperature changes, moisture movement or chemical action.

Good materials normally absorb these effects, but in excess they can cause deterioration and failure. A knowledge of these changes is therefore important. Selection of suitable materials and correct fixings and jointings during construction will assist in reducing the possibility of such deterioration.

Applied loads   Normally the simple extension or compression of a material under tensile or compressive forces is directly proportional to the imposed load (Hooke's Law), and also all materials under load change their shape and size to some degree according to the magnitude of the load. However, provided the elastic limit is not exceeded they should regain their normal shape when the load is removed, due to the natural elasticity of the material. Materials are therefore able to absorb the effects of stress. The elasticity of materials varies. *Figure 1.5* shows the different behaviour of materials under stress.

If a material is overloaded beyond its particular elastic limit, then either a permanent deformation will be produced or the material will fail.

Temperature variation   Almost all materials expand when the temperature increases and contract when the temperature falls. This change in size is measured by the coefficient of expansion, given by the equation

$$\text{Coefficient of expansion} = \frac{\text{Change in size}}{\text{Original size} \times \text{Temperature change}}$$

Different values for some typical materials are shown in *Table 1.1*.
Materials also absorb and emit heat in varying amounts, causing

10

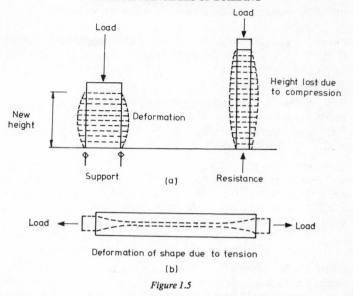

Figure 1.5

expansion and contraction, the amount of movement depending on the type of material and its absorptiveness, those of greater size being affected to a greater degree. The Forth Bridge is said to be 0.366 m longer in summer than in winter due to this expansion. Generally speaking, those of greater density are affected more than those lighter materials with insulating qualities.

The coefficient of expansion of each material, as shown by the above equation, is the amount of expansion per unit temperature rise. This allows calculations to be made in order that possible damage may be avoided. Allowances may be made by restricting lengths and areas of materials, and designing joints that allow movements to occur without causing damage (e.g. steel in concrete). Materials with high coefficients of expansion therefore require freedom for possible thermal movement (e.g. plastic guttering), because if restricted they will suffer deterioration or possible fracture.

Contraction may result in the permanent shrinkage of a material which is restrained at the ends and will cause shrinkage cracks to some degree.

Moisture content   All materials remain perfectly stable in dry conditions but the presence of moisture will change this situation (*Figure 1.6*).

11

Table 1.1 TYPICAL COEFFICIENTS OF EXPANSION (α)

Material	$\alpha(\times 10^5/°C)$
Aluminium	2.6
Brass	1.87
Copper	1.7
Glass	0.8
Invar	0.09
Iron	1.1
Lead	2.9
Tin	2.0
Zinc	2.9
Concrete	1.2
Steel	1.2
Brick	0.06
Stone	0.03–0.09
Softwood	0.05 (with grain) 3.4 (across grain)
Hardwood	0.4 (with grain) 5.0 (across grain)

The types of moisture encountered are:

Ground moisture. This is always present and will rise by capillary action.

Atmospheric moisture. This will tend to penetrate the structure, the severity depending on the amount of exposure and the rainfall.

Internal vapour. The internal conditions are affected by internal appliances and external conditions, which may result in condensation.

Materials, however, are affected by moisture in varying ways. Those of lower density are porous, while those of higher density are either less porous or non-porous. Porous materials allow absorption and possible expansion, both by heat and frost action, and on drying out there may be some contraction. These actions may occur quickly and continuously, but may be slow, and sometimes extreme conditions remain for long periods. The movements vary according to the type of material and are more noticeable on porous material. If the movement is restrained it may cause deformation in shape or fracture within the unit.

In order to avoid conditions that cause moisture movement it is wise to consider the choice of suitable materials and structures at the design stage or the remedial stage, the main consideration being that the porous type of materials need to be kept dry. In order to attain this it will frequently be necessary to provide protection, which can be produced by the design of the structure or by the introduction of some form of surface protection. All too often water is allowed to pass over porous surfaces.

The choice of suitable materials is a major consideration; it is concerned not only with the properties of the actual material but also the

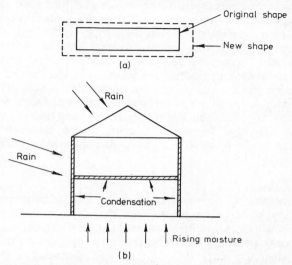

Figure 1.6   (a) Material becomes enlarged due to absorption of moisture; (b) Rising ground moisture

exposure conditions in which the material is placed. These may vary considerably according to the geographical situation and with the height of the property.

Chemical action   All materials contain basic chemicals which in isolation will remain unchanged but if allowed, accidentally or on purpose, to combine with others will take part in a chemical reaction. Normally, if materials are kept dry little or no chemical action will take place, but once moisture is present then chemical action is always possible. In building structures the chemical reactions with which we are mainly concerned are sulphate action and oxidation, which if allowed to develop will result in deterioration.

Sulphate action is the result of a reaction between sulphate and calcium aluminate combined with water. Calcium sulphate, magnesium sulphate and sodium sulphate are found in clays while calcium aluminate is found in Portland cement. They react to form a soluble compound called calcium sulphoaluminate, which is accompanied by

13

expansion. This can occur in concrete and mortars and the expansion causes surface erosion and disintegration.

Oxidation is the chemical reaction between basic metal elements, oxygen and moisture. The action differs according to the metal type. With non-ferrous metals oxidation causes the formation of oxides which adhere to the metal surface and produce a protective coating. In the case of ferrous metals, however, the situation is different. Iron combines with the oxygen and moisture, forming first the hydroxide and then the oxide. This process causes expansion in the moist state and as the moisture evaporates contraction takes place. The contact between the corrosion product and the metal surface is thus broken and further moisture is able to make contact with the metal surfaces, producing further corrosion. This action is continuous and will take place until all the metal has been corroded. A more precise discussion of the phenomena can be found in some booklets published by International Nickel.

Soil movements   Cohesive soils or clays are affected by ground water. In moist and wet conditions clays expand, in dry conditions they contract. This will occur during seasonal changes when the level of the ground water rises and falls. The greatest danger occurs during dry periods when the clays may shrink, causing considerable ground movement.

Tree roots from growing trees may have the same effect; roots will absorb ground moisture which if unchecked may cause shrinkage of the clay and hence ground movement.

Another source of ground movement is mining operations below ground level. They may cause subsidence of ground soils that may affect the support of the building.

Dimensional movements   All movements of expansion or contraction, which may be of small amounts initially, will if persistent develop into more serious and visible movement causing shrinkage cracks within the material or structure, loss of bond between material units, deflection of a structure or general expansion of part of a structure. Movements may be locally induced. The effects are more noticeable over greater areas or lengths. In order to avoid or reduce the possibility of movement, it is necessary to avoid materials that may be seriously affected, according to where they are used. Allowances should be made for movement by using expansion joints for larger areas, by providing joints that allow movement to occur without causing disruption and when possible by restricting unit areas or lengths.

Weather resistance

Another principle to be considered is that of weather resistance of materials. All buildings are, by definition, situated and exist in an open environment and are subjected to the effects of the weather.

As previously explained, water causes considerable trouble to both materials and structures as it is always ready to penetrate materials and structural units and cause defects. It is necessary to prevent this penetration and ensure that materials which are not impervious or water resistant are not allowed to come into contact with these conditions. The penetration that one is trying to prevent may be caused by absorption, capillary action, or through joints or shrinkage cracks. Weather penetration may be due to any of the causes listed below.

Ground water   Buildings stand in or upon the natural ground and in contact with ground water. The actual amount of water will vary according to the locality and the level of the water table. Building structures will absorb ground water by capillary action or electro-osmosis. The rise in ground water will continue for as long as the ground water exists and the material is still able to absorb it. If it is allowed to continue unchecked it will cause penetration and deterioration and a barrier will be needed to prevent this (*Figure 1.7*).

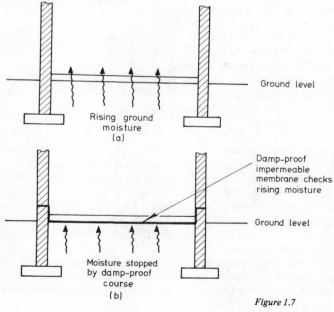

Figure 1.7

Exposure Buildings are constantly exposed to rainfall and winds. Rainfall will vary in amount and severity (as will other weather conditions) according to locality and season. An idea of the conditions to be expected may be got by consulting the record charts from the local meteorological office. These charts are similar to those shown in *Figure 1.8.*

Continuous rainfall helps to keep the material in a saturated condition, which is a serious situation, but the drier periods allow the absorbed moisture to evaporate from the material. Winds will assist penetration by driving rain on to the wall surface and holding it there for longer periods. This helps water to penetrate cracks or spaces, thus increasing the possibility of saturation. The degree of exposure will obviously differ according to the situation. In built up areas a certain amount of protection is afforded by other buildings, but in more open areas, buildings on high ground and taller buildings, the amount of protection is very small and buildings face the full brunt of the atmospheric conditions. It is essential that this problem is adequately considered, suitable materials are chosen, and protection provided when possible.

Vapours Atmospheres inside and outside buildings contain moisture in varying amounts. The sources of the moisture are the external

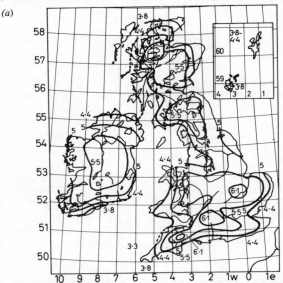

Figure 1.8 Climatological record chart maps (from Climatological Atlas of the British Isles and Meteorological Office Climatological Memorandum 43, *HMSO); (a) Average means of daily ranges of temperature in January, 1901–1930.*

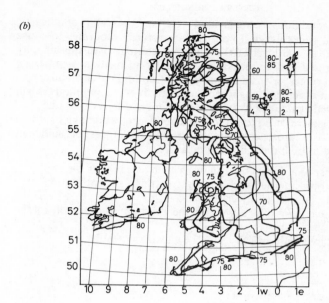

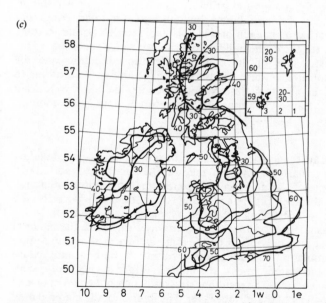

Figure 1.8 (b) Average means of relative humidity (per cent) at midday, 1921–1935; (c) Average annual number of days with more than 9h of bright sunshine, 1913–1932.

atmospheric conditions, rising ground water and the results of domestic and industrial water usage. In all cases moisture evaporates to cause moist air and as the level of the moisture content rises the air may become saturated and condensation begin. Condensation may persist at material surfaces or inside a material or compound structure, and may occur on other non-absorbent surfaces. If it is continuous it will cause saturated structures to the inconvenience of the occupants.

There is a general need to provide adequate protection against these possibilities. The most common is to use structures of sufficient thickness and to take the following measures.

Construct special forms of structures such as cavity walls.

Weatherproof external surfaces by treatment or application of a covering material.

Incorporate a layer material within the structure so as to control the movement of moisture.

Select suitable materials to resist the effects of weather.

Durability

The durability of materials and structures is most important, and this involves the quality of material units, bondings, jointings and fixings that make up the structures, each of which is liable to deteriorate to some degree during the life of the building. Durability varies according to the quality and structure of the material, climatic conditions and the amount of exposure. In turn, conditions of exposure vary according to location and the effect of atmospheric elements, including wind, rain and sun, which cause variations of temperature and moisture content.

Rain   Rain causes moist conditions in the atmosphere, on the building structure, particularly the material face, and also in the ground soils. In each case some of the moisture will penetrate into a porous material. The amount absorbed differs according to the material's porosity, the penetration obviously being greater in a more porous material.

Continuous absorption may result in the saturation of the material and drying out may only occur on the material face as shown in *Figure 1.9(a)*. Accumulation of the moisture within the material may cause expansion of the material mass, and limited surface drying causes contraction at the surface. The resultant stresses between the two may lead to a breaking away of the surface layer. The interior of the material may also soften and weaken.

Wind Wind varies considerably in both direction and velocity, and the variability increases as the height above ground level is increased. It adds to the problem of penetration as the additional wind pressure holds the moisture at the surface for longer periods and causes more rain to penetrate the surface and joints.

Frost action Frost affects saturated materials. The moisture within the material freezes and expands inside the structure, producing a pressure in this limited space which may break up the material, especially just under the surface layer. High density materials are more able to resist these pressures than low density materials (*Figure 1.9(b)*).

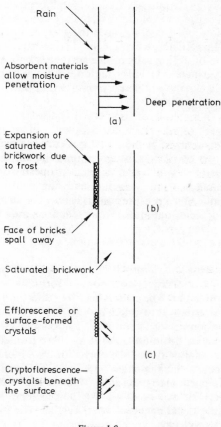

Figure 1.9

Sunlight Sun assists the drying out process, but rapid drying may cause too rapid a shrinkage at the material surface. This may affect the structure, the colour or the finish of the material.

Other non-porous materials may be affected by sunlight in different ways. A material may soften, melt or expand, processes which must be guarded against or allowed for. The durability of organic materials such as paints, plastics, asphalt, etc., is also affected by sunlight due to the removal of natural oils. This may cause drying out, brittleness, breakdown of surface coatings or the bleeding of coloured pigments which then appear to have faded or discoloured.

Efflorescence and cryptoflorescence The water-soluble salts found in clays and clay materials are mainly sulphates, which in moist conditions dissolve to form solutions which are absorbed into materials by capillary action and travel towards the surface, where evaporation of the moisture takes place, leaving behind concentrations of drying salts. The formation of drying salts on the surface is known as efflorescence. Beneath the surface, crystal formation is known as cryptoflorescence. These crystals expand and exert pressure that may cause surface erosion. (See *Figure 1.9(c)*.)

Chemical reactions Chemical reactions are the reactions which take place when two or more substances react chemically to form a new chemical substance which has different properties from the originals. Chemical changes affect materials and can cause corrosion or disintegration, affecting both the material and the structure, which may disrupt the adjacent materials. These reactions may be small and slow or may take place rapidly.

Corrosion can take place in two simple ways:

Oxidation. This has already been explained in simple terms. It occurs when metals and oxygen combine to form oxides, usually in the presence of moisture. The metals can be either non-ferrous (in which case they are usually protected by this oxide or some other type of chemical compound), or ferrous, i.e. iron or steel (when the corrosion does not stop after the initial coating has been formed). In atmospheres polluted with sulphur fumes the corrosion rate increases; zinc can be seriously affected, but the effect on copper and lead is very small and aluminium is particularly durable. With ferrous metals the action is more serious. Surface coatings are porous and allow moisture to penetrate to the metal beneath, where further oxidation takes place. In moist conditions oxides expand and during the drying period the oxide

20

coating will contract. The result is that the oxide becomes detached from the base metal and eventually the metal corrodes completely.

Electrolytic or galvanic action. This occurs between two dissimilar metals that are in contact and in impure rain water. (The oxidation described previously should strictly also be described in terms of ionic reactions but the explanation used is satisfactory for this book.) The action is similar to that in a simple cell where the anode gives up small deposits from its surface that go into electrolyte while the anode deteriorates.

In building work similar actions are able to take place between dissimilar metals and rainwater, which acts as the electrolyte. The degree of deterioration varies according to the type of metal. Only the one electrode will corrode, and a reference to the electrochemical list will reveal the metal likely to be affected. The one higher in the list will corrode, and the farther apart the two are the swifter will be the action. The electrochemical series, as it should be called, is shown in *Table 1.2* and lists chemical elements in their order of reactivity. The higher an element is in the table the more reactive the element and the more liable to corrosion. The table only refers to pure elements, however. For alloys and other building materials the galvanic table should be used. This is also shown in *Table 1.2*.

Table 1.2 (*a*) THE ELECTROCHEMICAL SERIES

Electromotive force series

Electrode reaction	Standard electrode potential, $E°$ V, 25°C	Electrode reaction	Standard electrode potential, $E°$ V, 25°C
$K = K^- + e^-$	−2.922	$Ni = Ni^{++} + 2e^-$	−0.250
$Ca = Ca^{++} + 2e^-$	−2.87	$Sn = Sn^{++} + 2e^-$	−0.136
$Na = Na^+ + e^-$	−2.712	$Pb = Pb^{++} + 2e^-$	−0.126
$Mg = Mg^{++} + 2e^-$	−2.34	$H2 = 2H^+ + 2e^-$	0.000
$Be = Be^{++} + 2e^-$	−1.70	$Cu = Cu^{++} + 2e^-$	0.345
$Al = Al^{+++} + 3e^-$	−1.67	$Cu = Cu^+ + e^-$	0.522
$Mn = Mn^{++} + 2e^-$	−1.05	$2Hg = Hg2^{++} + 2e^-$	0.799
$Zn = Zn^{++} + 2e^-$	−0.762	$Ag = Ag^+ + e^-$	0.800
$Cr = Cr^{+++} + 3e^-$	−0.71	$Pd = Pd^{++} + 2e^-$	0.83
$Ga = Ga^{+++} + 3e^-$	−0.52	$Hg = Hg^{++} + 2e^-$	0.854
$Fe = Fe^{++} + 2e^-$	−0.440	$Pt = Pt^{++} + 2e^-$	approx. 1.2
$Cd = Cd^{++} + 2e^-$	−0.402	$Au = Au^{+++} + 3e^-$	1.42
$In = In^{+++} + 3e^-$	−0.340	$Au = Au^+ + e^-$	1.68
$Tl = Tl^+ + e^-$	−0.336		
$Co = Co^{++} + 2e^-$	−0.277		

Table 1.2 (*b*) THE GALVANIC SERIES

Galvanic series
of metals and alloys in sea water

MAGNESIUM	
Zinc	
Aluminium alloy N3	
Aluminium alloy H20	Copper
Aluminium alloy H9	Aluminium bronze
Aluminium alloy N4	Composition G bronze
Low steel	90/10 Copper-nickel
Alloy steel	70/30 Copper-nickel—low iron
Cast iron	70/30 Copper-nickel—high iron
(Active) stainless steel: 13 Cr, 1 Ni	Nickel
(Active) stainless steel: 17 Cr	Inconel
(Active) stainless steel: 18 Cr, 8 Ni	Silver
(Active) stainless steel: 18 Cr, 8 Ni, 3 Mo	(Passive) stainless steel: 13 Cr, 1 Ni
Ni-resist	(Passive) stainless steel: 17 Cr
Muntz metal	(Passive) stainless steel: 18 Cr, 8 Ni
Yellow brass	(Passive) stainless steel: 18 Cr, 8 Ni, 3 Mo
Admiralty brass	Monel
Aluminium brass	Hastelloy C
Red brass	TITANIUM

Courtesy International Nickel.

Acidic action. Acidic substances appear in the form of soluble salts which are found in certain timbers such as oak, chestnut and western red cedar. Acid content varies. In moist conditions these soluble substances have a chemical effect on metals, causing stains on both the timber and the metal, and corrosion of the metal will follow. Oak causes the most trouble, and iron and steel are the metals most affected. It is necessary either to protect the metal, or to avoid use of such materials in damp conditions.

Atmospheric pollution   Atmospheric pollution is the result of combustion from either coal or other fuel burning in domestic or industrial sources or from the internal combustion engine, etc. This combustion produces carbonic and sulphuric deposits which are transmitted into the atmosphere. They finally come into contact with the material surface and in the presence of atmospheric moisture produce weak carbonic or sulphuric acids. The acids may have little effect, but over longer periods of time they may be sufficient to affect the material, causing surface erosion. The effect is noticeable with bricks, stone, mortar and roof coverings. Attempts are being made to reduce air pollution by creating smokeless zones, which will tend to reduce the problem. However, materials must be selected that are resistant to these chemical reactions.

Biological effects Biological effects occur in the following different ways:

Bacteria and rodents such as rats and mice, which will slowly destroy certain materials by devouring them.

Insects and beetles which devour cellular contents and structure, which may cause collapse.

Plant life in the form of ivy, moss and lichens, etc., which if allowed to develop will cause deterioration of material surface and jointing. The damage is done by root penetration which allows moisture into the structure. Moss and lichens are acidic and also affect metals.

Fungi will cause considerable deterioration if allowed to develop. They live on the cellular contents and structure of timber.

In all cases the effect is on the cellular and porous materials, especially when conditions are moist. Preservative treatments can be applied which may remove or deter this action.

Thermal insulation

An important requirement of a building is that of maintaining a satisfactory level of temperature at all times, and this will vary according to the use and the activities of the occupants. Heat can be obtained either from the sun or from the internal heating system provided. (See Chapter 10.)

Materials vary in their ability to prevent the loss of heat. Those of low density are able to absorb and retain heat and their resistance to the passage of heat is good, whereas those of high density will absorb and conduct heat. Air changes account for about one-third of the heat loss from a room and may be caused by deliberate or natural ventilation, or by leakages through structural units, warm air being replaced by cold. Good insulation is required in order to prevent this loss as it provides a barrier with a high resistance to heat flow. *Figure 1.10* illustrates the various ways in which heat is lost.

Sound

Noise in a building can be distracting and annoying to the occupier and

23

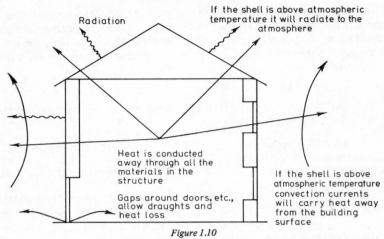

Figure 1.10

some noise abatement or control is therefore necessary. The problems of both noise insulation and absorption are covered in Chapter 11.

Fire

Many building materials and components are either liable to burn or are affected by heat, which in both cases is a source of danger to the building and the occupants. However, with reasonable care and protection most buildings remain safe.

The cause of fire may be one of several possibilities, such as:

Open fires, where actual fuels are a source of danger and cause direct heat and flame.

Heating units of various types such as electrical, gas, oil fired or solid fuel. They produce higher temperatures but are more easy to control.

Chimney flues, which are sources of high temperature and hot gases.

Electrical faults, which cause overheating and sparks and can be followed by ignition.

In all cases care and protection are needed to safeguard the building structure. Fires will occur if there is a high enough rise in temperature. The heat produced before the fire starts is initially absorbed by the materials, but eventually combustion occurs and is followed by flaming at even higher temperatures. This is the real danger, as the flames spread over the surface allowing the fire to spread to other parts. When the fire subsides, smouldering conditions remain, which are also a danger period as further ignition is always a possibility.

24

Fires cause considerable damage either by burning or from the effect of the heat, which can be absorbed causing expansion. Materials can also turn into a plastic state or soften, causing fractures, collapse and rupture of structures.

Fire protection   In order to provide safe conditions for the occupants it is necessary adequately to protect materials and structures. Many materials are non-combustible and will need to be protected to combat the possibilities of fire. Protection helps to reduce combustion, reduces or checks the spread of flame and provides a period of time before ignition occurs. This allows a period of escape for the occupants. It may be achieved in several ways:

Using a suitable design of construction such as providing dividing barriers to localize any fire (*Figure 1.11(a)*).

Using non-combustible materials whenever possible.

Protecting materials likely to be affected by fire, by surface treatment or by impregnating deterrent substances which will prevent the spread of flames.

Providing a covering of non-combustible substance to protect a vulnerable material, thus reducing the absorption of heat.

Building regulations require many precautions, all of which assist in reducing the effects of fire. They include:

The providing of materials and structures that have a resistance to fire of 30 min to 4 h, depending on the use of the building.

The localizing of fire by taking adequate precautions during construction and by dividing buildings into compartments both vertically and horizontally (*Figure 1.11(b)*).

Materials that are normally combustible or affected by heat, can by careful selection, treatment and protection, provide adequate resistance to fire.

Ventilation

The adequate ventilation of buildings is an essential requirement in providing satisfactory conditions for habitation. Ventilation involves the changing and circulation of air which will have the following effects:

Reduce the concentration of odours and gases by dispersing them.

Reduce or limit the concentration of dust and fumes by conveying them away.

Limit and control the rise of temperature.

Limit and control the humidity by helping to disperse any build-up of moisture content in the air.

While carrying out the above the risk of danger to health will at the same time be reduced. It can be achieved in the following ways:

Naturally, by relying on atmospheric conditions such as wind and air. Depending on their direction and intensity, pressure changes cause air currents to develop. These then provide a ventilating cir-

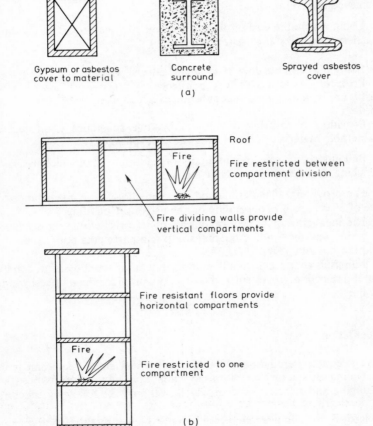

Figure 1.11   (a) Barriers to localize fires; (b) Compartments to localize fires

culation of air upwards through the chimney flues in conjunction with any windows or ventilators as shown in *Figure 1.12*.

Mechanically, where suitable ventilation conditions are provided and controlled mechanically as required, usually by extractor fan (*Figure 1.12(d)*).

All forms of ventilation require an inlet and outlet in order to function. Inlets may be doors, windows, air-bricks and other spaces, while outlets may be chimney flues, doors, windows and ventilation openings.

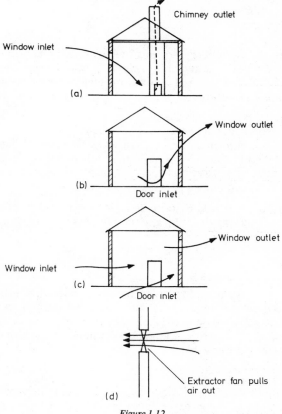

Figure 1.12

Differences of temperature and pressure between the outside and the inside of a building induce the air flow, which is from the higher to the lower zones. The natural action of warm air rising and cold air falling (convection) will also induce circulation.

27

It is necessary during construction to provide satisfactory standards of ventilation, and as a minimum the regulations require the area of opening windows to be at least equal to one-twentieth of the floor area. The position and distribution of ventilation inlets and outlets must therefore be carefully considered. Circulating air may cause cold draughts which are unpleasant and need to be stopped. High-level ventilation may be considered, which will provide an adequate circulation so that cold air has a better opportunity to mix with warmer air, thus reducing the risks of cold draughts at low level.

Lighting

Adequate lighting is necessary in order to provide satisfactory conditions for the health of the people working in and using the building. The amount of light required depends on several considerations, some of which are listed below.

The type of building and the intended use.
General conditions of comfort.
The desired performance of a given work operation. Some types of work need the maximum amount of light, others only a minimum.
The possible adverse effects upon a person's eyesight, the correct intensity and direction being necessary for health reasons.

Lighting is considered in more detail in Chapter 12 but *Figure 1.13* shows some ways in which the amount of daylight entering a room can be controlled.

Regulations   Building regulations require a minimum window area equal to at least one-tenth of the floor area, but normal requirements may need 15–20 per cent of the floor area. Another consideration is the height of window above floor level in order to admit the largest amount and spread of light possible.

Interior colour schemes   Colour can assist in room lighting because a suitable choice of coloured surfaces, walls and ceilings can provide reflected light (which is soft light) which will assist in gaining the maximum amount of light from limited window areas. White provides the best reflection, but other light pastel shades may provide an equal and more pleasing light, since a contrast of colour often gives satisfactory results.

28

Building cleanliness

A final consideration is that of the cleanliness of buildings. Regular cleaning will help to maintain the conditions that were planned and expected. This applies to the internal appearance, which must be good if living in it is to be enjoyed; and to the external appearance, for the same

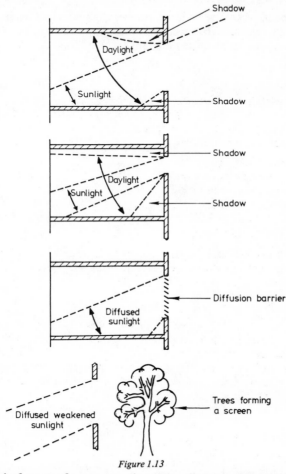

Figure 1.13

reason and of course for preservation. Cleanliness is also necessary for the efficient functioning of the building and for the health of the occupants. The requirements for cleanliness must be considered by the designer at the design stage when the choice of materials, finishes and structural forms is made, in order that easy access for cleaning operations is possible and so that accumulation of dust and dirt can be prevented.

Summary

This chapter has covered a large number of factors in brief and most of these as well as other factors concerned with maintenance and repair are discussed in much more detail in the chapters that follow.

CHAPTER 2

FOUNDATIONS

The foundations are constructed within the ground and then covered up so that they are no longer visible. It is then usually expected that all is well, and that the ground functions without any change. The only indication to the contrary is when there is a movement in the structure above ground level. It is then necessary to investigate the reasons for it, and decide what action should be taken. In order to make an assessment of the situation it is necessary to consider the basic requirements of a foundation.

REQUIREMENTS

The requirements of a foundation are as follows:

To provide support for the building. This means that the total load must be supported by the ground. The total load will include:

the dead load, i.e. the weight of all the walls, floors and roof;
the live load, i.e. the superficial load per square metre allowed by the building regulations.

To transmit the total load of the building on to the ground soils. For this it is necessary to transmit it to at least below ground level, so that the load is transmitted to stable, consolidated ground, and so that the foundations are not affected by the upthrust due to frost action.

To ensure that the bearing capacity of the soils is sufficient to support the building load, which will provide stable conditions. This is an important consideration when extension work may have upset the original calculations.

To prevent settlement or movements that may affect the stability of the building.

31

If all these conditions are maintained, the foundation will be successful and efficient, but conditions and situations can change. This can cause a breakdown of any of the requirements listed and may result in a foundation failure.

FOUNDATION FAILURES

Failures may be due to several causes which should be considered under the following headings: unstable conditions, changing ground conditions, ground movements and chemical reactions.

Unstable conditions

Unstable conditions may be due to the following:

Inadequate foundations. These can be due to the fact that the width of the foundation's spread is not wide enough to support the building load. This width can be calculated according to the following:

$$\text{Width of foundation (metres)} = \frac{\text{Weight of building load per metre run}}{\text{Safe bearing capacity of ground per square metre}}$$

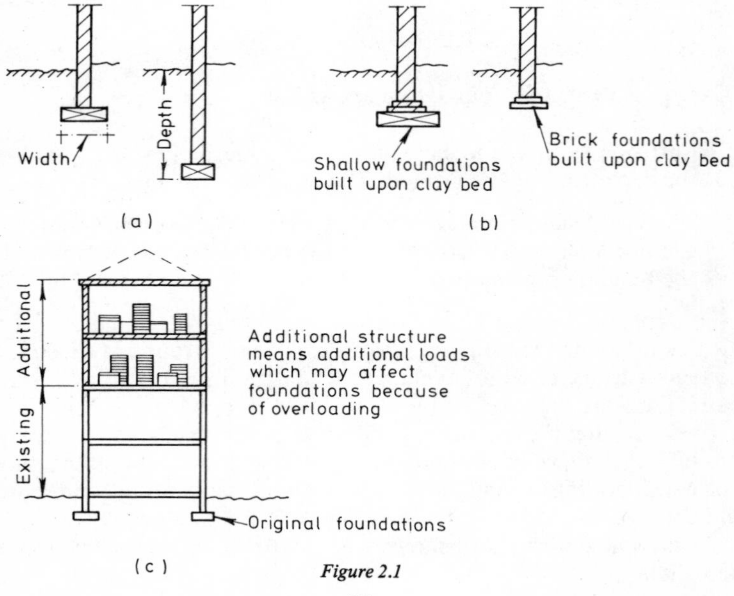
Width
Depth
(a)
Shallow foundations built upon clay bed
Brick foundations built upon clay bed
(b)
Additional
Existing
Additional structure means additional loads which may affect foundations because of overloading
Original foundations
(c)

Figure 2.1

It may be expensive to make the width of the foundation sufficient to support the building, so one should consider deeper excavation of the foundations to a point where the safe bearing capacity of the ground is greater (see *Figure 2.1(a)*).

No foundations, as may be found in older types of property. This situation may be due to the fact that the foundations were constructed upon loose rubble laid directly upon a clay bed, or brick footings used to spread the load instead of a concrete base (*Figure 2.1(b)*).

Overloading may occur, due either to additional loads being applied to the foundation because extension work has been constructed upon the original building (*Figure 2.1(c)*) or because the use of the building has been changed and the imposed loads upon the floors increased. In each case the loads imposed upon the ground soils are greater than those originally allowed for, and the building load then exceeds the bearing capacity of the ground.

Changes in ground conditions

Conditions may occur below ground level which may directly affect the bearing capacity of the soils, either improving it with no detrimental effect, or lowering it. In the latter case the effect may be noticeable and may cause foundation failures. These changes may occur because of:

Change in water content of the ground soils. The lower the moisture content the greater the bearing capacity, and consequently any increase in moisture content will cause a lowering of bearing capacity. The properties of cohesive soils vary according to moisture content. Dry hard clays have a high strength but, with an increase in moisture content, they become plastic and compressible. Sand may also be affected by moisture. Hard compact sand has a good bearing capacity, but loose sands may increase in bulk, with an increase in moisture content which will cause them to become less compacted. In a saturated condition they become as fluid as a running sand, which has no bearing capacity. Therefore the infiltration of water will ultimately affect the support of a building, and allow settlement movement of the structure.

Water penetration. This is caused in several ways. Investigation may show that the penetration is due to:

Surface water. This is caused by natural rainfall upon the ground, or paved areas draining into the ground soils. Small amounts cause no change, but continuous and concentrated amounts in areas of poor directional drainage can cause saturated conditions which will affect the bearing capacity of the soils.

Groundwater. Natural water is found in the ground at and below the water table. The depth will vary according to the location and the time of year, but it is much higher during the wet months.

Sloping ground. If the natural contours of the site are changed, so that the house is now at the lowest point, natural drainage of the water to these lower parts may be caused. This water may be ground water and local concentrations of water, which may be directed towards building foundations. The ground conditions will then change and cause structure movement. (See *Figure 2.2(a)*.)

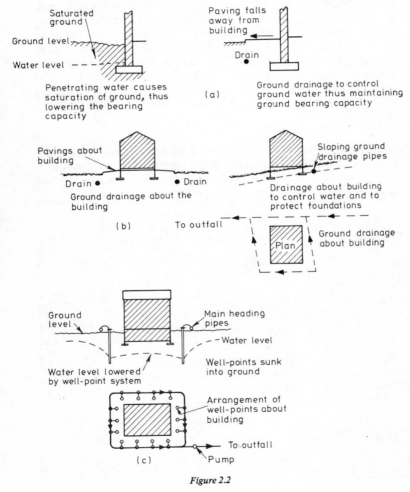

Figure 2.2

In all the above cases it should be apparent that ground water needs to be directed away from foundations by a system of pipes, so that they are protected. This can be achieved by site drainage and surface drainage.

Site drainage. A system of land drainage pipes will help to control and lower the water table level, and direct the water away to a suitable outlet (*Figure 2.2(b)*). In more severe conditions a system of well-point drainage can be installed. This system collects and transports the water to suitable outlets by means of automatic pumps (*Figure 2.2(c)*). It may be used as either a temporary or a permanent measure. Suitable outlets for site drainage are to water courses, dykes and storm drains.

Surface drainage. It is also necessary to control surface water around paved areas, which need to fall away from the building. The fall must be correct and suitable drainage channels must be provided. Roof water needs to be properly drained into storm-water drainage systems, making sure that leakage does not occur. If these precautions are not taken, water-logged conditions may cause movement of the structure.

Other causes of water penetration. Two other causes of water penetration are occasionally encountered. They are tidal conditions and flooding.

Tidal conditions. Land directly adjacent to tidal waters is affected by changing levels of water due to rising and falling tides. Precautions must be taken in these cases when designing such foundations. Suitable depth must be reached, and the use of a piling system would be a better solution (*Figure 2.3(a)*). It will also be necessary to prevent the washing away of ground soils from underneath foundations.

Flooding. This is caused by rising sea, or river waters breaking their normal banks and flooding adjacent areas of ground (*Figure 2.3(b)*). It only occurs for a short time usually and the water then recedes. However, while the situation exists the ground soils and the structures above and below ground level are affected. The effects are not always immediately apparent at the time of flooding, but may appear at a later date.

Ground movements

Any movement of the ground soils will affect the supports of the building and the actual structure above. The movements may be caused in several ways, such as geological faults, mining subsidence, vibrations and unequal settlements.

Geological faults

Occasionally there may be a movement or slip at a fault in the ground strata. This causes vibrations, or earth tremors, which are felt in the ground over considerable distances and could affect the stability of foundations. (See *Figure 2.4(a)*.)

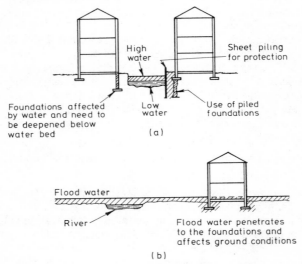

Figure 2.3

Mining subsidence

In many districts where underground mining operations are in progress, considerable ground movement occurs. When coal or any other mineral is removed from the mine workings, which are at a lower level than the foundations, the workings are supported by props. Eventually the mine supports are removed and the roof falls in. This causes the collapse of the ground above the workings, the effect of which is felt at ground level over a wide area. During the period of subsidence the ground surface is affected by a wave of tension and is forced up as a wave. This causes tensile stresses in the building foundations and, when they are on the crest of the wave, the building often splits down the middle (*Figure 2.4(b)*). When the wave passes, the ground subsides and becomes an

36

area of compression, and settles down at a lower level. By this time considerable damage will have occurred.

Some time must pass before remedial work is carried out in order to allow the ground to settle. Usually little is done to prevent settlement from occurring, but with new buildings the foundations are designed in the form of a reinforced concrete raft, which will ride the wave of stress without breaking up (*Figure 2.4(c)*). Alternatively, buildings are formed in small units.

Vibrations

These are waves of various magnitudes that travel within the ground soils. Although the damaging effect may be slight, movement may be caused over a period of time.

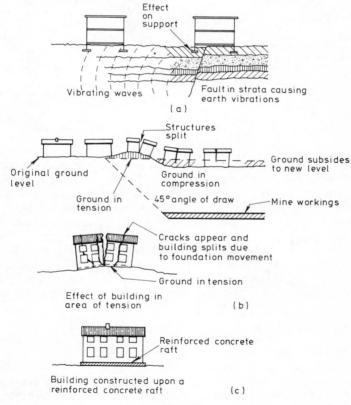

Figure 2.4

37

Continuous vibrations. These may be caused by traffic or machinery, and may be prolonged and at times violent (*Figure 2.5(a)*). They affect the older type of property because modern construction is normally designed to withstand ordinary vibrations, while older types of foundations may be affected especially if the house contains machinery, or is used for purposes other than that for which it was intended. Machinery and traffic can set up continuous vibrations which could cause a gradual foundation settlement.

Sudden shocks. These shocks, such as impact shocks, may affect foundations by causing vibrations (*Figure 2.5(b)*). Explosions cause sudden shocks, which may occur in all types of property as a result of the presence of gas, petroleum, spirits, explosives and other volatile

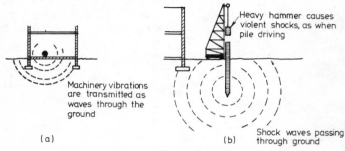

Figure 2.5

liquids. The shock can be serious and cause damage to the building structure and the ground support. Violent shocks in the ground may affect many foundations, though this may only be revealed a considerable time later. For this reason any building near a building damaged by an explosion should have its foundations carefully checked.

Various types of building plant can cause shock waves during site construction work. A good example of this would be the shock caused by pile driving machines (*Figure 2.5(b)*). For this reason great care should be taken when carrying out surveys on buildings that have had new buildings constructed nearby.

Unequal settlement

When general settlement of the ground about the building takes place equally and evenly, the effects are only slightly detrimental. However, if only part of the foundations is affected and unequal settlement occurs, part of the foundation remains stable while the remainder will move. This can cause a fracture of the concrete foundation and the structure above.

Shrinkable clays. Clays are affected by moisture and hence by wet and dry conditions owing to seasonal changes. Prolonged wet conditions lead to wet clays of low bearing capacity, but after prolonged dry periods moisture evaporates and allows the clay to dry and shrink. Shrinking clays affect the bearing capacity and permit ground movement, the effect being felt at depths of up to 1.5 m. This form of ground movement is common in clay districts and is often the cause of foundation movement. A precaution against it is to lay foundations at a satisfactory depth below ground level; a minimum of 1 m is considered a safe depth to be clear of atmospheric effects. (See *Figure 2.6(a).*)

Tree roots. Trees planted near to buildings can also cause unequal settlement. It is caused by the root system extracting moisture from the ground soil and clay which shrinks in the area around the root system.

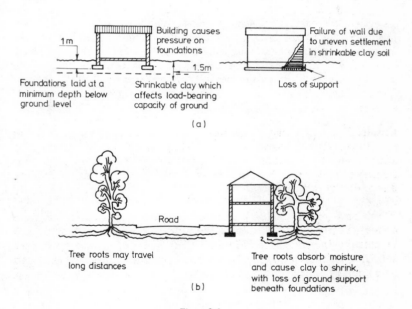

Figure 2.6

Tree roots can extend over considerable distances, and for this reason it is necessary to make adequate observations of the type of trees, their positions and possible effects upon foundations. (See *Figure 2.6(b).*)

39

Building on made up ground. Fill materials usually settle after they are placed, particularly when they contain organic materials or household refuse. The amount of settlement will depend on how well the fill was compacted while it was being placed, on the nature of the fill, and on the underlying ground. A fill containing a lot of household refuse, and tipped on to mud flats, could be expected to have very large settlements. On the other hand, crushed stone over rock would have very small settlements. Clay soils make very satisfactory fills if they are placed in layers (not more than 350 mm thick at a time), and compacted by proper equipment. Some materials, such as over-consolidated clay or unburnt colliery shale, may absorb water and expand after being placed. Burnt colliery shale has caused trouble when used as hardcore under house floors, through expansion resulting in heaving of the floors and displacement of enclosing walls.

Chemical reaction

The chemical reaction between ground soils and concrete foundations is basically that of sulphate attack upon the concrete. Sulphate, in the form of calcium sulphate, magnesium sulphate and sodium sulphate, is found in various types of soil and clays. They form solutions in the ground water and attack the 'set in' Portland cement. In fact, the sulphates react with tricalcium aluminate, one of the chemical compounds in Portland cement, to form calcium sulpho aluminate. This crystal is larger, and consequently expansion occurs which eventually causes complete disintegration of the concrete surface. The chemical action depends on:

The permeability of the concrete. The concrete needs to be fully compacted in order to reduce its permeability.

The amount and nature of the sulphate salts present in the ground soils.

The amount and level of the ground water.

The quality of the concrete in the foundation.

Although it is impossible to control the sulphates present in the ground, it is possible to produce concrete that can resist attack. This is by using sulphate resisting Portland cement, which contains only a small percentage of the tri-calcium aluminate compound. It is also possible to prevent the ground water coming into contact with the foundations by the use of drainage, or impermeable layers protecting the concrete. An analysis of the soils taken at a site investigation would reveal the amount of sulphate present so that appropriate action could be taken.

INSPECTION OF FOUNDATIONS

Indications of foundation failures are usually found in the structure above ground level, when movement cracks may indicate movement at foundation level. Under these circumstances it is necessary to ascertain the cause of failure.

Above ground level the development of cracks may be observed visually, and stickers or tell-tales, in the form of paper or glass, secured across the movement crack will indicate whether the movement is still active or not. It will also be necessary to carry out observations below ground level. This can be done by digging a trial hole adjacent to the suspected position of the failure, to the level of the underside of the foundations and possibly further. Observations can then be made of the actual ground at the lowest level at which the structure rests. At first visual observation will be made, then sample tests can be carried out by knocking an iron bar into the soil, or by dropping it into the soil from a height of about 1 m. Later, more detailed laboratory tests can be carried out on samples of soil for moisture content, bearing capacity and loading. In the latter case, the test is carried out by simulating conditions at foundation level, and the soil in excess of the building load over an area of 300 mm square. Any settlement is measured on a gauge. A check loading will enable an assessment of the foundation design to be made.

The initial inspection will reveal conditions as they are, but they will need to be carefully studied and observed on several occasions over a period of time, before a decision can be made as to the actual cause and course of action to be taken. The decision must, after all, be the correct one and must not involve the owner in any unnecessary expenditure. It may be necessary to dig the trial hole on adjacent ground belonging to another owner, in which case permission must first be obtained.

REMEDIAL ACTIONS

When there are no foundations, and the walls are built of rubble, the building will need a new concrete base. The building load must be ascertained and the concrete foundation designed. The base must be of adequate width and thickness, and must be placed at a suitable depth below ground level. It must be mass concrete and laid in short working lengths.

Inadequate foundations

In cases where foundations are inadequate they will require reforming in order to provide stable conditions, in which case the following actions may be necessary.

Provision of a greater spread of the load over a wider area of ground. This can be done by placing mass concrete under the existing concrete. Where there is poor ground, then as a precaution lateral reinforcing bars can be used across the width of the foundations (*Figure 2.7(a)*).

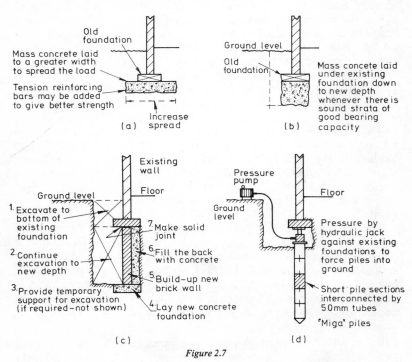

Figure 2.7

Foundations can be taken to a greater depth in order to reach ground of better capacity. This could be a short distance from the surface or several metres down, and could be achieved by:

Using new concrete as a mass beneath the existing concrete (*Figure 2.7(b)*).
Underpinning to a greater depth. Deep trenches are dug in short lengths and new concrete is laid. Then brickwork is built up to support the existing foundations (*Figure 2.7(c)*).
Using a system of short piles driven down to greater depths which will support the existing foundation base (*Figure 2.7(d)*).

In all cases it is important to remember that the safe bearing capacity of the ground at the new depth, and the weight of the building load, need to be calculated. Then the dimension of the foundations can be determined (*Figure 2.8*). The ground soils need to be consolidated before the new concrete is laid, and work on the new foundations must be carried out in lengths not greater than 1.200 m, in order to prevent further movement.

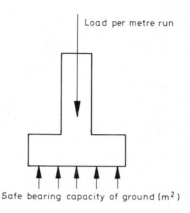

Load per metre run

Safe bearing capacity of ground (m²)

Width of foundations= $\dfrac{\text{Load per metre run}}{\text{Safe bearing capacity of ground}}$

Figure 2.8

Last, but by no means least, it must be remembered that before carrying out foundation remedial work temporary timber support must be provided for the main building structure. This is usually done by propping and shoring it. Temporary timber support should also be provided in all excavations below ground level. It is better to take as many precautions as are practical at this stage rather than risk any possibility of further movement occurring, which could cause the building to collapse, with danger to occupants and workmen.

In all cases where buildings are undergoing structural alterations, underpinning or other forms of remedial work, it is necessary to provide temporary support. This is provided by shoring and propping which will transfer all structural loads to the ground.

Raking shores

Raking shores are a means of giving support to the main wall structure from the ground (*Figure 2.9(a)*). The system is composed of a wall plate secured to the wall by means of timber needles fitted into the wall at each floor level. The support is given by raking shores supported from a grillage base and secured under each needle. Folding wedges are used to tighten up the shores so as to give maximum support. Riding shores can be used when the distance at the base is restricted. Raking shores are placed to coincide with internal cross walls, in order to maintain stability and strength.

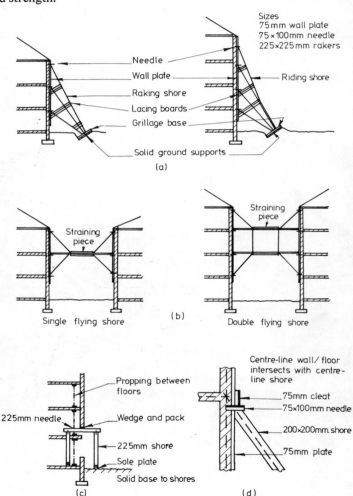

Figure 2.9

44

Flying shores

Flying shores are a means of providing support to wall structures by placing horizontal shores between buildings to prevent the bulging or movement of walls (*Figure 2.9(b)*). Wall plates are fixed to each wall and are secured by needles, the main supports being provided by a horizontal shore fitted at floor levels between the buildings. Raking struts are fitted and folding wedges are used to tighten and provide maximum support. (See also *Figures 2.10* and *2.11*.)

Dead shores

Dead shores are used to give support to a vertical load (*Figure 2.9(c)*). Large horizontal needles are placed through the wall, which in turn are supported by vertical shores placed on solid bases. These are braced

Figure 2.10   Flying shore constructed of scaffolding tubes

and wedged against the wall structure above. When the shores are in position, work can proceed below, either in removal of a wall or in the placing of steel beams in position. Propping is carried out between floors, starting at a solid base to the first floor, then each floor is propped in line above. The props can be made up of timber or steel and should be adjustable. They support the floor load and relieve the load on the wall.

45

It is also necessary to strut the window and door openings as a precaution against movement. This is done by placing uprights against the jambs of the openings and then wedging struts between the uprights.

Underpinning

To shallow depths

Underpinning to shallow depths may simply mean that trenches are dug beneath the existing foundations in short working lengths (about 1.0–1.5 m long). The trench would then be filled with concrete up to the existing concrete foundations. The trench should be dug deep enough to

Figure 2.11   Traditional flying shore constructed of timber sections

reach the type of ground that has the correct bearing capacity (*Figure 2.7(b)*). When it is necessary to increase the width of the foundations in order to spread the load over a greater area of ground, the trench is excavated to the required width and filled with concrete up to the existing foundations. In this case it may be necessary to place reinforcement bars across the width of the foundations in order to take up any bending stresses that may be induced in the foundation concrete.

To greater depths

Where foundations need to be taken to much lower depths, the existing structure must be supported by a wall or series of brick legs built from a new concrete base as shown (*Figure 2.7(c)*). The following sequence of operations will be necessary in order to underpin the total length of wall without causing any movement:

Excavate a shallow trench to the level of the underside of the existing foundations, and to the total length of the wall.

Excavate to the new depth in short lengths of approximately 1.35 m.

Provide temporary timber support to the sides of the excavation and to the existing foundation if required, in order to prevent movement.

Excavate for and lay a concrete base (a 1:2:4 concrete mix).

Build a brick wall from the new base up to support the old foundation base in lengths of approximately 1.30 m.

Infill behind the new wall with concrete (a 1:10 concrete mix).

Make a solid joint between the new wall and the old foundation with fine concrete rammed in tightly.

To greater depths using piling systems

Where a considerable depth of underpinning is required, a system of short piles can be sunk into the ground beneath the structural walls. This is shown in *Figure 2.7(d)* which is an example of the use of short-precast Miga piles. The following operations are necessary when this type of pile is used:

A shallow trench is dug along the length of the wall to the level of the underside of the existing foundation.

A further, deeper excavation is made to a short length of the existing foundation.

A short-precast Miga 750 mm is then placed under the old foundation. It is then jacked down from under the old foundation into the ground, by means of a hydraulic jack attached to a pressure pump. Additional sections are added until the resistance to further penetration indicates that a level has been reached where there is soil of adequate bearing capacity.

The top of the pile is wedged with short steel sections to the underside of the old foundation. Then each pile is finally connected with concrete caps.

Whenever remedial work of this nature is being carried out, it is essential to take adequate precautions at each stage, and to carry out the job thoroughly so that the maximum amount of support is given to the building structure and further movement is prevented.

Bibliography

Building Research Establishment Digests, HMSO:

    Series 1, No. 3, 'House Foundations on Shrinkable Clays'
    Series 1, No. 9, 'Building on Made Up Ground or Filling'
    Series 2, No. 78, 'Vibrations in Buildings'
    Series 2, No. 63, 'Soils and Foundations No. 1'
    Series 2, No. 64, 'Soils and Foundations No. 2'
    Series 2, No. 67, 'Soils and Foundations No. 3'
    Series 2, No. 90, 'Concrete in Sulphate Bearing Soils and Ground Water'

'Mining Subsidence', Special Report No. 12, *National Building Studies*
'Sites and Foundations', *Factory Building Studies No. 5*
Franki Miga Piles, Franki Piling Co. Ltd.

CHAPTER 3

EXTERNAL AND INTERNAL STRUCTURAL WALLS

General structural considerations

Walls generally enclose a building and provide support for other elements of the construction. They can be constructed of bricks, stone or concrete blocks, and are classified as being load bearing (giving support), non-load bearing in the form of partitions or panels, and finally as external or internal walls.

The materials used for construction vary considerably according to the type and intended use of the wall. They may be light or heavy depending on the density of the materials. The strength of wall units, their structure and ability to give adequate support differ, and the performance varies according to the situation and use to which they are subjected. The appearance and finish of the chosen materials will vary according to design requirements. It should also be remembered that jointing mortars, which are an important element of the structure, must have similar properties to those of the bricks or blocks.

It is therefore apparent that a number of considerations are necessary before choosing a structure or a material. The following basic requirements of wall structures must always be considered when analysing a situation. They must be:

Stable so that they remain in position without movement, and therefore give rigid support.

Capable of supporting loads, because these walls normally support floors and roofs.

Formed of durable materials that will withstand the climatic conditions and deterioration in general.

Capable of protecting the building against climatic conditions.

Capable of providing adequate thermal insulation in certain cases.

BRICK WALLS

Brick walls are constructed of small brick units which are built together to form larger structural areas. The materials used are subjected to atmospheric conditions and other variables and differ considerably in performance.

Brick types vary from hard durable engineering bricks to less durable lightweight bricks. They may be made of clay, sand, lime or concrete and each undergoes different chemical reactions. Mortars vary in mix and react to conditions differently depending on consistency. There are various ways in which brickwork can deteriorate and fail, which are considered below.

Movement of brickwork

Wall structures rely upon foundations for their support and so the two react mutually together. Any cracks which may appear in structures must be carefully studied, as it is not always easy to detect the cause. When making observations of movement it is necessary to observe the shape and direction of any cracks which are apparent. They are the result of stresses set up within the structure and careful study may reveal states of tension, compression or shear stress.

Settlement cracks

It has been described in Chapter 2 how failure of the ground support will cause settlement of foundations. If the building settles as a complete unit it will suffer little or no damage (*Figure 3.1*). If, however, the

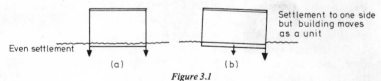

Even settlement

Settlement to one side but building moves as a unit

(a)   (b)

Figure 3.1

building settles unevenly, cracks will arise which are basically of two kinds:

Small cracks which require further observation in order to determine whether they are still active or not. This can be ascertained by placing tell-tales across the crack. The cracks may occur as a result of the initial settlement of a new construction and may be no longer active. If they are still active then further investigation is needed, followed by remedial action to prevent them from developing further.

Larger active cracks indicate more serious movement, the cause of which needs to be ascertained and corrected before more serious conditions arise.

The common types of uneven settlement are illustrated in *Figure 3.2* and the types of cracks that they give rise to are best understood by referring to these diagrams.

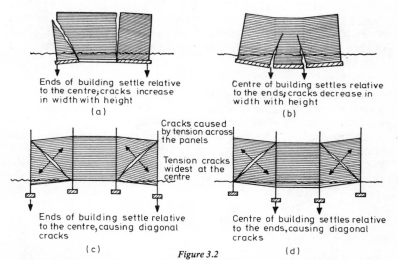

Ends of building settle relative to the centre; cracks increase in width with height
(a)

Centre of building settles relative to the ends; cracks decrease in width with height
(b)

Cracks caused by tension across the panels

Tension cracks widest at the centre

Ends of building settle relative to the centre, causing diagonal cracks
(c)

Centre of building settles relative to the ends, causing diagonal cracks
(d)

Figure 3.2

Settlement cracks are usually diagonal and frequently appear at the weather parts of the structure such as door and window openings. The cracks are usually due to a lack of support in the structure in addition to failure of the ground support. An example of the result of movement due to inadequate horizontal support in framed building is shown in *Figure 3.3*.

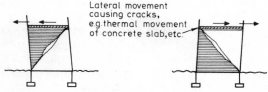

Lateral movement causing cracks, e.g. thermal movement of concrete slab, etc.

Figure 3.3

Remedial work Remedial work can only be carried out when the work in correcting the failure of the foundations has been completed. It will usually involve rebuilding the wall structure, either totally or in part, cutting out and replacing either fractured bricks or areas, then repointing the brickwork. The extent of brick replacement will of course depend upon the seriousness of the situation.

Bulging, buckling and spreading

Bulging and buckling These mainly involve external walls. They are caused by the spreading outwards of the wall structure, either vertically between ground level and the roof, or horizontally between the walls (*Figures 3.4(a)* and *(b)*). They may be due to a lowering of the stability of the structure which can be caused by:

Vibrations from machinery, building plant or traffic.

The overloading of the structure, e.g. by increasing loads on floors or by building on additional structures such as floors.

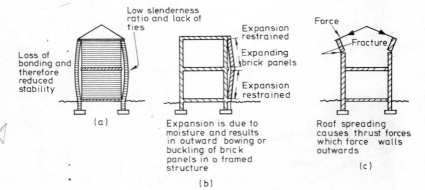

Figure 3.4

The wall having a low slenderness ratio, i.e. insufficient thickness in relation to the height.

The lack of cross-ties between the outer wall structures and the cross walls. This is when the floor joists or beams are parallel to the outer wall and therefore do not provide ties to the outer walls. Bulging normally occurs in older types of property, especially those built using lime mortar, which may have deteriorated because of damp conditions or age. This type of defect must be checked in time, because if allowed to continue it could lead to a collapse of the wall. First indications of this defect is when a space appears between the wall and the floor at the first-floor level.

Spreading Spreading occurs at roof level when the roof sags. The sagging action produces a horizontal thrust on the external supporting walls which may cause them to fracture (*Figure 3.4(c)*).

Remedial work The measures taken to prevent or counteract the above defects may be either of a temporary or of a permanent nature. In both cases it is necessary to provide temporary support either by shoring the outer walls in order to prevent any further spreading (*Figure 3.5(a)*) or by introducing propping between floors in order to give continuous support from the ground.

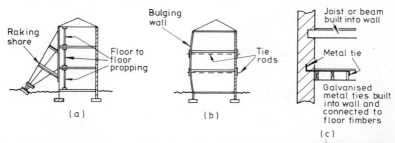

Figure 3.5   (a) Temporary support needed in rebuilding front wall; (b) Use of tie rods for temporary support; (c) Methods of tying structure

Temporary measures will only prevent the continuance of the action and usually take the form of cross-tie rods connecting the opposite outer walls. The rods are fitted at or beneath the first-floor level and will prevent further spreading. It is then necessary to check and to provide a bond with the cross-walls (*Figure 3.5(b)*) and cross-ties with the floor structures (*Figure 3.5(c)*).

Permanent measures involve the re-building of the wall. First of all temporary support is provided, then the affected part of the wall is taken down and re-built from a sound base. It is essential to build in adequate ties with the cross-walls or floor and beam units. This is achieved by building and bonding the components together, or by providing metal ties which make connections between units and therefore provide stable conditions.

Thermal movement of brickwork

Variations of temperature cause a number of different reactions on brickwork. For example, excess expansion in long continuous lengths of brickwork may cause differential movement fracture on contraction (*Figure 3.6(a)*). Lateral movement may also occur along horizontal damp-proof courses such as at parapet walls. Here expansion forces brickwork outwards, but when it contracts on cooling it does not return to its original length but causes tension cracks to appear (*Figure 3.6(b)*). Similar action will take place in structures that absorb excess heat and then cool quickly.

Remedial work Remedial work will involve the re-building or repairing of damaged brickwork, but an important consideration should be the prevention of a repetition of the fault. This can be

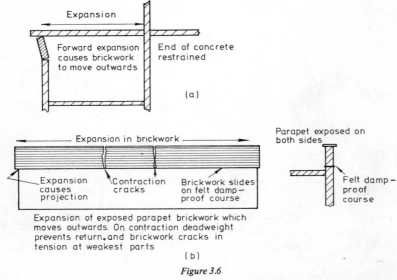

Expansion

Forward expansion causes brickwork to move outwards

End of concrete restrained

(a)

Expansion in brickwork

Expansion causes projection

Contraction cracks

Brickwork slides on felt damp-proof course

Parapet exposed on both sides

Felt damp-proof course

Expansion of exposed parapet brickwork which moves outwards. On contraction deadweight prevents return, and brickwork cracks in tension at weakest parts

(b)

Figure 3.6

achieved by the introduction of expansion joints in the brickwork at strategic positions. If there is a natural vertical joint in the brickwork elevation, the joint can be filled with a suitable jointing material that will allow for the expansion. If one is not available then the expansion material should be 'toothed in' the vertical elevation, which will allow for expansion and avoid causing a fracture.

Moisture content

The moisture content of brickwork depends on whether the walls are external or internal, because external walls are affected by atmospheric conditions but internal walls are not. Bricks themselves vary in their ability to absorb moisture and some are considerably more permeable than others; they may absorb sufficient moisture to cause expansion, in which case they would probably also dry rapidly and shrink (*Figure 3.7*). Excessive expansion and contraction can produce shrinkage cracks which can be very pronounced in certain instances.

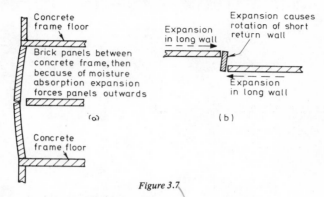

Figure 3.7

Effects of moisture on brick structures

Normally, materials in dry situations will not tend to deteriorate, but when moisture is present there is always a possibility of deterioration, and brickwork is no exception. Damp conditions likely to have an effect are those of rising moisture which causes damp walls. Rising moisture may either rise from the ground or penetrate downwards from roof level. In both cases moisture movement occurs due to capillary action, and it will continue to spread to other parts of the structure if there is an inadequate damp-proof barrier or no damp-proof barrier at all. In the latter case it will be necessary to insert an efficient barrier to check and control moisture movement.

Damp-proof barriers

Damp-proof barriers can be provided in several ways which will involve the introduction of a continuous layer along the total length and thickness of the wall.

1st Method—two courses of blue engineering bricks
This consists of cutting out two courses of brickwork to the full thickness of the wall and then building in blue bricks, two courses deep, with the vertical joints left dry so as to prevent capillary action in the vertical direction (*Figure 3.8(a)*).

2nd Method—continuous layer of felt or sheet copper

A horizontal mortar joint is cut through the full thickness of the wall, using a brick cutting saw, for lengths of 1.3 m at a time, and then a bituminous lead-cored damp-proof felt or copper sheet is inserted and the joint above made solid with cement mortar. It is necessary to overlap all joints by about 150 mm (*Figure 3.8(b)*).

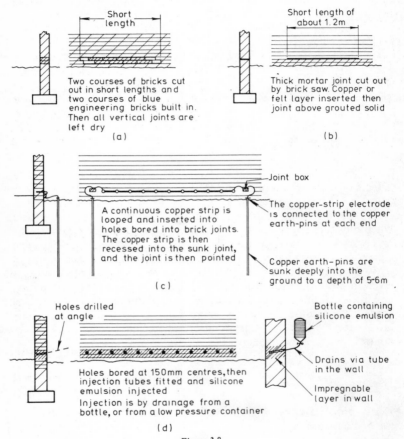

Figure 3.8

3rd Method—the electro-osmatic process

Ground moisture normally rises by capillary action through porous materials as the result of upward acting surface tension forces. The upward movement is accelerated by the existence of a small electrical potential difference which acts between the water molecules and results in rising damp conditions. This may be controlled by the technique of electro-osmosis, a method of short circuiting the cause, to reduce the surface tension and hence the rise of moisture. It is effected by fitting a continuous copper electrode strip into holes which have been drilled into the full thickness of the wall at 225 mm centres (*Figure 3.8(c)*). The continuous copper strip is inserted into a horizontal joint about 150 mm above ground level, and the ends connected to copper earth rods driven into the ground to a depth of 5–6 m and spread 10–12 m apart.

4th Method—latex siliconate pressure grouting
Holes are drilled at an angle into the wall at 150 mm centres along a horizontal line to the extent of the full thickness of the wall. Tubes are fitted to each hole and a solution of silicone emulsion is injected under pressure. The silicate diffuses into the damp wall, and the joint and the holes are then pointed (*Figure 3.8(d)*). This provides a continuous layer of non-permeable material which will check the rise of moisture. The work of providing a new damp-proof barrier is best carried out during the summer months when the walls are reasonably dry.

General moisture penetration

Besides moisture movement up from ground level and down from the roof there is the problem of moisture penetrating into the brickwork when it is exposed to normal climatic conditions. In extreme conditions of driving rain it is possible for moisture to penetrate through brick walls 225 mm thick. Good cavity wall construction has led to the successful solution of this problem but in older property damp walls may be the result of:

Solid brick walls built with porous bricks or porous mortar joints (*Figure 3.9(a)*).

Incorrect construction details, i.e. water from sills, copings and parapets allowed to drain on to the wall surface, which results in brickwork saturation and penetration (*Figures 3.9(b)* and (c)).

Leakages from gutter and rainwater pipes (*Figure 3.9(d)*).

Leakages from service water pipes.

Poor cavity wall construction such as vertical and horizontal damp proof courses around window and door openings, full thickness concrete lintel without damp-proof cavity trap (*Figure 3.9(e)*). Wall ties incorrectly fixed or mortar droppings allowed to collect on ties during construction (*Figure 3.9(f)*), or mortar dropping, forming a bridge over cavity at the level of the damp-proof course (*Figure 3.9(g)*).

Each of these can cause deterioration of brickwork, internal finishes and decoration. It is therefore essential to provide some form of protection in order to improve the resistance of the wall to moisture penetration.

Reducing moisture penetration There are various methods of reducing moisture penetration:

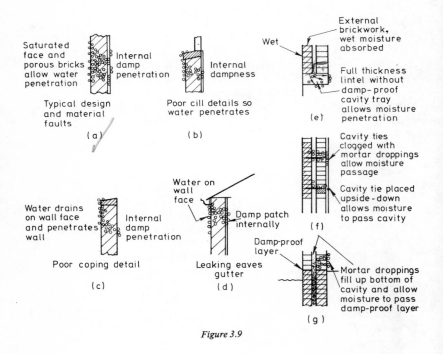

Figure 3.9

Repointing the mortar joints of the wall. They must be raked out to a depth of 12 mm, cleaned out and repointed with a good mortar.

After repointing the wall a useful extra precaution is to apply two coats of silicone water repellant solution (*Figure 3.10(a)*).

Applying a rendering coat to the wall surface after first brushing down all loose particles and mortar joints. This will seal the brickwork with a jointless surface. An extra precaution could be the addition of a water proofing compound to the cement and sand rendering mortar (*Figure 3.10(b)*).

Fixing weather covering to the external surface such as:

Horizontal painted weather-boardings to the wall surface (*Figure 3.10(c)*).
Tile or slate hanging (*Figure 3.10(d)*).
A coal tar or pitch coating to external surface.

Cut out external layer of old brickwork, 112 mm thick, and replace this with good quality pressed bricks of low permeability. (See *Figure 3.10(e)*.)

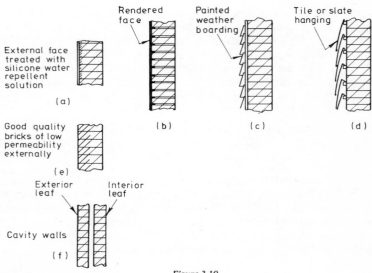

Figure 3.10

As above, but this time construct a cavity at least 50 mm thick (*Figure 3.10(f)*). Care must be taken to prevent defects mentioned on page 57.

General weathering of brickwork

During wet periods moisture is continually absorbed by brickwork and if there is only a limited drying by evaporation this can cause the brickwork to deteriorate in the following ways.

(i) *Frost action.* The water held in the saturated brick changes to ice when the external temperature falls below 0°C; when this physical change takes place the ice expands to approximately 9 per cent of its

59

volume. This force of expansion causes internal stresses within the small crevices of the brick which may be sufficient to cause spalling of the brick face.

(2) *General erosion of the surface* (*weathering*). When the water is held within the brick it may cause it to expand. Later the external surface may dry by evaporation, which will cause contraction of the surface layer during which the surface hardens. This action sets up stresses which may affect the less durable, soft or unburnt bricks, causing particles to spall from the brick or mortar face.

This general weathering of brickwork is most serious in exposed structures such as chimney stacks, parapet walls, retaining walls, boundary walls and exposed elevations. It is here that selection of suitable bricks is essential and that periodic inspection of the exposed areas is carried out in order to maintain a satisfactory structure. If they are left without regular maintenance they could progressively deteriorate to such an extent that remedial work will be very expensive. In any case the remedial work might involve any of the following:

Rebuilding the area of brickwork seriously affected.
Cutting out and replacing defective bricks.
Raking out joints and repointing with sound mortar.

In remedial work it is important to use good quality materials, e.g. bricks that are sound and well burnt, and mortar that is made with clean sand, cement and lime and allowed to set slowly. In all cases where moisture penetrates from the external environment the repair work can be improved by painting the brickwork with two coats of silicone water repellent solution to prevent further deterioration.

Deterioration by soluble salts

Water-soluble salts are commonly found in clay and clay materials; the salts are burnt into anhydrous compounds during the brick manufacture. When the bricks are built into the structure the moisture reacts with the compounds to form a solution which travels by capillary action through brick structures until the salts eventually arrive at the wall surface. This may cause:

The appearance of white deposits on the wall surface, a phenomenon known as efflorescence.
If these salt crystals are formed just below the surface in the small brick crevices they cause a surface erosion known as cryptoflorescence.
If the supply of salts solution is such that cryptoflorescence can con-

tinue indefinitely it will lead to the decay of individual bricks. The soluble salts usually encountered are those of calcium sulphate, sodium sulphate and magnesium sulphate. They are found in varying amounts in:

Ground soils (especially clays) with which all foundations have contact.

Clay bricks which are formed from ground clays.

Natural limestone; atmospheres contaminated with sulphur oxides attack the calcium carbonate (limestone) to form calcium sulphate, which can affect adjacent brickwork.

Contact with sea water or sea spray.

In most cases the solution will evaporate from the material surface, leaving the salts upon the wall face. This is efflorescence, which is not serious but does cause discolouration of the brick surface. Some salts, especially magnesium sulphate, may crystallize beneath the surface of the brick, and the expanding crystal causes surface erosion. This is cryptoflorescence which affects the softer bricks and mortar. Efflorescence is often apparent on the face of new construction, where water used in the construction has evaporated at the surface, leaving the salts visible behind. This is short lived, however. When efflorescence persists with heavy deposits, then close inspection is necessary. Whitish crystals forming behind flaking erosion indicate a serious attack.

Remedial work   The following remedial work is necessary:

The first operation should be to check the source of moisture, and if possible to provide a suitable damp-proof course in order to stop moisture movement.

Always brush away surface efflorescence from the brick face.

Cut out and replace any deteriorated bricks with new ones.

Rake out eroded joints and repoint as necessary.

Avoid using bricks of high soluble salt content in parts where moisture or efflorescence exists. A simple test is to leave the brick partially immersed in distilled water. Salts will form on the brick surface if they are present in the bricks.

Ensure that brickwork in close contact with limestone is constructed of good quality hard-burnt bricks in order to resist surface erosion.

Other forms of chemical attack

Chemical attack may appear in the form of:

Sulphate attack on mortar joints.

Atmospheric impurities that affect the material face.

The oxidation of ferrous metals, causing expansion and hence the cracking of wall structures.

Sulphate attack This is a chemical reaction resulting from the combination of sulphate salts in the brick, the tricalcium aluminate constituent of Portland cement in the mortar, and water which is necessary in promoting the reaction. This forms a new compound called calcium sulpho aluminate, the crystal of which causes considerable expansion and results in loss of strength and disintegration of the mortar joints, together with distortion of the brick structure (*Figures 3.11(a)* and (*b*)). This action is particularly noticeable in brickwork in exposed positions such as gable and parapet walls, chimney stacks, free standing and retaining walls (*Figure 3.11(c)*) and external walls in more exposed conditions, especially those covered with dense renderings (*Figure 3.11(d)*).

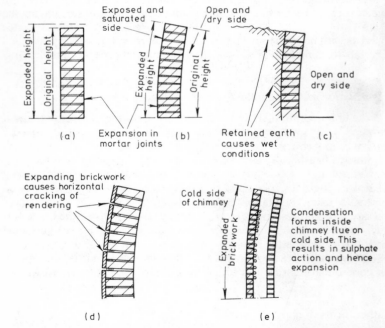

Figure 3.11 (a) Expansion vertical when whole of brickwork is exposed and saturated; (b) Expansion uneven when one side of brickwork is exposed and saturated and the other side dry; (c) Brick retaining wall which causes uneven expansion; (d) Effect on rendering face; (e) Effect in chimney flue

62

Sulphate salts cause expansion and lifting of the structures, which in wet conditions may lift completely apart. If they are wet on one side only, expansion will occur to that side, causing a curvature of the wall surface. Chimneys are affected in a similar way, with a gradual curving and leaning of the stack structure (*Figure 3.11(e)*). In this case heavy condensation may form on the cold side within the flue and it is then absorbed into the sides of the bricks which increases the action. With densely rendered brickwork horizontal shrinkage cracks appear along the line of expanding mortar joints and water may enter these cracks and assist to increase the chemical action.

The necessary remedial work involves locating and eliminating the source of moisture and rebuilding the affected brickwork using a less dense mortar. However, if the action is only slight, repointing may be sufficient. As a precaution against re-occurrence the following steps should be taken:

In considerably exposed positions where wet conditions are expected, bricks of low sulphate content should be used.

Mortar containing a low cement content but an increased lime content should be used. (*richer mix*)

The source of water should be completely removed.

Chimney flues should be lined and insulated in order to reduce condensation to a minimum.

Gypsum plaster should never be mixed with Portland cement.

Atmospheric impurities These are usually in the form of dust particles from coal burning appliances. They come into contact with material surfaces and moisture and form weak sulphuric and carbonic acid solutions. The resulting acid, although diluted, may collect and become concentrated in areas where it causes the deterioration of brick surfaces, especially of softer or under-burnt bricks which will allow surface erosion. Mortar joints are affected.

The necessary remedial work involves removing surface dirt by washing, thus eliminating possible sources of trouble. In addition, cut out all defective bricks and rebuild the wall with new, sound bricks as required. The whole of the wall should be repointed. In the case of extensive surface deterioration consider the possibility of rendering the whole surface after preparing a sound base.

Oxidation of ferrous metals When a ferrous metal oxidizes the oxide expands and exerts a pressure within the brick structure. This results in movement cracks and the fracture of brick units around metal sections or fixings.

General considerations

When carrying out remedial work on brickwork the following points should always be considered:

When sections of brickwork are being cut out, taken down or removed, great care should be taken to ensure that the adjacent construction is not damaged or disturbed.

Brick and mortar must be suitable for the existing structure from the point of view of quality and colour matching.

New work must be bonded into existing structures correctly. It must be well bedded and all joints must be filled with mortar, as it is very easy to create conditions that may induce further deterioration.

STONEWORK IN EXTERNAL WALLS

Stone was very popular in older buildings, where it was used either on its own or in combination with bricks. Today, however, the use of stone is restricted owing to cost, though it is still widely used in natural stone districts.

Natural stone was formed in two ways: firstly from solidified molten materials, which produce igneous rocks including granite and other durable stone; secondly from deposited particles from fragmentation of igneous rocks, which compacted and hardened under pressure to form sedimentary rocks which include limestones and sandstones. It is within these two groups that we find the building stones.

Defects occur in natural stone, and the durability depends on carbonate content and the action of the acid constituents of the atmosphere and rainwater. The amount of carbonate in natural stones differs. Some contain either calcite or calcium carbonate, others dolomite (a double carbonate of calcium and magnesium) and there are even some that contain almost no carbonate at all; these are the most durable.

Common building stones

Limestones

Limestones vary in density and porosity. They consist of particles of carbonate of lime (calcium carbonate) cemented together with calcite under pressure. Limestones differ in hardness and structure, and consequently the weathering properties vary considerably. The carbonates in the stone deteriorate, and some stones react with atmospheric impurities and general weathering, while others have a high degree of durability.

Sandstones

Sandstones consist of fine grains of sand cemented together under pressure to form a cohesive mass. Their textures vary from fine to coarse and they form a range varying from soft calcareous sandstones to hard siliceous sandstones. Sandstones differ in hardness and durability, and react to atmospheric conditions, chemical impurities and weathering. The softer and porous stones are less durable, and the sandstones with a calcium carbonate cementing compound are affected by atmospheric acids.

Granites

Granites are very durable stones and some contain a small amount of calcite which may slightly increase the durability. Since they are very durable in damp conditions they are very often used as plinth stones.

Durability

Moisture of the atmosphere is an important factor when considering the durability of stone, because in a very dry atmosphere the stone will not deteriorate. The subject is considered below under various headings.

Atmospheric pollution

Air nearly always contains impurities of sulphur and carbon as a result of fuel-burning appliances, though the effect is more pronounced in urban and industrial areas. The carbonaceous particles constituting smoke cause the disfiguration of buildings with soot deposits, and sulphurous particles cause the decay of building materials (*Figure 3.12(a)*). These sulphur compounds, mainly sulphur dioxide with smaller amounts of sulphur trioxide, will join with the moisture of the atmosphere to form acidic solutions, which in turn react with the dolomites, the carbonates in the limestone, the carbonates in the calceous sandstones, and mortars. The reaction causes the formation of calcium sulphate at the material surface, which causes surface blistering and sealing, loss of cohesion of surface particles and similar effects in adjacent materials.

Pollution deposits may be very heavy in certain districts, while in others they may be almost negligible. The deposits travel with the wind and are widely dispersed. Buildings are often washed by atmospheric rain which keeps certain parts of the building free of deposits although other parts may be heavily contaminated. The Clean Air Act which is being enforced in many districts is intended to reduce the sources of air pollution and should help to alleviate the problem.

Solubility

Many limestones are slightly soluble in water, especially if the water contains dissolved carbon dioxide and/or sulphur dioxide. Surfaces exposed to rain may slowly dissolve away, giving a weather-worn appearance (*Figure 3.12(b)*). This form of erosion is normally encountered with the softer types of limestone, the harder ones being only

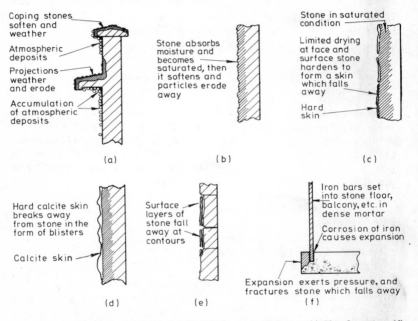

Figure 3.12   (a) Atmospheric deposits; (b) Solution and weathering; (c) Skin formation; (d) Blistering; (e) Contour scaling; (f) Expansion by corrosion

slightly affected. The washing of stone by rain will tend to remove soot particles and clear away unsightly stains. On the sheltered surfaces, however, coatings of sooty deposits accumulate and become firmly attached, thus giving the well known black and white patchy appearance common to buildings faced with limestone.

66

Sheltered surfaces may also collect hard deposits of calcium carbonate and sulphate. They are left behind when the water evaporates out of the solutions that are formed when the rain washes the surface. In polluted atmospheres the surfaces of granites and sandstones bonded with silica or iron oxides tend to collect hard adherent deposits which are insoluble and extremely difficult to remove. On the other hand, surface deposits on limestone, although hard, can normally be softened and removed with water.

Skin formation

Calcium sulphate causes the formation of a hard glossy skin on the surface of limestone (*Figure 3.12(c)*). This skin may be more harmful than protective, and although some stones offer good resistance others allow the development of the following undesirable effects:

Blistering and scaling of the surface (*Figure 3.12(d)*).
Development of cracks at arrises and areas of decay.
Hard glossy surfaces over a layer of friable stone.
Scabbing of the surface skin.

Magnesium limestone under similar conditions will form both calcium sulphate and magnesium sulphate, which can be extremely damaging from the point of view of decay. Calcareous sandstones are often affected in a similar manner. The regular washing of stone will help to keep the surface clear of atmospheric deposits, thus reducing or preventing the formation of the hard sulphate skin.

Contour scaling

Contour scaling occurs in sandstones and less durable limestones. It is a form of weathering in which the external layer of the stone remains sound but the layer of stone beneath becomes friable. Eventually this thin external layer will fall away (*Figure 3.12(e)*). This is caused by the repeated wetting and drying of the stone which leaves the internal layer in a moist condition; here it dissolves part of the cementitious matter which in turn causes loss of cohesion. This internal layer of the stone becomes soft and friable, and then the harder surface of the stone falls away as a layer.

Soluble salt action

This is a similar type of action to that which occurs in brickwork. The intensity of the effect depends on the actual salts present and the type of stone involved, but the effects can be serious, continuous and progressive. It is also very difficult to rectify. The effects are caused by:

Crystallization of salts from solution.

Changes in the state of hydration of the salts, depending on temperature and humidity.

Production of sulphates by the reaction of carbonates and acids of sulphur from the atmosphere.

Salt from sea water or sea spray.

Lack of precautions during construction to prevent the passage of solutions.

For prevention it is necessary to provide adequate damp-proof barriers in order to check capillary paths that will allow the passage of moisture from the ground or via brick backings.

The removal of surface salt deposits is best carried out after first removing or checking the source of water. It is then necessary to brush away all surface salt deposits and to follow this by washing with clean water. This tends to bring any further salts to the surface. The operation must be repeated until it clears completely.

As mentioned above it is important to prevent the penetration of moisture and the saturation of walls, and certain procedures must be followed during construction. Copings and sills made of porous stone require a damp-proof barrier to check the passage of moisture. Defective copings, projecting cornices and sills may need to be protected by lead or copper flashings. Masonry backed by brickwork can be coated with bituminous paint at the rear, to provide a barrier between the materials.

Frost action

Stones in a saturated condition may be damaged by frost action in the same way as bricks are damaged (see page 59). Limestones and many sandstones are generally resistant to this action but there are many softer types that are liable to be damaged, especially if they are highly saturated. Saturation may result from:

Sufficient atmospheric rain being absorbed.

Leaking rainwater from gutters and pipes.

Leaking parapet gutters.

Bad construction.

As a general rule, horizontal surfaces such as copings, cornices, plinths, sills and other projections provide catchment surfaces for water. They become saturated, and then frost action is likely to occur. In cases where saturation is likely it is necessary to select stone that possesses a high resistance to moisture penetration and frost action, and to provide cover flashings to most types of projections.

Staining

Organic staining   Organic matter may be present in limestones. When fixed it tends to be drawn towards the surface, especially when new stone is drying out, producing brownish coloured stains at the surface. This is a result of the presence of alkaline solutions, the source of alkali being either mortar, grey Portland cement or hydraulic lime. The correct choice of mortar will help to reduce the problem. Mortars of white cement and lime putty are less likely to cause staining.

Metallic staining   In nearly all situations where metals are attached to stone the problem of staining the stone surface occurs. It is more noticeable on lighter coloured stone, and as a means of prevention metals may be coated with silicone and wax. Stains may be removed by washing with a solution of ammonia and then brushing when dry. This will have to be repeated several times, finally washing thoroughly with clean water.

Oil staining   This may be removed by using a volatile organic solvent, preferably carbon tetrachloride, but white spirit or benzene can also be used. They evaporate after drawing the oil to the surface without leaving further stains. The application will need to be repeated several times.

Vegetation

Mosses and lichens grow on stone surfaces and normally cause little damage, though they can damage metal gutterings. To kill and remove the growths a treatment of magnesium fluoride solution can be applied, and when dry the stone can be brushed clean. Ivy growing on walls can cause damage to masonry, because its aerial roots grow and penetrate into the mortar joints. If this is allowed to develop it will cause considerable damage and permit moisture penetration.

69

Cleaning stonework

Buildings normally require some form of surface cleaning in order to remove coatings of atmospheric impurities. It can be carried out in several ways.

Periodic cleaning   This is carried out by hosing the building with water and then brushing down with a stiff brush. This simple cleansing process is very effective.

Water spraying   This process is carried out with the application of a fine spray of water directed on to the coated stone surfaces. The calcium deposits, being soluble, will soften and can be removed by brushing. The period of spraying required for adequate soaking may be 15 min to several hours before the deposits soften sufficiently to be removed.

The staining of stone surfaces may occur after cleaning operations have been completed. This is caused by soluble salts being brought to the surface by absorbed water which evaporates at the surface. However, these clear after brushing or atmospheric washing.

Steam cleaning   In this process steam is applied from a jet under high pressure on to the surface of the stone, where it softens and removes calcium sulphate deposits reasonably quickly. Less water is used in this process, so there is less inconvenience to the public and occupants of the building.

Sand blasting   This has the advantage of being a dry process. It is carried out by blasting fine angular quartz particles under pressure from a nozzle on to the surface of the stone. The force of the particles striking the stone surface will remove the deposits.

In each case a scaffolding will be required in order to provide adequate protection for the public passing the building. Special care should be taken when protecting door openings, where water will be able to penetrate through cracks or spaces in the sheeting. These areas should be covered with polythene sheeting, with any joints taped.

Repairs to damaged stonework

Redressing old stone surfaces

Where the depth of decay is not excessive it is possible for the whole surface of the stone to be dressed down to a new depth (*Figure 3.13(a)*).

This can be accomplished by cutting back the decayed and blemished surface to a depth of 12–25 mm. The method is suitable for plain and straight surfaces and it is possible to restore surfaces at reasonable cost.

Replacement with new stone

Where the depth of decay is greater, other methods are necessary: either cutting and replacing complete stone blocks, or cutting out stone blocks and replacing the surface stone with a suitable thinner stone facing about 50 mm thick (*Figure 3.13(b)*). Replacement stone blocks need to

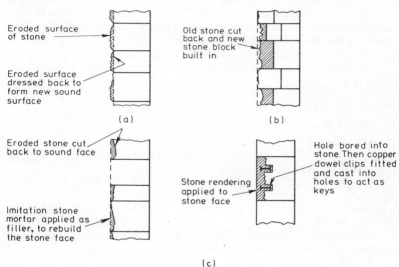

Figure 3.13

be of a similar stone to the existing wall in type, colour and texture. It is often found to be satisfactory to use old stone for replacement, which can be cut, prepared and then built in. When cutting out the defective stone care must be taken not to disturb surrounding masonry.

Plastics repairs

This method is suitable for the repair of superficial damage of stones that are otherwise sound. It provides an artificial stone face that can be finished to resemble the existing wall. However, it may not always be entirely suitable and much depends on the type and position of the building. It does, however, provide a method of repair much cheaper than replacing with new stone.

In order to be successful, the work needs to be carried out by skilled operatives under strict supervision, and the preparation of a good sound base and use of good quality materials are essential. The stone must be cut back to a sound base and all loose fragments and dust removed, as it is essential to secure good adhesion between the plastics repair and the stone base, to which the repair must be well keyed (*Figure 3.13(c)*). Mechanical keys can be provided by drilling holes into the stone base, or by grouting copper clips or dowels into the drilled holes.

The mortars that can be used for plastics repair are based on:

Portland cement, sand or crushed stone and lime additives. Depending on the type of finish required, white or coloured cements should be used to 'shade in' with the existing stonework.

Zinc oxychloride cement, sand or crushed stone.

Crushed stone or sand with silicon ester as a binder.

It is essential to adhere to the following points when carrying out plastics repairs:

Good adhesion on first application is essential.

Too thin a coating is to be avoided.

Greater thickness should be built up gradually in thin layers, and kept moist during the hardening period.

Each block of stone must be treated separately, with the correct jointing made between blocks.

Rapid drying must be prevented. The repair must be kept moist during the curing period.

After repair, projecting features must be protected with cover flashings.

Mortars for jointing masonry

Masonry mortars used in rebuilding and repairs should be composed of white or tinted cement, lime and crushed stone or sand to the following mixtures:

Masonry work: 1 part cement
3 parts lime
10 parts crushed stone or sand.
Rubble walling: 1 part cement
1–2 parts lime
6–9 parts crushed stone or sand.

Stone preservatives

Stone walls that are of a porous nature can be treated with a preservative coating in order to reduce the absorption of moisture. In all cases it is first necessary to allow the wall to dry so as not to trap moisture or salts beneath the surface; entrapped moisture will, on evaporating at the surface, cause deterioration of the preservative coating. For this reason treatments are best carried out during the summer months.

Types of stone preservatives can be classified as follows:

Paint coatings. If the nature of the stone face is not too important, paint coatings can give suitable protection. This treatment will require regular maintenance to prevent deterioration, and it will also be necessary to seal the face and edges of the stone in order to prevent paths for moisture penetration. Many stone textured paints are available and suitable for this work.

Silicon esters. Application of silicon esters to the stone surfaces improves the weathering effect of the stone.

Silicon water repellents. These also reduce rain penetration, but as in the case of silicon esters, they have only a limited value unless surface coverage is complete. If moisture and salts are trapped beneath the treated surface then the scaling of the stone or silicone film may follow.

Generally, stonework is a stable and durable material and deterioration usually occurs at the face only. Before carrying out treatment and restoration work it is necessary to decide what the cause of the defect is, what cleaning methods and remedial work are required, and whether any preservation treatment is needed. The remedial work will normally be carried out by specialist masons and great care is needed in carrying out preparatory work and surface treatments. Maintenance work is also important, and the adequate cleaning of stone surfaces and keeping the joints in good condition will usually be sufficient.

REINFORCED CONCRETE FOR EXTERNAL WALLS

Concrete, or reinforced concrete, has been used in all forms of construction from the beginning of this century. Concrete is a material that is strong in compression but weak in tension. To overcome this weakness mild steel reinforcing bars are included to resist internal stresses. The reinforced concrete is then strong in both compression and tension and as such it is used successfully in construction work in the form of columns, beams, floors, walls, roofs and foundations. It can be used either internally or externally where it is exposed to atmospheric conditions.

The success of a concrete structure depends upon:

Good design and detailing of the structure.

The use of good quality materials that are clean and free from impurities.

The correct measurement of all ingredients (either by volume or weight) to the specified mix proportions.

Adequate mixing of ingredients. With modern mixers a problem only occurs if the mixing time is too short.

The correct placing and resultant compaction of the concrete. This is especially important around reinforcing bars and any external exposed faces.

Durability

Reinforced concrete structures constructed to the specifications listed above will be durable, permanent, and will require little maintenance for a period of many years. However, some may not live up to expectations. Deterioration may occur and develop requiring either extensive and costly repairs, or, if only the surface has deteriorated, provision of some form of surface treatment.

In extreme cases the structure may be in such a condition that it is best to write it off as dangerous or not worth restoring.

The conditions of exposure will have varying effects on the structure itself and the structural surfaces. It is important, therefore, that investigations and testing should take place to estimate the suitability of the building, and of the materials themselves for that particular environment.

Materials tested in areas of severe exposure such as coastal regions, chemical plants, gas works, etc., will in most cases show some form of surface deterioration. Under these conditions the life of the structure is likely to be shorter (even with well made concrete) unless the exposed surfaces are adequately protected and maintained. Materials tested in areas of moderate exposure will normally remain in good condition without any adverse effects. However, the life of the structure will be considerably shorter if the concrete protecting the reinforcement is insufficient. This usually occurs when the bars and wires are near the surface, or the concrete is poor and porous. Defects such as these can be avoided or corrected in future structures so that maintenance work is kept to a minimum. The defective structures can generally be repaired and given a new lease of life at a fraction of the cost of rebuilding.

Defects

Chemical failure Chemical failure is caused by the redistribution of chemicals in cements or aggregates, resulting in unwanted compounds. Set Portland cement sometimes contains an excess of free hydrated lime, which may become soluble in water and therefore able to move to other parts of the concrete. Calcium and magnesium sulphates are reactive and cause expansion of concrete. (This chemical action is described on page 40.) Concrete may also be exposed to the aggressive effects of atmospheric impurities, similar to the way in which these impurities cause stonework to deteriorate (see page 67). Chemicals in liquid or solid form used during various types of manufacturing processes may cause surface deterioration if they come into contact with the concrete structure.

Electrolytic action Electrolytic action is possible in connection with the mild steel reinforcing bars, and will cause them to corrode. The corrosion can become excessive at the intersections of reinforcements and cause 'pop outs' of the concrete. It is encouraged if the bars are of different types or unevenly stressed. Moisture is necessary for electrolytic action to take place; if, however, the moisture happens to be a salt solution, e.g. sea spray, it may cause saturated conditions in the concrete structure which would result in aggressive corrosion of the reinforcement bars.

Over-stressing. Over-stressing can cause internal or surface disruption of the granular structure of the concrete. Over-stressing can be caused by compressive, tensile or shearing forces. Tension, caused by overloading, produces 'clean' cracks in one place or occasionally a complete fracture. Compression, however, normally produces cracking or occasionally tearing and usually in several places, but not usually a complete failure. Shearing follows a similar pattern.

Failure of cover concrete This occurs when its contact with the main core is not strong enough to be able to resist expansion forces caused by corrosion of the reinforcement, thermal expansion and moisture stresses, including the effect of frost (*Figure 3.14*).

Faulty design Faulty design may lead to structural deterioration and other partial or complete collapse (*Figure 3.15*). The most serious fault

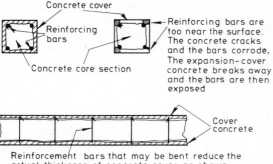

Reinforcement bars that may be bent reduce the
actual thickness of concrete cover as shown

Figure 3.14

in design would cause overloading, dealt with on page 75. However, the
following structural design and detailing can cause deterioration. For
example, it is essential to include some means of removing rainwater from
horizontal surfaces such as copings, sills, projections, etc., that allow
moisture to collect and ultimately penetrate (*Figure 3.15(a)*). Reinforcement should not normally be used at projections as this may lead to its
corrosion and cracking of the concrete edge (*Figure 3.15 (b)*). Structures
should not be designed so that it is difficult to pour concrete around the
reinforcing bars properly unless the concrete is overwetted (*Figure
3.15(c)*). The poor control of mixing and curing of wet concrete will also
produce shrinkage and cracks.

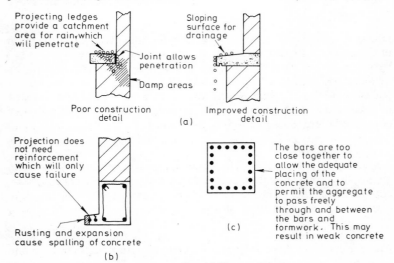

Figure 3.15

Inappropriate materials   It is often found that deterioration is caused by the materials used in the formation of the concrete. Durable concrete can only be produced by using good quality materials that are free from impurities. For example:

Clay particles make contact with the surfaces of aggregates and prevent the adhesion of cement, which causes loss of strength in the concrete. River and pond water contains suspended clay and organic particles and should never be used.

Crushed-brick rubble that contains gypsum plaster should never be used, because the calcium sulphate will react with cement as described on page 40.

Sea water or unwashed seashore sand which contains sodium chloride will increase the risk of corroding reinforcing bars.

High alumina cement should never be mixed with Portland cement. In fact, difficulty can be experienced in using this type of cement, because during the first 100 h of the hardening process a great deal of heat is given off. This can cause excessive expansion if the cement is used casting large sections. Its use is best confined to applications underground, where high resistance to chemical attack is required, and in refractory work.

Faults in concreting practice   These faults will obviously affect and reduce the durability of concrete and hence the structure. Typical faults that occur may be the result of:

The use of too much water during mixing, which results in shrinkage and lowering of strength.

The careless placing and insecure fixing of the reinforcing bars is often the cause of their being too near the concrete face. Corrosion of the bars results.

Insecure formwork, which allows the leakage or bleeding of wet concrete, especially the cement content. This causes honeycombing and hence permeable concrete, and it may also permit the movement of the actual formwork.

Insufficient consolidation, which results in porous concrete. This is usually due to air voids being left in the concrete or the use of unsuitable vibrations that cause segregation with a concomitant loss of strength and surface shrinkage. Mechanical vibrators may be used, and help to produce good quality durable concrete. They can be either secured to the outside of the formwork or, in the case of immersion poker vibrators, placed in the concrete. Surface vibrators can be used for use on floor slabs. However, if a vibrator is used the concrete should be of a drier mix and lower workability in order to prevent segregation, and it should always be used with care and only for limited periods to remove any entrapped air pockets.

Carelessly made construction joints will result in a poor appearance, give insufficient bonding or tying and produce capillary paths for moisture.

Typical defects

There are numerous defects that can occur in concrete structures.

Scarred surfaces. These surfaces will often reveal rusting reinforcing bars in areas where the cover concrete has spalled or cracked or has been forced away by expanding iron oxides (*Figure 3.16(a)*). Tapping the concrete surface may reveal other loose areas where the concrete has lost its bond with the main core concrete.

Thermal expansion. Differential temperature changes, especially if they are rapid, can cause movement cracks, but if the temperature rise is slow then the concrete will absorb the expansion without cracking (*Figure 3.16(b)*). Provided that any movement is unrestrained, no damage will be done, but if there is restraint the resulting stresses will

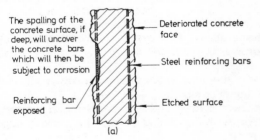

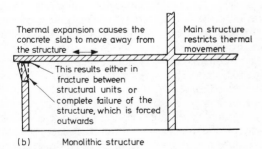

Figure 3.16

78

cause either cracks or the fracture of the unit. This can occur in long walls, parapets and monolithic structures, and in such structures expansion joints must be provided in order to allow controlled movement.

Cracks. Cracks can be caused either by structural movement or by the foundations' support being at fault. The latter can cause diagonal cracks, which if continuing down into the ground would suggest settlement of the foundations. It may be difficult to determine the cause of cracking. If it is of long standing and not progressive it would suggest settlement before the concrete had matured. If it is a new development and active it may suggest thermal movement, or something more serious.

Etching of surface. This is caused by atmospheric and industrial conditions. The result is a roughening of the surface. It is normally a slow process and is the result of the slow chemical breakdown of the concrete surface previously described. This type of attack will occur in atmospheric conditions around gasworks, chemical plants, railways and other industries that produce sulphurous compounds and dust particles. In some cases and under certain circumstances surfaces may be subjected to leakages of water, the effects of condensation, sea water or spray, and also spillage of fats and/or acids at processing plants, all of which will result in surface deterioration.

Frost damage. This results in the spalling of the concrete face due to the expansion effect of ice crystals. It normally occurs in concrete of low strength.

Abrasion. If materials and concrete are allowed to rub together, the surface of the concrete will wear progressively, depending on the strength of the concrete.

Fire damage. Fires produce excessive temperatures which are absorbed by concrete and the reinforcing bars. The bars absorb a greater amount of heat, which results in expansion, the amount of which is greater than that of concrete. The resulting stress causes the bars to buckle and the cover concrete to spall. Deflection in beams and floor slabs may cause cracks to appear and concrete may disintegrate during a fire if it is doused with cold water. Certain aggregates such as crushed granite chippings tend to become unstable in high temperature fires, causing an explosion of the concrete surfaces. The most suitable aggregate to use where there is such a high fire risk is in fact crushed clean clay bricks.

Remedial work

Defects can be classified into two different types: those that can be rectified by partial rebuilding and those that can be remedied by repairing the surface.

Partial rebuilding. This can cure various structural failures, foundation settlement, periodic thermal movement and overloading of the structure. In each case the defect may be either partially rebuilt or totally replaced. In addition, it is essential to remove the cause of any movement responsible for failure. Concrete damaged by chemical action, fire and inherently bad concrete sometimes requires limited rebuilding, the extent of which depends on a thorough investigation of the defect in question. Poor concrete may be left as a backing, provided it is cleaned down and a new weather resistant surface layer is added to the exterior. A new rendering of Gunite can be added. First a layer of reinforcement is fitted and layers of Gunite are added in order to provide a new sealed protective cover, the reinforcement being well secured to the concrete core.

Walls containing deleterious chemicals which have been absorbed from the atmosphere would be an unsafe background for the application of wet surface treatments, and precautions are necessary. Rebuilding of the structure may be required, or alternatively, the concrete should be allowed to dry thoroughly and then a coat of bitumen applied and the surface coated with an application of Gunite and reinforcement. If the chemical action is severe, it may be better to demolish it completely and rebuild with a less absorbent concrete. Concrete damaged by fire can be repaired in a similar way, i.e. first remove doubtful concrete and then replace it with a new concrete, but not before adding to or replacing the damaged reinforcing bars.

Repairing the surface. This will cure surface erosion, cracks that are no longer progressive, honeycomb patches, concrete that has cracked and become detached, and similar defects. In these cases loose concrete, and loose concrete around reinforcing bars, is removed and then cleaned. Additional reinforcing bars can be fitted and deteriorated bars can be cut off. New bars should be fitted and welded to the existing bars in order to provide a good sound base for the new cover concrete.

In all the above cases it is essential that the concrete surfaces are firstly thoroughly cleaned of all dirt, dust and loose particles in order to obtain a good bond. It is also necessary to prepare the surface as a key for bonding the new concrete to the old. Surface preparation may be carried out with a wire brush, scabbling hammer, chipping hammer or sandblasting, after which it should be doused and washed with water.

Methods of repair

Application of mortar by hand This is done as a filling and a cover rendering. The method is carried out using two coats and any greater depths are built up in thin layers (*Figure 3.17(a)*). The two coats are an undercoat of 1:1 or 1:2 parts of cement and sand, and a finishing coat of 1:3 parts cement and sand finished with a wood float. Small areas treated in this way may produce a patchy appearance, in order to improve which it may be necessary to clean down and treat the whole surface with a rendering or to apply a coating of stone-based paint when

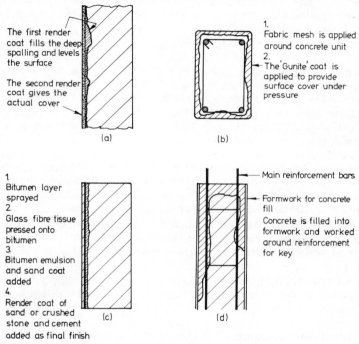

Figure 3.17

the surface has dried out. A water proof additive can be added to the render to improve its weather resistance.

Application of fine concrete under pressure   This method, known as the Gunite method, involves the application of fine concrete in the form of a spray on to structural surfaces at high velocity through a cement gun, in layers 10–50 mm thick (*Figure 3.17(b)*). Concrete deposited in this manner forms an instant bond with a good suction. The Gunite is a mixture of 1:3 or 1:2½ parts of cement, dry sand and water. The constituent materials are applied at a pressure of approximately 43 N/m² from a pressure machine via separate tubes to the nozzle of the gun. At the nozzle the cement, sand aggregate and water mix together and are then blown into place.

Existing surfaces are first sandblasted in order to clean and roughen the surface. The mixture is then blown on to the concrete face, which then builds up a dense layer of Gunite. The surface is built up and not worked in any way, and then left to dry. In the case of thick layers, a wrapping of fabric mesh reinforcement is required around the concrete unit before Gunite is applied.

Sprayed bitumen, sand and cement coating   A coat of bitumen is applied to concrete surfaces, on to which a layer of bitumen emulsion and sand is applied (*Figure 3.17(c)*). It is then finished with a final coat of cement, sand or aggregates mixed with water.

This method is able to hide bad areas and cover fine cracks and defects and is carried out as follows.

All loose concrete is chipped away, the bars are exposed as required for key and then a mixture of bitumen and sand is applied by spraying, in order to fill hollows and defects.

All other surfaces are cleaned down with a wire brush.

Bitumen emulsion primer is applied to all surfaces, and a tissue of glass fibre is then pressed into the bitumen layer before it dries.

A second coat of bitumen emulsion mixed with sand is then sprayed on.

A final coat composed of sand, or crushed stone aggregate mixed with cement and water, is sprayed on to give the final textured finish.

Concrete cast into position   In situations where repairs are required to be of greater depth, it will be necessary to provide formwork to enable a mass of concrete to be poured into position (*Figure 3.17(d)*). The deteriorated concrete is first removed and loose concrete chipped away from the face and from around reinforcing bars. Additional reinforcement can be added which must be securely fastened to existing bars. A formwork is built around the structural member and adequately supported; concrete is then poured and consolidated into position. It is vitally important carefully to pack the new concrete around the steel reinforcing bars so as to ensure a good key and bond.

Some demolition, followed by rebuilding   In this case it is important to ensure unity of the reinforcement and watertight jointing. Reinforcing bars will need to be renewed and it will be necessary to make good connections either by wiring or by welding joints. The joint with the old concrete will need to be well prepared and it will be necessary to provide ties and bond by washing the existing concrete with cement grout prior to pouring the new concrete.

In all cases of repairing concrete the structure to be repaired must be kept in a moist condition during the period of curing, i.e. for about seven days after the completion of repair.

Bibliography

Building Research Establishment Digests, HMSO:

Series 1, No. 21, 'The Weathering, Preservation and Maintenance of Natural Stone Masonry'
Series 1, No. 128, 'Stone Preservatives'
Series 2, No. 58, 'Choice of Mortars'
Series 2, No. 113, 'Cleaning External Surfaces of Buildings'
Series 2, No. 125, 'Colourless Treatments for Masonry'

'Concrete Masonry', *Concrete,* **4,** 144–148, 1970
'Recommendations for the Production of High Quality Concrete Surfaces', *C & CA Advisory Booklet 29*
'The Properties of Cement Paste Compacted under High Pressure', *C & CA Research Report 19*

CHAPTER 4

FINISHES TO EXTERNAL AND INTERNAL WALLS

EXTERNAL RENDERINGS

Wall structures are constructed in various materials, many of which have a natural finish that offers suitable resistance to the effects of the atmosphere and also provides a satisfactory and pleasant appearance. There are several materials frequently used that require further treatment such as block, brick and no-fine concrete walls. They require the application of external renderings.

The purpose of the rendering is to provide a decorative wall finish and to exclude the weather, moisture in particular. This is achieved by the application of a continuous and durable coating to the wall surface. It usually consists of two coats to ensure that joints are overlapped as a safeguard against penetration. In effect it seals the surface of porous brickwork, both the mortar joints and if correctly applied the many gaps and passages that can allow the moisture to pass through.

Types of finish and material

Finish

Renderings may be finished in various ways, depending on the materials used, the way in which they are applied and the tools or machines used. The following are the more common types:

Pebble-dash or dry-dash, which can be defined as a rough finish in which small pebbles or crushed stones are thrown on to a freshly applied coat of mortar and left exposed.

Rough-cast or wet-dash (known as Harling in Scotland), where the final coat containing coarse aggregate is thrown on as a wet mix and left rough.

Scraped finish, a mortar finishing coat, which after levelling and allowing to stiffen for some hours is scraped with a steel straight edge or other finishing tool.

Textured finishes, named according to the type of treatment given, such as ribbed stucco, torn stucco, stippled stucco, fan texture or English Cottage texture.

Smooth (floated) finish, produced by the use of a wooden float.

Crazing or the occurrence of a network of fine cracks is one of the defects experienced in these renderings. Smooth finishes craze, but on the other hand a rough surface will tend to collect particles of harmful atmospheric dust which may affect its durability.

Materials

Renderings must be of good quality and made of pure materials, including cements, limes, sand and gravels, as unclean or contaminated materials lead to defects and will themselves deteriorate. The materials generally used are:

Cements. Ordinary Portland cement or waterproofing cement.

Limes. Hydrated, quicklime or any non-hydraulic lime run to putty is normally used with gauged mortar. Hydraulic lime (Roman cement) is used without Portland cement for repairing old stucco work.

Sands. Natural sands which are clean and free of clay particles, silt, all forms of organic matter and soluble salts, are used. Medium and larger particle size sand is better than the finer type, which tends to cause shrinkage and surface crazing.

Aggregates. These include gravels, granite chippings and marble chippings which are less than about 12 mm in diameter.

Colour pigments. These should comply with the requirements of BS1014, *Pigments for cement, magnesium oxychloride and concrete*, 1961. However, a coloured cement is preferable to the use of pigments since it is easier to obtain uniformity of colouring with such a material.

Mix proportions

Mix proportions depend upon the type of background or backing material, the degree of exposure and the type of treatment. Suitable mixes are listed in *Table 4.1*.

Table 4.1 SUITABLE MORTAR MIXES FOR EXTERNAL AND INTERNAL USE

Background	Backing coat	Finishing coat
Brickwork and hollow clay tiles	A or D	a
	B, C, E, F or G	a, b, c, d, e or f
Concrete cast *in situ*	E	a, b, c, d, e or f
	None	c or e
Building blocks	A or D	a
	B, C, E, F or G	a, b, c, d, e or f
Metal lathing	A or D	a
	E, F or G	a, b, c, d, e or f
Gypsum plasterboard	E	c
	None	c
Fibre building board (insulating board)	E	c
	None	c
Wood-wool slabs	A or D	a
	B, E, F or G	a, b, c, d, e or f
Cork slabs	E	c or d
	None	c

KEY TO SYMBOLS

Backing coats	Finishing coats
A Cement-gauged lime/sand (1:2:9) B Cement-gauged lime/sand (1:1:6) C Cement/sand D Gypsum-plaster gauged lime/sand E Retarded hemihydrate gypsum-plaster/sand* F Anhydrous gypsum-plaster/sand* G Lime-gauged anhydrous gypsum-plaster/sand	a Lime putty gauged with gypsum-plaster (1 part lime to $\frac{1}{4}-\frac{1}{2}$ plaster) b Lime putty gauged with gypsum-plaster (1 part lime to 1 part plaster) c Retarded hemihydrate gypsum-plaster d Anhydrous gypsum-plaster or Keen's or Parian cement. e Retarded hemihydrate gypsum-plaster gauged with lime f Anhydrous gypsum-plaster gauged with lime

* Lightweight aggregates may be used instead of sand.

Application of renderings

A rendering is never applied in one coat directly on to the wall surface because it would lead to all types of defects. The correct method is to apply the rendering in several coats to build up the required thickness. These coats are referred to as undercoats (or render coats) and finishing coat.

The undercoat is applied directly to the wall surface to provide a base coat to receive the finishing coat. It is also a means of straightening out and levelling uneven wall surfaces and of sealing the structural wall. The thickness of this coat should be 10–15 mm. It can be applied in one or two coats, each coat being scratched in order to provide a key for the next application. Each render coat needs to be of slightly less strength than the next coat to be applied.

The finishing coats are applied directly to the undercoats and are finished flat and smooth. The finish may have a plain or smooth-trowelled surface. It is best finished with a wooden float which produces a very satisfactory surface. If finished with a steel float, over-trowelling brings the cement content to the surface, which encourages excess shrinkage and surface crazing. Plain surfaces may be scratched, scraped, combed or textured in order to give a satisfactory decorative appearance. The finishing coat can also be a rough-cast layer composed of a mortar containing coarse aggregates to give a roughened appearance. It can be applied by hand or thrown on by a trowel. Alternatively, a splatter machine can be used. When a handle is turned the mix is automatically thrown out on to the base coat.

In order to obtain a satisfactorily rendered surface a number of points must be considered:

The preparation of the structural base surface is necessary and important. A good sound base is essential for the correct application of render coats.

It is often necessary to rake out mortar joints or to hack the background surface in order to provide a suitable key, especially on concrete surfaces.

All backgrounds need to be cleaned down and made free of dust and loose particles.

Old walls need to be brushed and washed down before rendering.

All surfaces need to be wetted before the application of render coats. Washing carries away loose particles and dampens down suction, thus reducing excessive absorption of the render mortar. It will also reduce drying shrinkage.

Undercoats of renderings need to be scratched before hardening in order to provide a suitable key for the next coat.

Dense renderings are not considered to be good. They cause shrinkage, and hence cracks that will allow moisture to penetrate and collect behind the render coat. This trapped moisture is unable to escape and will give rise to serious defects.

Renderings of cement, lime and sand are to be preferred. They produce less shrinkage and will permit the evaporation of any entrapped moisture.

It is unwise to apply renderings during extreme weather conditions as they often prove to be unsatisfactory afterwards.

Renderings can be applied to various types of structural surfaces and each needs to be separately considered.

Dense, strong and smooth surfaces, such as dense concrete and some clay bricks or blocks, may give rise to adhesion difficulties because of their smooth surface and low porosity. Hacking or the use of grooves in the backings is one way out of this difficulty; another method is the stapling and plugging of a light metal mesh or the use of a stipple coat consisting of Portland cement, sand, water and p.v.a. emulsion.

Moderately strong porous material surface, such as most clay bricks, sand lime bricks and concrete or clay bricks, normally provide a suitable key, especially when the mortar joints are raked out. Rendering is normally carried out without difficulty.

Moderately weak porous material surfaces, such as lightweight concrete (pumice, foam slag, or clinker concrete) normally provide good adhesion but require a rendering of lower strength than the material base to which it is applied, in order to reduce or prevent possible shrinkage.

Protection of renderings

The completed rendering will only remain in a satisfactory condition if certain precautionary measures have been included during building of the structure. For example, renderings are particularly vulnerable at the edges and angles. The following protective measures will assist in maintaining durability:

Eave projections will provide protection along the top edges of rendered areas (*Figure 4.1(a)*).

Parapets must be of good design. They should have projecting coping stones that include an effective drip, weather adequately, and have an effective damp-proof layer beneath (*Figure 4.1 (b)*).

Sills which are situated at various openings will require adequate protection and an effective drip in order to throw the surface water clear of the rendering below (*Figure 4.1(c)*).

Effective and durable flashings should be provided at various projections and exposed edges of rendered panels (*Figure 4.1(d)*). This will assist in controlling moisture penetration at these positions.

Brick projections of about 15–21 mm should be provided at the edges of abutments to provide a definite finish for the render area and satisfactory protection (*Figure 4.1(e)*).

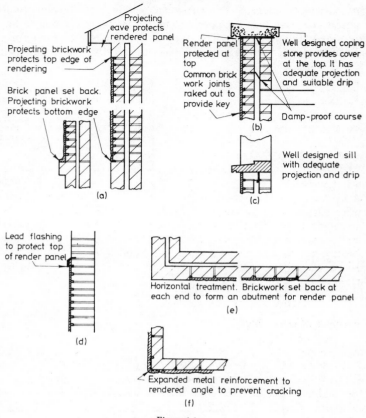

Projecting eave protects rendered panel

Projecting brickwork protects top edge of rendering

Brick panel set back. Projecting brickwork protects bottom edge

(a)

Render panel protected at top
Common brick work joints raked out to provide key

(b)

Well designed coping stone provides cover at the top. It has adequate projection and suitable drip

Damp-proof course

Well designed sill with adequate projection and drip

(c)

Lead flashing to protect top of render panel

(d)

Horizontal treatment. Brickwork set back at each end to form an abutment for render panel

(e)

Expanded metal reinforcement to rendered angle to prevent cracking

(f)

Figure 4.1

The external angle of rendered panels needs special attention during the application of the render. Any flaws between the two surfaces may allow moisture penetration. Deterioration will then follow and the angle may develop serious cracks. It then remains a weak feature. (See *Figure 4.1(f)*.)

Rendering defects

The principles and practice behind the application of satisfactory and stable renderings have already been described. However, a number of apparently unexpected defects may occur.

89

Weak backing structure The structural backing may be constructed of unsuitable materials of poor strength, or materials which have deteriorated (*Figure 4.2(a)*). This type of backing is unsuitable for an application of a rendering as it will allow the render coat to pull away

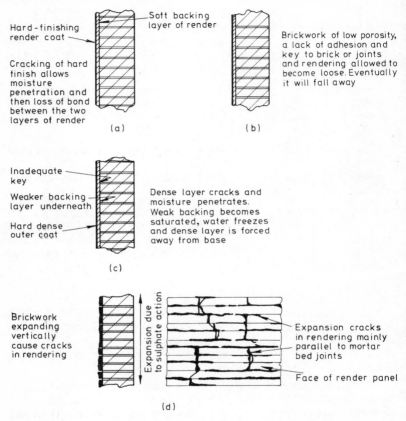

Hard-finishing render coat

Soft backing layer of render

Cracking of hard finish allows moisture penetration and then loss of bond between the two layers of render

(a)

Brickwork of low porosity, a lack of adhesion and key to brick or joints and rendering allowed to become loose. Eventually it will fall away

(b)

Inadequate key

Weaker backing layer underneath

Hard dense outer coat

Dense layer cracks and moisture penetrates. Weak backing becomes saturated, water freezes and dense layer is forced away from base

(c)

Brickwork expanding vertically cause cracks in rendering

Expansion due to sulphate action

Expansion cracks in rendering mainly parallel to mortar bed joints

Face of render panel

(d)

Figure 4.2

and fail completely, thus allowing moisture penetration. It may be necessary to rebuild the structural backing with sound materials.

Weak bonding to the base This causes the loss of adhesion and hence very little bonding, which may allow areas of rendering to fall away (*Figure 4.2(b)*). This may occur on backing materials that afford little or no absorption and therefore provide little or no bond.

Weak rendering undercoat   Where weak rendering undercoats are used in conjunction with a dense hard-finish coat, there is a difference in the amount of shrinkage of the two layers. This may result in the dense layer breaking away from the softer base.

Surface shrinkage cracks   These appear due to shrinkage or differential movements and may initially be small or slight, but will invariably develop and allow moisture to penetrate to the rear. Other defects may develop.

Moisture trapped behind a dense finishing coat   Moisture may collect behind render coats as a result of:

Rising moisture, the result of capillary action upwards from the ground, or downwards from higher levels.

Moisture penetration through the surface cracks in a dense rendering surface.

Moisture trapped in this manner and unable to evaporate from the surface will cause the undercoat to become a form of 'solution'. This will soften further and result in the loss of bond with the hard, dense finishing coat which may then fall away, leaving the soft base coat open to further deterioration.

Frost action   Moisture that is entrapped behind render coats or within surface cracks may cause saturated conditions and will be subjected to frost action during periods of low temperature. Expanding ice may cause dense renderings to be forced away from the structural base, especially where little or no bonding exists (*Figure 4.2(c)*).

Unsuitable materials   The use of unclean materials leads to deterioration and so does the incorrect mixing of the materials in forming the render mortar. Poor application of the rendering will cause several types of defects.

Failure of protection   Various protective edges, damp-proof layers and protective flashings may become faulty as previously described, or no longer perform their protective function efficiently. They may then allow the passage of moisture.

Chemical attack The cause of chemical attack is soluble salts that may be present in the structural unit, or atmospheric impurities. Soluble salts will cause efflorescence and crystallization with similar effects to those of brickwork. Sulphate attack causes horizontal and vertical cracks in the render surface (*Figure 4.2(d)*), which are the result of sulphate action causing expansion in the brick backing material. The rendered surface breaks up into rectangular areas which indicates action behind. Polluted atmosphere as described on page 63 contain sulphur dioxide and carbon dioxide which in diluted forms may attack rendered surfaces—particularly those of poor quality—causing surface erosion.

Impact damage This type of damage is usually accidental and normally results in local damage around the area of impact.

Remedial work

Initial inspections should reveal the cause of the defect, the nature of the existing renderings, including both the backing and finishing coats, and also the extent of the damage. It should then be possible to decide on the remedial work, which may be carried out in one of the following three ways:

Repairing small patches.

Repairing several small patches together. This is better dealt with by forming several small areas into one large area.

Removing the total area, preparing for and rendering the wall area.

The decision on action to be taken will depend on a number of factors, such as what is actually essential, the appearance required and the money available. To repair small and large areas it is essential, in all cases, to hack away the defective rendering back to the wall surface and to brush away all loose mortar, dirt and dust in order to leave the base clean. Mortar joints must be raked clear and square edges must be cut to the original rendered area ready to receive the new rendering. The wall areas must be sprayed with water to wash away dust and dirt. This will also reduce the amount of absorption so that too much moisture is not extracted from the new rendering. The new render mix is then chosen. If it is to be used for patches it will need to be of a similar strength and porosity to the existing rendering and must of course match it in all other respects. Plain smooth finishes are best obtained with a wood float which provides a satisfactory surface for decorating. A steel float gives a smooth finish but should not be used because it produces a surface of high cement content that is liable to shrink and give rise to surface crazing.

Cracks in rendered surfaces may be the result of structural movement in the wall backing. If this is the case, it must be corrected first. It may also be the result of failure of adhesion. It is then necessary to test the existing renderings for hollowness by tapping and sounding the surface. This will indicate any loss of adhesion. Hollow areas and cracks must be cut out, the latter to about 30–75 mm, and the edges cut square, brushed out and washed with water before the application of the new rendering.

The stopping or facing of shrinkage cracks is not really a satisfactory method unless the cracks are correctly cleaned out and prepared before stopping.

Decoration of external finishings

Newly rendered surfaces may be left in their natural state, reliance being placed on their quality to weather atmospheric conditions without deterioration. However, rendering may be decorated in order to provide a satisfactory appearance and to seal the outer surface with a protective coating. Coloured surfaces may also be obtained by including coloured cements in the mix.

In all cases the rendered surfaces will need to be in a dry condition before the application of decorative finishes. All new work must be delayed as long as possible until all moisture has evaporated. It is best done during the summer months, when wet conditions are less prevalent.

Typical paints for use on external surfaces may be chosen from the following:

Cement paint. This is composed of white Portland cement with added pigments, an accelerator, water repellents and other additives mixed together with water, and applied in two coats. The paint can be difficult to apply owing to the density of the materials which, being in suspension, tend to settle unless continually stirred. The application may therefore be patchy, with thick and thin areas of paint. The paint forms a hard dense surface covering, so care should be taken to avoid trapping any moisture behind it, because it will be difficult for it to evaporate into the atmosphere. This can result in deterioration of the surface coating, which will flake away.

Oil paint. This is applied in two or three coats and it is necessary for the rendered areas to be completely dry before the paint is applied. Any moisture present in the rendering eventually evaporates to the surface causing the paint to peel and flake away. This is an expensive but very satisfactory method of protection. The paint surface needs to be well maintained in order to maintain a sealed surface.

Oil-bound distemper. This is an alternative to the previous method, but the coating needs renewing more frequently. Before application it is essential to remove all loose fragments from old coatings. It is not a particularly good or durable method and is little used.

External grade emulsion paint. This is a resin emulsion paint. It is a good material to use, is easy to apply and produces a more positive covering. It is normally applied in two coats, and any moisture beneath is able to evaporate to the surface without detrimental effect. It provides a satisfactory covering at an economical cost and is easy to maintain.

Stone paint. This is a resin emulsion paint containing fine grit aggregate particles. It is applied as emulsion paint in one or two coats. The covering is durable and provides an imitation stone appearance which is pleasing and satisfactory for application to external renderings.

All loose paint must be removed and the cracks rebuilt with oil mastic, mastic putty or fillers. The edges of the old paint surfaces must be treated with stopping or filler, prepared and repainted. The edges of the paintwork should then be rubbed down with a pumice block to a sound base, prepared and repainted. The paint is then stripped off and again rubbed down and repainted. These steps are taken in order to lose the thick edge which would otherwise always be visible.

Stucco covered walls of earlier periods are nearly all protected by paintwork. These surfaces contain numerous layers which are very often 3–4 mm in thickness. They may be found to have cracked in numerous places with the possible lifting of the paint edges at the crack. The paint may then fall away. The cracking of the paint film is often combined with the cracking of the stucco beneath. In this case it is very important to carry out the procedure described above.

General conclusions

Renderings must always be treated in a correct manner in order to provide a durable finish; deterioration will always be encouraged by incorrect application and the slipshod treatment of materials. Adequate preparation of bases is always of prime importance.

When renderings are applied to a structure that may allow movements between different materials, or within a material mass, whether it is new or remedial, then the application of some form of reinforcement will be required. This can be expanded metal lathing, chicken wire, or open weave hessian, each of which will help reduce deterioration.

Finally, an alternative to rendering can always be considered. This can be some form of cladding such as vertical or horizontal boarding, slate or tile hanging or plastic covering.

PAINTING AND DECORATING

Decorative treatments as applied to component surfaces have two purposes, one decorative and the other to provide a protective covering. Both are concerned with the maintenance of structures, the general appearance of the building being an aesthetic necessity and the provision of a protective coating essential to many of the material surfaces.

Many building materials are durable and others are less durable and likely to deteriorate; it is these that require protection in order to prevent deterioration. The basic cause of deterioration is atmospheric conditions and the presence of moisture which affects materials such as iron, steel, timber, renderings and others. If such materials are protected and kept dry, then little cause for decay will arise, so that protection needs to be a complete seal around the material in order to keep the moisture out.

Conditions of exposure differ between external and internal situations:

External conditions are high exposure, atmospheric moisture and impurities, each of which tends to cause the protective coatings to deteriorate. In these situations there is need for greater protection.

Internal conditions are normally dry and unaffected by atmospheric conditions, so that a protective coating is less important than a decorative appearance, there being less possibility of deterioration. However, internal moisture does occur in certain cases and some protection will be required. The moisture is caused by:

Atmospheric moisture or vapour.
Condensation forming on material surfaces.
Moisture rising from ground sources.
Moisture penetration through walls or roof.

Paint deterioration

Paint deterioration is due to atmospheric conditions such as the effect of the sun, wind and rain, and temperature changes causing expansion and contraction of the material base with the resulting loss of bond between paint and the material surface. Atmospheric dust, dirt and chemical impurities must also be taken into account, since they cause deterioration of the paint surface, resulting in a weathered appearance.

Deterioration also occurs when the first coat is not adequately bonded to the material surface and allowed to dry before succeeding coats of paint are added. Moisture penetration into a material will cause wet and saturated conditions, this moisture will eventually find its way to the material surface, where it evaporates, and in doing so it will cause the paint film to lift from the material base.

In the first place protective coats should be applied to all surfaces of a material before fixing, but afterwards only visible surfaces receive treatment. It is not possible, therefore, to maintain the complete seal and deterioration may occur via the unprotected surface.

Maintenance

All decorative and protective coverings require constant maintenance in order to preserve good durable surfaces. This usually includes:

The regular washing of surfaces to remove dust and dirt particles in order to prolong the life of the paint covering.

The washing down of surface coverings and the addition of further coats of paint.

This maintenance work requires to be carefully considered and dealt with by experienced operators; this is necessary so that maximum preservation can be obtained for economical maintenance costs. When the maintenance work includes the addition of further coats of paint then the treatment can be detailed as:

A detailed preparation of the material surface.

The application of the first or priming coat, requiring adequate bond to the material base, acting as a seal.

The addition of further paint coats which will protect the priming coat and provide the main protective layers.

The application of a final finishing coat which is a paint layer of better durability, offering greater resistance to detrimental conditions.

All of the above operations should be carried out in suitable atmospheric conditions by skilled craftsmen, because treatment incorrectly applied is a waste of time and money, and deterioration will rapidly re-occur. This is especially so when paint is applied to damp surfaces, because the dampness trapped beneath will break the bond between each coat of paint. No work should be carried out unless the surfaces are dry.

A detailed consideration of the method and practice of painting and decorating, surface preparation, priming and painting application to various materials follows. In all cases the first consideration is that of preparing the material surface by cleaning and washing to remove dirt, dust and grease, ready to receive the initial coat of paint.

Treatment of timber surfaces

Timber is classified into softwoods, which are easy to paint, and hardwoods, some of which are difficult to paint. Much depends upon the ability of the timber to absorb the paint and thereby provide a suitable base from which to work.

In painting dry, well seasoned timber few difficulties arise, but when timber is unseasoned or laden with moisture, the effect upon the applied paint is sufficient to break the durability by blistering, peeling or flaking of the paint, and mould growth. During construction, timber units on site are often inadequately protected and are liable to absorb moisture rapidly. For this reason all units will need to be well primed before leaving the manufacturers' works, and to be protected on site.

Preparation of old painted surfaces

The method of preparation of old painted surfaces will depend upon the condition of the actual surface.

Surfaces in good condition will only require a good rub down using one of the following:

Sandpaper—a dry method
Abrasive paper—a wet method with water
Pumice or soda block—with water

after which surfaces are allowed to dry completely before applying paint.

Surfaces in poor condition require the complete removal of the paint in order to provide a satisfactory surface. This may be carried out by burning off the paint, using a stripping knife and the heat from a blow lamp or calor gas torch, or by the use of a chemical remover which is brushed on to soften the paint, which is then removed using a stripping knife and wire wool.

Exposed timber that is unpainted may become brittle and open-grained. The surface should be scraped and well papered and then a thin primer paint applied. Alternatively, the surface should be washed with soap and water or solvent, rubbed down with abrasive and then a thin primer paint applied.

One of the following primer coats should then be applied to seal the surface and provide a sound base for a decorative coating: a lead based oil primer, either white lead or pink lead—the pink is better because it has greater durability; an acrylic waterborne wood primer undercoat, which is a modern durable primer; or an aluminium wood primer, which is especially useful on resinous timber.

Preparation of new timber surfaces

Treatment will depend on the variety of wood.

Seasoned softwoods require to be rubbed down with sandpaper, knotting applied to knots and resinous flaws, and the timber should be primed.

Unseasoned softwoods will contain moisture that should escape by evaporation; in this case the timber should be left to season and dry. However, if it needs to be painted immediately, then either a coat of water paint or a thin oil-based primer paint should be used as a buffer coat. After twelve months the surface can be prepared, primed and painted in the normal manner.

Hardwoods that are less absorbent than softwoods are difficult to prime because of the lack of adhesion. The application of the priming coat is helped by thinning the primer with a thinner or white spirit.

Oily timbers such as teak, iroko or cedar, have an oily or greasy surface which will affect the paint coatings. This is best dealt with by applying a coat of teak oil and then leaving it with no further treatment for twelve months. If the surface then requires to be finished with paint or varnish, the following procedure should be used. Degrease the surface by washing with acetone, petrol or turpentine; prime with a mixture of varnish and turpentine of equal parts, and finally apply either a full coat of varnish or a coat of enamel paint.

Bitumen painted or creosoted timber will be difficult to paint if the treatment has been freshly applied because the bitumen or creosote will bleed through the finished coating. In these conditions the timber must not be painted; however, when it has aged, say after twelve months, it becomes less troublesome and can be painted. In this case it will be necessary to clean the surface and apply either a sealer coat of spirit media and shellac knotting, say in two coats, or apply a coat of aluminium primer.

In each of the foregoing cases surfaces have been prepared and coated with a suitable primer so as to form a good base. Once this has been established, normal paint coats can be added, such as one coat of undercoat paint and two coats of gloss finish (or similar) paint, or two coats of undercoat paint and one coat of gloss finish (or similar). Both will provide a decorative finish and protective layer.

Timbers having a decorative surface are usually treated so that they can be shown to the best advantage. In order to do this and at the same time give them a protective coating, a coating with a clear finish is applied. This treatment is often referred to as varnish coating.

In many existing cases old varnished timber is of a yellow to brown colour and not particularly attractive. This type of surface may be washed clean with soap and water, the surface abrased and then re-coated.

Modern treatment demands a much clearer finish in order that the natural timber shows. This can be difficult when retreating a varnish discoloured with age. This type of surface can be treated by one of the following methods:

1. Clean down and wash to remove dirt and grease with a detergent or suitable solvent, then rub down and dust.

2. Remove old varnish with a paint remover and stripper.

3. Sand the surface down with a sanding tool to remove all varnish and leave a clear timber base. One of the following finishes may then be applied: (a) an oleoresinous varnish, which is quick drying and hard wearing, for external use; (b) a catylic wood finish, based on catalysed formaldehyde resin, which is very durable and used for external work; or (c) a polyurethane varnish, which is quick drying and has a hard surface. In each case two coats will be a minimum, three coats better. Externally three coats will be the minimum. This may require to be renewed every two years.

Treatment of metal surfaces

Ferrous metals

Unprotected iron and steel will, in damp conditions, corrode rapidly; the rate and severity of the attack varies according to atmospheric conditions. Atmospheric impurities usually contain sulphur compounds which are particularly injurious; the attack will be more severe in industrial than in rural areas.

The maintenance problem is to prevent or reduce the possibility of corrosion by covering the iron or steel with continuous protective coats of paint. For this reason it is particularly important to pay special attention to the preparatory work before painting commences, and to use the best quality priming paint; this works out to be the most economical in the long run. The number of coats and the quality of the finish of the paint will, of course, depend on the severity of exposure.

Preparation of metal surfaces   The effective life of protective paint coats will be longer on well prepared metal bases than on poorly prepared surfaces; for this reason it is necessary to remove all traces of rust by one of the following methods:

Chip the surface with a hammer or scrape the surface and then brush with a wire brush. It may be difficult to remove pitted rust by this method.

Grit blast the metal clean. This is a good method.

Apply a chemical de-rusting solution to remove the rust. This needs to be washed clean with white spirits or solvent to remove grease before the priming coat is applied.

Heat the metal by gas or similar torch, and then brush with a wire brush.

Priming metal surfaces   It is necessary to prime the metal as soon as the cleaning operation has been completed and the metal is clean. When repainting existing work, all bare patches and areas will need to be touched with primer paint first. The following priming paints are suitable for metal surfaces:

Red lead paint
Chromate priming paint
Zinc dust primer (this is best but the most expensive).

When the priming coat is completely dry and hard, then follow with the normal coat of paint.

Non-ferrous metals

As stated on page 125, non-ferrous metals do not corrode to any great extent. However, most surfaces are affected to some degree depending upon atmospheric conditions. Many of these metals have surfaces that are difficult to paint, each will therefore need different treatment.

Zinc and galvanized iron or steel   Zinc has a smooth surface that affords little key, and it is therefore difficult to apply a coating of paint.

To overcome this the surface requires to be roughened or et
order to provide a base on which the paint will adhere.

Etching may be carried out by the application of a pre-galvo
for 15 min, which is then washed off with water. Another meth.
paint it with an etching primer paint which will cause its own etching
and provide an adhered base for further painting.

On the other hand, if the metal is left to weather in its natural form the
surface will become roughened. For this reason existing weathered surfaces will already be in a condition suitable for application of the
priming paint. Suitable priming paints are calcium plumbate primer for
zinc and zinc chromate primer for galvanized iron.

Aluminium   Aluminium has a particularly smooth and shiny surface
which is greasy and requires the following pre-treatment to acquire a
key for paint. First de-grease the metal by cleaning with white spirit,
then etch with an etching primer paint, followed with a priming coat of
zinc chromate primer.

Copper   Copper has a smooth surface which is acidic and may affect
the paint. The following treatment is necessary. Wash the surface with
white spirit, then etch with an abrasive paper and follow with a coat of
synthetic varnish. In some cases the gloss paint may be applied direct.

Brass and bronze   Brass and bronze have a similar greasy and smooth
surface which will need to be de-greased with white spirit, then etched
with an abrasive paper and primed with a coat of chromate primer.

Bitumen coated metals   Such materials as cast-iron pipes, which are
heavily coated with bitumen, may if painted direct show surface crazing
or the possible blending of bitumen through the paint. In this case it may
be better to re-coat with bitumen paint, or seal with one or two coats of
aluminium sealer paint before applying the normal coats of paint.

Metal pipes carrying hot water or steam   These are difficult to paint
because the paint is affected by high temperatures unless they are given
the correct initial treatment, which varies according to the pipe
temperature.

First the pipes should be de-greased with white spirit and then primed
with a chromate primer for temperatures up to 93°C. The pipes should

be finished with gloss paint in the usual way. For pipes with temperatures above 93°C it is better to use aluminium primer and finish with aluminium paint.

In all the above cases, unless stated otherwise, normal paints can be added after the priming coat has dried, such as one undercoat and one gloss coat, or one undercoat and two gloss coats.

Treatment of brickwork, masonry, concrete, rendered and plastered surfaces

Deterioration due to presence of moisture

Brickwork, masonry, concrete and rendered and plastered surfaces, which are mainly naturally formed or with little manufacture process, are porous by nature. For this reason moisture may be present in the materials by natural means, or it may be absorbed during building operations, in which case it is necessary that the moisture dries out before decorative paint coats are applied. If water is sealed in behind the paint there is the risk of blistering, peeling and mould growths, each causing deterioration. Most paints seal the material surface so that moisture is unable to evaporate through and escape. However, gloss paints are less permeable than flat paints, and oil paints are less permeable than water paints or emulsion paints. The latter then are more likely to allow moisture to escape from the seal.

There is also the possibility of moisture being absorbed into the dry structures of older properties through defective damp-proof courses, flashings and other water-proof barriers. In this case the decorative surfaces will deteriorate in the same way. (See *Figure 4.3(a)*.)

Deterioration due to presence of alkali

Brickwork, concrete and cement renderings are each of an alkaline nature, while gypsum plasters are not alkaline, although it is possible, through free lime being present in the wall, for alkaline salts to be brought from the brick or concrete backing to an alkaline free surface during the wet situation and the subsequent drying out period.

In the presence of moisture, alkaline salts become soluble to form caustic and corrosive solutions that attack the paint vehicle and varnish content, causing a softening of paint. The solutions also attack paint pigments which causes a discolouration of the finished colour.

In all cases it is necessary to leave the surfaces as long as possible in order to dry out completely, then decorate with water paint which is more permeable and less likely to be attacked. If an oil paint finish is needed then the surface should be primed with an alkaline resisting primer paint (*Figure 4.3(b)*).

Deterioration due to efflorescence

Soluble salts are brought forward to the surface during the drying out of building work. These salts crystallize, leaving a deposit of white salts on

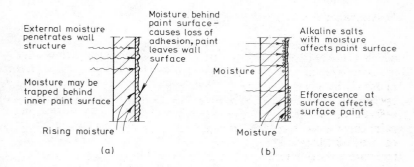

External moisture penetrates wall structure

Moisture behind paint surface – causes loss of adhesion, paint leaves wall surface

Moisture may be trapped behind inner paint surface

Rising moisture

(a)

Alkaline salts with moisture affects paint surface

Moisture

Efforescence at surface affects surface paint

Moisture

(b)

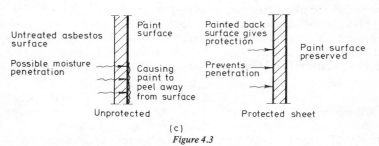

Untreated asbestos surface

Possible moisture penetration

Paint surface

Causing paint to peel away from surface

Unprotected

Painted back surface gives protection

Prevents penetration

Paint surface preserved

Protected sheet

(c)

Figure 4.3

the surface which cause little harm. This is called efflorescence. If, however, the crystals grow beneath the plastered or rendered surface it can force the paint from the wall surface, and this is called cryptoefflorescence.

To treat this defect the wall should be allowed to dry out completely before decorating, and the salts then removed with a coarse abrasive paper. The wall is then re-damped and left to dry, which should bring the remaining salts to the surface. These should again be rubbed off with an abrasive paper and the process repeated until the action ceases. Decoration can then be carried out in the normal way.

Treatment of gypsum plastered surfaces

Gypsum plastered surfaces being porous in nature, they are affected by moisture, so before paint is applied they must be dry in order to avoid the effects of evaporation and subsequent deterioration of the paint. They are divided into classes, which should be treated as follows:

Class A and B (hemihydrate plasters). These are porous plasters of the quick setting type which are commonly used and form a satisfactory surface to decorate. They require to be rubbed down and coated with a thin oily primer.

Class B plasters with a lightweight aggregate such as Carlite do not require any further treatment. They only need to be rubbed down and lightly abrased, then a plaster primer paint applied.

Class D (anhydrous plasters) such as Keene's or Parian cement dry very hard indeed with a glassy dense surface to which paint does not adhere. In this case, when the finishing coat is applied it should not be allowed to dry completely before surface preparation has been made. This takes the form of application of a coat of sharp primer within two to four hours of the plaster being finished. The sharp coat consists of white lead paint mixed with white spirit and a little gold-size as a binder. This coat helps adhesion. Then after the normal drying period it can be primed with a plaster priming paint. If the surface is old or dry then it can be wetted and abrased with an abrasive paper in order to form a key, primed with a plaster primer paint and finished with paint or emulsion paint.

Treatment of cement renderings

The treatment of cement renderings has been covered on page 93. It is, however, necessary to consider the redecoration of old surfaces.

If the surface is plain it may be reasonably clean, but if it has a rough texture it may be dirty and contain injurious atmospheric deposits which need to be removed before new paint is applied. If the surface is neutral then cement paint, emulsion paint or oil paint can be used, the latter proving to be a costly method. Emulsion paint is best, being economical in cost, easy to apply and affording a more positive cover. Cement paints, however, should not be coated with paint or emulsion unless the whole of the cement paint is first removed.

Treatment of lime rendered surfaces

The lime rendered surfaces of older type property are normally coated with oil paints for protection and maintenance needs to be continued in this manner. In all cases of remedial work it is first necessary to clean and wash the surface with soap and water to remove dirt and grease, then to make good any flaws with good stopping, and prime with an alkaline resistant primer. This is followed with normal paint coats. Glossy surfaces must be rubbed down with a water-proof abrasive paper whilst wet. If the surfaces are liable to have soluble salts present they should be treated with cement paint or emulsion paint which will allow the moisture to evaporate.

Decoration of wall boards and other sheet finishings

Wall boards are in various forms of structure and surface finish, so that treatments and effects will differ. Many boards are thin and made of pulp or fibre which can be seriously affected by warping and buckling in moist conditions. This may be because one face only is painted, the other being unprotected; in order to avoid this the reverse side must be painted. Fibres of some boards tend to lift when coated with a water based paint, in which case the surface requires a sealer coat first.

Softboards of soft fibre texture These may be coated with emulsion paint direct. If a sealer is required, a primer sealer, emulsion varnish, or acrylic primer undercoat may be used.

Medium pressed boards These require a primer sealer, acrylic primer or emulsion paint direct.

Hard pressed boards of hardboard type These have a smooth face, and require a proprietary hardboard primer coat, or a primer with varnish additive. Some wall boards have a sealed surface and do not need site priming. However, once the initial priming coat is established, normal wall paint or emulsion paint can be applied as required.

Fireproofed boards Fireproofed boards, and wall boards or ceiling tiles of the flame retardant type, are impregnated with fire resisting solutions. These must be considered when decorating, because the fire resistant coating or content may be brought out or covered up with the new decoration and so reduce their effectiveness. In order to retain the required resistance they should be coated with a fire retardant paint, and an alkaline resistant primer coat will reduce the risk of salt movement at the face.

Acoustic boards These require careful treatment so as not to fill or seal the material's surface perforations, which would reduce the acoustic qualities. Emulsion paint applied in thin coats, with a spray, is the best method of application.

Foamed polystyrene This may be decorated with water-borne paints or paints thinned with white spirit. Emulsion and acrylic paint may also be used. Care in the use of solvent or thinners must be exercised because some types may dissolve the polystyrene.

Plastics sheets with a high pressed surface Such sheets provide little or no mechanical key, so that the surface needs to be abrased with abrasive paper, after which a thin coat of enamel paint should be applied. When this is dry normal paint coats may follow.

Asbestos Asbestos and similar sheets are of an alkaline nature and in a moist or damp condition will affect painted surfaces. It is also necessary to paint the back of the sheets, otherwise moisture will penetrate from the rear to the front and beneath the paint layer, causing paint to peel off. For this reason the back of asbestos sheets may be painted with bitumen or similar paint, and the face and sides primed with an alkaline resistant primer paint or emulsion paint applied direct (*Figure 4.3(c)*).

Wallpaper and wall coverings

Wallpaper and wall coverings provide decorated coverings to wall surfaces; necessary operations include preparation of the wall surface, and treatment and the hanging of the wallpaper.

Wall surfaces must be sound, dry, smooth and clean before hanging wallpaper, and new plaster surfaces must be dry so as to provide a suitable base. If the wall surfaces are troubled with penetrating or rising moisture, then this must be corrected and allowed to dry out before decorating. Wall surfaces that are troubled with continuing dampness and mould growths should be treated with an antiseptic solution or a wash of 2 per cent solution of mould inhibitor, and then allowed to dry.

Surfaces must be free from dirt, and loose and flaking particles, and cracks, joints and other imperfections must be made good with a suitable filler. Existing papered surfaces will need to be stripped off. This may be done with a stripping knife after the paper has been softened by soaking with hot water, steam or wallpaper stripping solution. When dry, the surface will need to be rubbed with sandpaper, and then sealed with a coat of glue size or a coat of wallpaper adhesive.

The wallpaper should be hung by applying it direct to the prepared wall surface or by first applying a cross-lining, then hanging the wallpaper over the lining. A cross-lining of wallpaper is applied by hanging the lining paper horizontally, the wall paper being hung vertically. Linings provide a good base for the main paper, and especially for good quality papers, when it is a necessity. Cross-lining is a useful method to use on bad or cracked wall surfaces, where it will cover and bind the imperfect surface together.

Lining papers are of various types such as:

Brown or white paper, for walls that are badly cracked, and plastered breeze block walls.

Linen backed paper, being reinforced with fine calico gauze. This is used on cracked ceilings, walls and battened partitions.

Linen backed tape, which is used for covering cracks and joints in wall boards.

Ingrain paper, which may be applied to any surface and may be decorated with emulsion to give a textured surface.

Bitumen backed paper, which may be applied to damp walls in order to keep the paper dry. (It must be remembered that this does not cure the cause of the dampness.)

Wallpapers are of various types, designs, patterns and colours, but they may be classified under the following headings:

Pulps. The cheaper type of paper, being soft and easy to tear. The pattern is printed directly on to the paper.

Grounds. These are of a better quality paper, the paper being coated or grounded with colour or preparation before the design is printed, to give a finish such as coloured, satin-like or silk finish, etc. They may be hand or machine printed to produce various finished papers such as:

Hand printed papers.
Machine printed papers—these are general purpose papers.
Embossed, woven, textured and relief type papers.
Wood grain papers.
Washable papers, some being plastics or synthetics coated to produce surfaces resistant to steam and water.

Flocks. These have a raised pile and a velvet look. They are a good class decorative paper.

Vinyls. These are papers coated with a vinyl face which has the printed pattern fused into the vinyl surface.

Paint defects

Modern materials are carefully manufactured with the best of materials and are carefully checked, so that there is only a slight possibility that faults will occur in the material. Manufacturers also issue instructions as to the use of their materials, and these must be followed. However, defects do occur in various conditions and by different causes, which may be classified as:

Poor quality workmanship in preparing surfaces and applying materials.

Insufficient knowledge of materials, which are incorrectly applied, or chosen for the wrong situations.

Lack of adhesion to surfaces by material coatings, often connected with moist, humid conditions.

These result in a number of defects which are listed below.

Blistering   Blistering of the paint surfaces may be due to imprisoned moisture, or resin pockets, which force up the paint film into little bubbles or blisters. These prevent the film from making contact with the base again. The defective paint coat must be removed down to the timber surface.

Bleeding   Bleeding is the diffusion of colouring matter such as bitumen, creosote, resinous deposits and black japans from the sub-base to the paint surface. It requires the removal of the cause and an application of a sealer, styptic knotting, or aluminium primer paint.

Blooming   Blooming is the formation of a surface mist, haze or milkiness due to the presence of moisture in the atmosphere, or chilling of surface gloss coat, or varnish. It may be removed with a soft rag, or washed with clean water and then polished. It may eventually destroy the surface gloss, in which case it would be necessary to flat down and re-gloss.

Chalking   Chalking is the powdering of surface paint due to external exposure and lack of a paint binder and/or vehicle. It will require washing and rubbing down to provide a sound base for adhesion, then sealing and application of a new coat of paint.

Cissing Cissing is the partial creep-back of the surface paint film due to differences in surface tension; it may result in lack of adhesion over small areas. It may be caused through oil or grease on the surface of the base being painted over, silicones of polished surfaces being painted over, or an over-oily undercoat surface. It will be necessary to rub down the area that has cissed and to clean with turpentine, or in bad cases to burn off and start again from the base.

Crazing or surface cracking Crazing is due to a hard drying paint coat being applied over a soft or oily undercoating, or one that is not fully dry causing irregular cracking of the surface paint coat. This is sometimes referred to as 'crocodiling'. Remedial treatment will be to strip the affected areas and re-paint.

Curtaining or sagging Curtaining occurs when paint runs down a painted surface in drips or with a curtain effect. It is due to bad workmanship, i.e. the uneven application of paint, too thick in parts, which causes it to run. When these runs are thoroughly dry they can be rubbed down and recoated.

Efflorescence White crystalline deposits form on the paint surface or immediately beneath; they will have evaporated from the brickwork base. Efflorescence will cause disfiguration and disruption of the paint film. It should be allowed to dry, then wiped down, stripped and left until the development has stopped. It will then be safe to re-decorate.

Flaking Flaking is the lifting up and peeling away of the paint, usually from small cracks in the paint film, due to loss of adhesion at the surface. It is caused by applying paint over a moist, greasy, chalky or any other insecure surface. The defective areas will have to be removed, the paint stripped down and the surface refinished with all the paint coats.

Grinning Grinning is due to the poor opacity of a paint film which allows the paint coat beneath to show through the finishing coat. It is the result of poor workmanship, incorrect thinning of paint, or use of incorrect colours. The cure is to add further coats of paint until a satisfactory surface is obtained.

Livering or gelling   Livering or gelling results from a chemical change in the paint, which reduces it to an unstable jelly-like mass. It is caused by using unsuitable thinners, or long storage. It should be washed down with white spirit or other suitable solvent. When dry the remaining paint should be rubbed down and new coats built up to gloss finish.

Loss of gloss   Loss of gloss or the sinking of the gloss finish is due to the action of surface moisture, atmospheric moisture or condensation that affect the drying of the paint film, especially during fog or frost periods. A porous undercoat may cause a similar effect. Remedial action requires the surface to be rubbed down and re-glossed when perfectly dry.

Mould growths   Such growths are due to damp conditions in old buildings, when condensation causes the disfiguration of the painted or decorated surface. The mould becomes active in moist conditions, causing dark blemishes and patches. To cure this defect it is necessary to prevent further dampness, then completely to strip off decorative materials, wash down the wall, and then sterilize the surface with an antiseptic solution before re-decorating. If the surface is to be painted then a fungicidal paint should be used.

Saponification   Saponification is a soapy formation of paint due to an attack by alkalis upon the paint media. It usually occurs on plaster or cement surfaces due to their high alkali content. It will require the complete stripping and cleaning of the surface before the re-application of decorative paint. The surface must dry out and become neutral, and should then be coated with an alkali resistant primer followed by the normal coats of paint.

Bibliography

'External Rendered Finishes to Walls', *National Building Studies Bulletin No. 12*
'Rendered Outside Walls', *M.P.B.W. Advisory Leaflet No 27*
The Decorator's Handbook, Imperial Chemical Industries Ltd.
Building Research Establishment Digests, HMSO:

   Series 1, No. 41, 'Treatment of Damp Walls'
   Series 1, No. 131, 'External Rendered Finishes'
   Series 2, No. 51, 'Painting Walls 1'
   Series 2, No. 56, 'Painting Walls 2'
   Series 2, No. 57, 'Painting Walls 3'
   Series 2, No. 70, 'Painting Metals in Buildings 1'
   Series 2, No. 71, 'Painting Metals in Buildings 2'
   Series 2, No. 38, 'Painting Asbestos Sheets'

CHAPTER 5

ROOFS

The requirements of a roof are, first, to provide a suitable weather resisting covering made from durable materials, and second, to provide suitable insulation. With these two points in mind this chapter analyses the various forms of roof and roof coverings. It is important to know the composition of the structures and the materials and methods of fixing that can be used, in order to be able to appreciate the conditions and failures that can occur.

PITCHED ROOF COVERING

The pitched or sloping roof can be covered with various materials such as slates, tiles, corrugated sheets and timber shingles, or it can be thatched.

Slates

Slates are usually made from natural slate and cover many older buildings. There are a number of types:

Welsh slate. This has been used widely throughout the UK. Such slates are blue-grey in colour, about 4–5 mm thick and of regular size. They are normally very durable and strong.

Westmorland slate. These slates are used in random or diminishing sizes and in greater thicknesses, i.e. 8–10 mm. They are greenish-grey in colour and have a decorative and pleasing appearance.

Cornish slate. This is used in either random or diminishing sizes, of 6–10 mm thickness. It has a pleasing decorative appearance that is brownish-grey in colour.

Swithland slate. These slates are also used in random or diminishing sizes but are 10–15 mm thick. They are extensively used throughout the Midlands.

Stone slate. This is natural stone which is split into thin pieces. It has been widely used in England in districts along the limestone ridge.

Concrete slate. This is a modern manufactured slate. It is used in larger sizes and in thicknesses of 12–15 mm and is manufactured from concrete. It can be produced with various attractive 'slate' colour finishes.

The slates are secured to battens using two slate nails to each slate. The slate nails themselves are made of galvanized iron, which has limited durability; zinc, which is soft and difficult to fix but which has reasonable durability; or copper, which is the most durable and costly of the three. The lengths of the nails vary from 38 to 50 mm, depending on the thickness of the slates being used.

Tiles

Tiles are now rapidly becoming the more economical type of covering and they are widely used. There are two main types:

Clay tiles. These are clay products that are either hand made or machine made. They are either plain, single lapped, double lapped or interlocking, and are of various profiles and colours.

Concrete tiles. These are made from concrete and are of similar types, profiles and colours to clay tiles.

They are secured and held by their nibs from battens; in plain tiling they are nailed every fourth or fifth course.

Corrugated sheets

Corrugated sheets are widely used for industrial buildings and are of various profiles. The main types used are:

Corrugated asbestos sheets. There are various types such as Standard sheets or Big Size sheets. They are secured to timber or steel purlins by either galvanized drive screws or hook bolts. They are of standard widths of various lengths and have good durability.

Corrugated galvanized-iron sheets. The standard corrugated sheets have a limited durability only. They are secured to timber purlins with galvanized nails and require regular maintenance. This type provides a cheap covering, but it is now being superseded by corrugated asbestos.

Timber shingles

Timber shingles are made from Western Red Cedar which is cut and split into thin timber slates or shingles. They are laid in a similar manner to slates, i.e. they are nailed with two aluminium flat-head nails, to either slat deck or boarding. They are not widely used in the UK but provide a very durable covering.

Thatch

Thatch is a rural type of covering constructed from reed thatching. It is laid over timber battens and frame by craftsmen called thatchers. This form of covering is very satisfactory but also very costly, though it has a long life. It is used mostly in rural areas.

Structural frameworks

Structural frameworks are the frameworks which support the roof covering. They are normally constructed of softwood or steel frames and comprise rafters, ridge plates and supporting purlins (*Figure 5.1*).

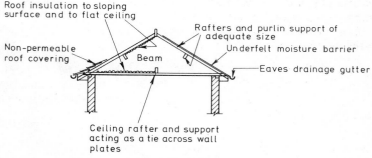

Figure 5.1

The size of the timber members is important as it is essential to use economical sizes which are governed by the span of the member and the load it carries. This can be obtained by calculation. They also need to be protected against fungal decay, beetle attack and fire. In addition, the following must also be included:

A moisture barrier in the form of an underfelt which is laid over the rafters, correctly lapped, and fitted into the eaves gutter.

The insulation of the roof areas in layer form, which can be either:

113

a layer of expanded polystyrene or glass-wool fibre which is laid upon the ceiling or included in the roof coverings, or
loose infill granules as a layer upon the ceiling; these may be either cork, expanded polystyrene or vermiculite.

The securing of ceilings to joists, in order to close the roof space, by using joists of adequate size, supported by beams and plates, and covered on the underside with plaster boarding finished with plaster, or lath and plaster. The latter is the oldest method.

Other components

Gables and verges

Gables and verges can be made either from timber barge-boards, which are secured to bearers and purlin ends, or in the form of a verge with a tile or slate undercloak, infilled with neatly pointed cement mortar.

Hips and valleys

Hips and valleys are made either from sheet lead or copper fitted upon a softwood-boarded timber base or from special tiles.

Ridges

Ridges are made with ridge tiles which must be correctly bedded in mortar and pointed. They can be either half-round or angular in shape and up to 250 mm wide. Both hips and ridges can also be made by dressing lead over a timber roll.

Gutters

Horizontal and inclined gutters are made from sheet lead, sheet copper or asphalt, which is laid upon softwood gutter boards (*Figure 5.2*). The edges are turned over tilting fillets and the lining at the wall abutments is taken up to a height of about 100 mm and made watertight with an additional cover fillet. This type of gutter finish is normally used behind a parapet wall or the junction of two sloping roof surfaces. A more common finish is provided by the use of purpose-made half-round gutters manufactured from cast iron, asbestos or plastics.

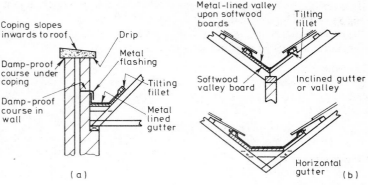

Figure 5.2

Defects of pitched roofs and their structural timbers

The timber used in the construction of pitched roofs is mainly softwoods, which is liable to fungal or insect attack. Fungal attack can be either wet rot, as a result of continuous exposure to excess moisture caused by leaking roof covering, or a dry rot in more confined conditions such as beneath flatroof coverings and gutters. Insect attack is usually caused by the Furniture Beetle in softwood and occasionally the Powder Post and Death Watch Beetles in hardwoods. In certain areas of southern England the House Longhorn Beetle has caused considerable damage in roofing timbers, so much so that the Building Regulations make it compulsory to pretreat all such timbers with a preservative. A more detailed consideration of timber decay and deterioration is given in Chapter 6.

Another important point is the strength and stability of the timber framing. A deterioration in strength may result in the sagging and spreading of the roof. This may be the result of:

The failure of purlins to support the roof framing.

The load of the roof causing the spreading of the outer walls when there is nothing to stop it.

The failure of beams or purlins which are undersized.

Inadequate ties to the outer walls; cross-walls are necessary for support. The wall plates which are secured to the wall and frame may not be tied together.

The purlins and rafters themselves may sag or deflect when fully loaded and this may be due to:

The timbers being undersized.

115

The roof being overloaded. This often happens when lighter weighted slates are replaced by heavier plain tiles.

The failure of fixing due to the corrosion of nails, screws or bolts, which may permit the movement of the roof frame.

Remedial work for structural timbers

Remedial work is usually carried out from the point of view of making the structure both stable and safe. Any deteriorated or mis-shapen timber is always replaced. In the case of sagging and spreading it is first necessary to prevent further movement by:

Providing temporary shoring and propping.

Providing and fixing members across the width of the roof. Using timber ties or adjustable tie rods fixed to either wall plate, with care it is possible to pull the wall plates together and at the same time lift the roof with jacks which are placed under the ridge.

Rebuilding any defective brickwork and providing bonding and ties between the cross-walls.

In order to stabilize a roof structure, and where timbers are found to be either sagging or deflected due to a loss of support, or the timbers being undersized, then:

Introduce additional purlins to support the rafters.

Replace any rafters that are permanently deflected.

Provide additional support to the purlins by either building up the cross-walls, or by adding small trusses or strutting.

Defective roof coverings

Slates

Slates are generally durable materials but are nevertheless susceptible to deterioration, which can take the following forms:

Chemical erosion as a result of atmospheric pollution. With poor quality slates this causes a softening of the laminated layers and surfaces, resulting in a breakdown of the bond between the layers so that the slate erodes away.

The appearance of cracks along the grain of the slate for no apparent reason. However, small cracks may develop at the quarry when the slate is being cut, which may later open up either as a result of frost action or some other form of surface pressure which has not been accounted for.

The fixing nails, depending on the type being used, may corrode and allow the slates to become dislodged.

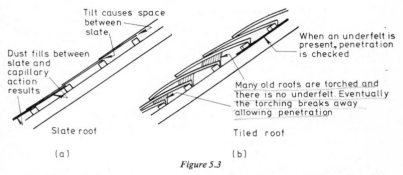

Figure 5.3

Capillary action may occur between slates. The space between them fills with dust and dirt that accumulates and allows absorbed moisture to pass upwards by capillary action (*Figure 5.3(a)*).

Remedial work   The following courses of action may be taken:

Re-nail loose slates. Single slates may be either fixed or replaced and should be secured in position with copper clips.

Strip off areas of defective slates, re-nail the sound slates and make out with new slates.

Strip off all the slates on the roof, re-slate with new ones or use the existing sound slates and make out with new ones as required. In both cases it will be necessary to renew the softwood battens and to fix a layer of underfelt.

Strip off defective slates and re-roof with either clay or concrete tiles. This is often the most economical method.

In addition, if the fixing nails show signs of corroding, the slates will eventually become dislodged. Because this is a continuous process over a period of years, it is more economical to consider re-roofing as soon as possible.

Tiles

Roof tiles are normally durable, but although they are thick they are nevertheless brittle. Deterioration occurs in a few situations, and usually takes the following forms:

The tiles break across their width and fall away. This may be due to:

Damage as a result of pressure on the surface causing a fracture.
Damage due to small shrinkage cracks developing.

The softening of the tile structure which permits surface deterioration. This can be caused by the action of atmospheric impurities and general weathering. It would be particularly active in the case of underburnt clay tiles.

The presence of laminations. Clay tiles, especially plain machine made tiles, will contain laminations owing to the form of clay preparation used. Deterioration results when the surface laminations break away with the assistance of atmospheric moisture and frost, the whole tile eventually falling apart.

The loss of nibs. The tile nibs that suspend the tiles from the battens may be faulty and break off, so that the tile is free to slide away.

Wind dislodgement. During high winds, tiles in certain areas of the roof may well be dislodged, often as a result of suction. Areas around hips, ridges, and gables are particularly affected.

Leakage. This is liable to occur at single-lap joints at the head and sides of the tile, especially when they are not correctly fixed or seated together. Tiles may also be slightly lifted, causing a gap or space through which leakage conditions are made worse by the action of the wind (*Figure 5.3 (b)*).

Remedial work   It is a fairly simple and easy operation to repair a tiled roof. The tiles are self-supported by their nibs and can easily be lifted and removed from the battens. The choices are to:

Re-fix the loose tiles or replace with new ones of a similar type.
Remove the deteriorated tiles and then re-lay and fix that particular area of tiles to whatever extent is thought necessary.
Re-roof the total area with new tiles of a more suitable type if laminations have occurred, depending on the size of the area involved.
In addition, the renewal of timber battens may be required, together with a layer of underfelt.

Corrugated sheets—asbestos

Corrugated asbestos sheets are composed of asbestos fibre and cement

118

and are generally satisfactory, but are nevertheless liable to deteriorate in the following ways:

They are damaged easily, being weak and unable to take a load. They therefore crack or break when subjected to pressure.

Small shrinkage cracks may develop into large cracks which eventually break completely.

Moss and lichen growths may cause surface deterioration, and continuous contact with their acidic waste products and the cement content of the sheets may cause a slight softening of the sheet surface.

Rainwater made acidic by atmospheric pollution may attack and soften the material surface by chemical action.

The fixing screws or bolts may corrode.

Remedial work Corrugated asbestos sheets cannot successfully be repaired, but it is a comparatively easy operation to replace damaged sheets or to fit new bolts or drive screws.

Corrugated sheets—galvanized iron

A galvanized zinc protective coating to iron lasts for a limited time only and galvanized iron corrugated sheets require regular protective maintenance in the form of a red oxide or a bituminous paint. The galvanized sheets usually deteriorate as a result of the corrosion of the basic metal after the protective coating has failed. This also applies to the fixing screws and bolts.

Remedial work Galvanized iron corrugated sheets are comparatively easy to replace. New sheets should be given the necessary protective coats of paint before they are placed in position so that all the laps have complete protection. A final coat should then be applied to seal the laps.

Shingles and thatching

Shingle tiles are normally very desirable but if only slight deterioration occurs then a large area may need to be re-laid, as such shingle is nailed directly to the slat deck. Unprotected nails will corrode and allow the shingles to move. It is therefore necessary to use rust resistant nails with either aluminium or zinc coats. Shingle tiles require an underlay of building paper and the tiles themselves form an insulation layer.

Thatching is normally a durable roof covering with a long life. It has exceptionally good insulation and resistance to atmospheric conditions. However, it may become brittle with age and deteriorate slowly. Deterioration is then assisted by the natural habits and functions of bird life, but birds can be kept away by wire netting fitted over thatchings. Thatch repairs can be carried out, but re-thatching may be required. Special attention is required when forming flashings to abutments. This is normally done with mortar with oversailing bricks above.

Defective roofing details

Modern roofs contain a layer of underfelt which acts as a second water-proof layer. It may be absent in older types of roof, where torching will have been used.

Torching is an operation carried out after the roof covering is completed. It is a mixture of lime mortar with cow hair which is added as a binder. It was daubed behind each batten to fill the spaces between the slates or tiles and was an attempt to seal the roof space against wind and driving rain. When slates are disturbed the torching falls away, and a lot of trouble may be caused by drifting snow passing through the spaces between the tiles where torching is missing (*Figure 5.3(b)*). The result is that snow collects upon the ceiling, melts and percolates through it.

Valleys and roof gutters   Valleys and roof gutters can be of various pitches and made from materials such as lead and copper. Lead is a very heavy, durable material, but is subject to thermal movement, for which allowances must be made. Movement must not be restricted or else folds and cracks will appear. It will therefore expand noticeably on heating, and has a habit of 'creep' which is exhibited when, due to its own weight, it is unable to return to its original position on cooling. If this occurs on sloping surfaces, all fixings should be checked, as lead has the habit of tearing away from its fixings.

Copper is lighter in weight, of good durability and is an alternative to lead. It is virtually trouble free.

Both lead and copper may be affected by acidic products from moss and lichen growths that occur on roof surfaces, as mentioned above. Solutions of their chemical waste products in water drip on to metal gutters and the action causes the deterioration of lead, resulting in per-forations and leakages. These perforations may result in the general deterioration of the metal and its consequent reduction in thickness, and it may need to be replaced either totally or in part. In addition, any decayed boarding should be replaced, and all fixings checked and made good. Slates and tiles should have sufficient overlap to provide water-tight conditions. Small cracks and holes can, however, be repaired by soldering and replacing fixings.

Hips　There are various types of hip and they all require special treatments and close inspection.

Half-round hip tiles. These may become dislodged due to high winds that cause suction, or they may slip due to the corrosion of the hip iron base. The hip irons will require a protective bituminous or galvanized coat; if corroded they should be replaced. The hip tiles can be replaced or re-bedded in gauged mortar, and jointed and pointed to make them watertight.

Bonnet hips. These are made with a special angular tile and are bedded and neatly pointed in gauged mortar. The securing fixing nails may corrode and allow the tile to slip and the bedding mortar to fall away, in which case the tiles must be re-laid and secured with non-corrosive nails.

Close-mitred hips. Slates are cut and mitred together and a lead flashing is fitted beneath. Cut slates may break away and slip, or the flashings may become dislodged. The slates and flashings can be refixed or replaced as required, but the use of small pieces of slate should be avoided.

Lead-roll hips. Sheet lead is fitted over a wood roll and bedded over the roof covering on either side. The lead may be found to slip down owing to its weight, and it may also lift away from the roof surface during high winds. Many hips of this type are found on the older type of slated roof.

Ridge tiles　Ridge tiles may become dislodged and the bedding mortar may deteriorate. They may be either re-bedded and pointed with gauged mortar or replaced with new tiles of the correct angle.

Verges at gables　Verges at gables are normally bedded and fitted with mortar, but the mortar often deteriorates by general weathering and falls away. The verges must be re-built, filled solid and pointed with gauged mortar, or high winds may lift and displace the verge tiles or slates.

121

FLAT ROOFS

Flat roofs are defined as being those with slight falls of less than 10°. They comprise a standard base of timber or concrete decking to provide the falls and then a final weatherproof covering (*Figure 5.4(a)*). The coverings may be metal, bituminous felt or asphalt, and these are considered separately below.

Roof coverings

Metal

Metal roof coverings are usually in the form of copper, zinc, aluminium or lead sheets (*Figure 5.4(b)*). Copper provides a very satisfactory and

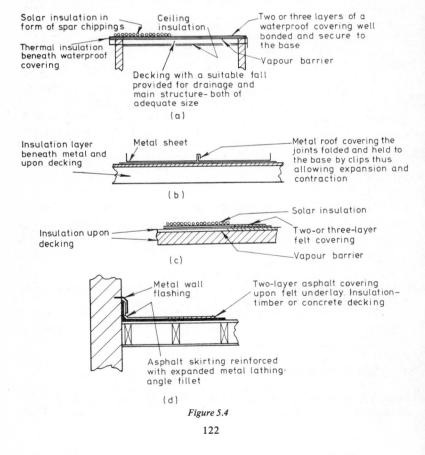

Figure 5.4

durable roof, but is costly. It is comparatively light in weight and is replacing lead on many public and similar buildings. The thickness of the sheet used is 24 gauge and it is laid in maximum widths of 675 mm. It is jointed by folded welts or drips, and is secured by fixing clips or tacks to the base.

Zinc provides a reasonably satisfactory roof, although it is a little less durable. It is much stiffer than copper and is laid in maximum widths of 850 mm and jointed with rolls and welted drips.

Aluminium, like zinc, provides a lightweight roof covering, but should be of the super-purity grade to give greater durability. It is a much softer metal, is laid in maximum widths of 530 mm and is jointed with folded rolls or seams and welted drips.

Lead is a costly covering that is little used today, but is still encountered during alterations and remedial work. It is very heavy and durable, but becomes brittle with age. Milled lead sheets are normally used for most roofs and are laid in maximum widths of 675 mm. They are jointed with drip and rolls. Cast lead sheets are often encountered on ancient buildings and are of greater thickness and weight, which gives better durability.

All sheet metals are subject to thermal expansion and contraction, and it is therefore essential that allowance for movement is provided. All joints must be made by folding or overlapping the metal to provide watertight connections, with the minimum of fixings being used to facilitate this movement. The covering metals are laid upon an underlay of felt or building paper and the surfaces are provided with adequate falls to enable any surface to drain towards outlets.

Bituminous felt

Bituminous felt is a modern and more economical type of covering. It consists of several layers bonded together with bituminous adhesive (*Figure 5.4 (c)*). A built-up felt roof constructed under ideal conditions and with good workmanship provides a satisfactory covering, but many things can go wrong and therefore it is not considered to be the best durable covering. A top protective layer of a mineral surface finish to combat the effects of solar heat, and a vapour barrier beneath to protect the covering from condensation, are needed.

Asphalt roof covering

Asphalt roof covering is a semi-plastic material which is applied in hot mastic form and laid in two layers (*Figure 5.4(d)*). It provides a jointless covering, of good durability. The provision of reinforcement at all angular joints and angle fillets is required, as these are positions where deterioration may occur. Some form of protection against condensation from beneath is also required. Laid by skilled craftsmen, this material has proved to be an economical medium-priced covering that is widely used.

Structural base

The structural base is the decking and the support to the waterproof covering. It can be made from either reinforced concrete or timber.

Reinforced concrete. This is concrete slab reinforced with mild steel bars of size and spacing depending on the span. The thickness of the concrete slab is also proportional to the span but, as a general rule, it equals one thirtieth of the span. Precast concrete beams can also be used to form the base and screeds of 25–50 mm in thickness are provided on the top surface to give adequate falls for rainwater drainage.

Timber base. This is composed of a decking supported by a system of beams. The system can be softwood joists, plywood or boxed beams, or latticed beams in metal or timber for larger spans. Each beam spans from the wall bearings and the size and depth varies according to the length of the span. Firring strips are fitted in order to give the decking the required falls. The decking is then fitted to the main structure, and it can be softwood boarding, plywood sheets, wood-wool slabs or ribbed metal sheets.

In the construction of flat roofs it is necessary to provide a vapour barrier in the form of a polythene sheet and an insulation layer immediately above it. The insulation layer is provided by either a quilt of fibreglass or by expanded polystyrene, or a similar material. The ceiling beneath is normally attached directly to the structure in the form of a lightweight plaster to the slab floors, or plasterboards fixed to timber joists. In the case of latticed beams, additional timber rails are fitted, to which are fixed fibre or gypsum ceiling tiles. In all cases a ceiling provides additional insulation. Special attention is required at eaves, gutters, kerbs, abutments and outlets in order to control and carry away surface water by suitable forms of drainage.

Defective metal roof coverings

Copper   Copper is the most durable of metal coverings. As is the case with most metals, it exhibits considerable thermal expansion, for which an allowance must always be made; it must not be restrained, as damage by thermal expansion is always a possibility. It is therefore important to keep a check on the sheets for splits and cracks and the welted joints and drips.

Another problem is the accumulation of atmospheric dust in the form of a silt around the various jointings of the sheets which may allow water to penetrate by capillary action and so must be cleared. The metal will also corrode by contact with the oxygen, water and other chemicals of the atmosphere. This chemical action produces a green patina on the metal surface which, if left undisturbed, will act as a protective coating, because as it gets thicker the more difficult it is for the chemicals to penetrate through to the pure copper.

Zinc Zinc is a rigid metal but is not widely used because its main defect is that it can be attacked by acid solutions that may be present in polluted atmospheres. Other acidic solutions will also attack it, such as that produced by wet oak. In addition, when zinc is in contact with other metals there is the probability of electrolytic action, which results in the sacrificial deterioration of the zinc.

Aluminium The best grade of super-purity aluminium is highly durable, but other grades are less so. Pure aluminium is a soft metal but the alloy used has a percentage of other metals added to it to give rigidity. This means that electrolytic action is a possibility and lower grade metal sheets may deteriorate. This also occurs when aluminium comes into contact with many other metals, and the aluminium is subject to sacrificial corrosion.

Lead Lead is a very durable and a very heavy metal. However, under certain conditions deterioration may occur, resulting in a breakdown of its watertight properties. One of the main problems of lead roofs occurs in situations where it is laid in sloping positions. Because of its weight it pulls on its fixings and may tear. This is aggravated by thermal expansion effects which cause 'creep'. Wherever thermal expansion occurs and the sheets are restrained at the edges, folds will appear in the sheet. These will remain in the raised position and with age they harden and become brittle. In time cracks will develop which will allow moisture to penetrate.

Joints which are in the form of drips to horizontal joints, or edges at right angles to the roof fall, and rolls to joints parallel to the roof fall, may become defective owing to either the movement of the lead sheet which causes the unfolding of the lead, or dirt and silt collecting about the joints, resulting in a source of capillary action.

Fixings in the form of nails and clips in another metal can cause problems because of electrolytic action. If the fixings are of copper, and lead sheet is being used, the effect is only slight, but it would be greater with other combinations.

The oxidation of the lead results in a white-grey coating of lead oxide, which, like copper, protects the metal from further attack. It should therefore be left undisturbed.

Remedial work

Small defects such as cracks and perforations can be repaired with solder joints or dots. If the perforations are spread over a wide area, then the replacement of a panel of sheet metal should be carried out. All metal sheets are fixed in small individual areas, which if defective can easily be renewed. Care should be taken when replacing a sheet, as the lifting of adjacent sheets may cause further defects such as cracks, folds, etc. Flat roofs require a minimum fall of 38 mm in 3 m. This may be insufficient and it will therefore be necessary to provide a greater fall in order to provide adequate drainage.

In the case of metal sheets that are affected by thermal expansion, it will be necessary to check that the sheet area is not excessive, and to make sure that the sheets are free to move and that the joints are correctly made. If there is evidence that electrolytic action has occurred, check for the presence of dissimilar metals, and either use similar metals by replacing one of them, or add a coating of bituminous paint between the dissimilar metals. In addition, check for corrosion or movement of fixings, joints and flashings, and renew or refix them as required. Collections of silt and rubble should be cleared and the affected area cleaned down.

When replacing sheet metal coverings, durability and cost must be considered carefully. Copper is the most durable but also the most costly. Lead is also durable but it is very costly owing to the high labour costs involved. It will probably be more economical to use either aluminium or asphalt as a replacement.

Other defective roof coverings

Bituminous felts   These are composed of built-up layers of felt bonded together with a bituminous adhesive. If correctly treated and maintained it provides a durable roof covering. The durability can be affected in the following ways:

Incorrect use of materials, e.g. unsuitable bonding adhesive and methods of laying felt (*Figure 5.5(a)*).

Neglecting to take precautions against the movement of the substructure, and the drying and shrinkage of the base due to thermal changes, which may result in cracks and tears.

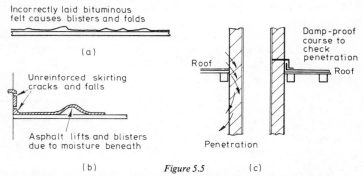

(a)

Unreinforced skirting cracks and falls

Asphalt lifts and blisters due to moisture beneath

Incorrectly laid bituminous felt causes blisters and folds

Roof

Penetration

Damp-proof course to check penetration

Roof

(b)   *Figure 5.5*   (c)

Moisture being entrapped beneath the felt layers as a result of excessive condensation. It will cause the uplifting of felt in the form of 'bubbling'.

Long term exposure, which may result in crazing and pitting. Eventually moisture will penetrate into the felt fibres, and deterioration will then be accelerated.

Excessive exposure will cause loss in flexibility. The felt is then liable to crack.

Pressure on blistered or folded surfaces will cause cracks and leakages.

Insufficient fall will cause deterioration on the flat surface, especially if the water is allowed to gather in pools, which may permit pimpling and blistering during summer and frost damage during winter. A greater fall than the minimum of 50 mm in 3 m is preferred so that positive drainage is provided.

A poor finish at upstands and at flashings at vertical wall abutments (*Figure 5.5(c)*).

Asphalt This is normally durable, impervious and satisfactory, especially when correctly laid with the necessary precautions. However, it can be affected in several ways:

Excessive moisture may collect beneath the impervious layers

127

(probably as a result of excess condensation) and may cause the lifting of the asphalt layers to give the 'bubbling' effect. Moisture which is entrapped and unable to escape will absorb heat and then expand, resulting in pressure on the asphalt and the formation of bubbles. These may develop and result in cracks and perforations (*Figure 5.5(b)*).

Thermal expansion may cause slight lifting.

Asphalt applied to vertical areas such as skirtings, upstands, kerbs, etc., requires special attention as it will fall away owing to its weight, and there is also a possibility of cracking and breaking along the horizontal joints.

Internal and external angles are areas where cracking may occur, and vertical and horizontal angles must be reinforced with angle fillets and expanded metal lathing in order to prevent any recurrence.

Asphalt skirtings may often be found to be defective, especially when they are turned into a horizontal mortar joint. This is more apparent with a timber-base roof structure. With timber bases there is always the likelihood of movement, and so asphalt should not be turned into wall joints but should be left vertical with a metal cover flashing fitted.

Asphalt may be affected by acids which come into contact with and attack the limestone filler.

Asphalt may be affected by contact with petrol, oils, fats and greases.

Remedial work

Bituminous felt roofing   It will be necessary to check the main areas of felt for any of the above defects, paying particular attention to joints, overlaps and edges of felt roofs such as turn-ups, turn-downs, abutments, kerbs and flashings. Small areas can be repaired with new felt layers, but care should be taken when lifting and jointing up to the existing felt. If the condition of the roof shows signs of general deterioration, then recovering the total area will be necessary.

The treatment of the edges may require the laying of new felt strips and re-jointing. Skirtings at turn-ups can be renewed, making sure that there is a good watertight joint with the wall. Felt will require to be wedged and pointed; good quality felts and bitumen compounds are essential, and it will require a high standard of workmanship. The final surface treatment is important: a layer of mineral chippings bonded to the base felt with cold bitumen will provide protection from solar heat.

Asphalt covering   Repairs to the asphalt layers are reasonably easy to effect. Asphalt melts when heated and small areas or cracks can be softened by applying hot asphalt to the deteriorated surface. The old surface can then be removed. The area is then cleaned out, prepared, and the new asphalt laid, special attention being given to the joint with the old surface. Both the old and the new will anneal together successfully.

In order to overcome excessive condensation beneath the asphalt layer, small paravents may be fitted at suitable intervals. These will allow expanding moist air to escape.

If the total area of asphalt is to be re-covered then precautions must be taken to keep the insulation dry by incorporating a vapour barrier beneath the insulation. Skirtings can easily be re-laid, a layer of expanded metal lathing and a thickening-out with an asphalt angle fillet being included. The inclusion of a suitable mineral finish provides some protection against solar effects.

ALL TYPES OF ROOFS—OTHER FEATURES

Roof lights provide high level lighting and are useful when side windows are not available. They are found in forms such as fixed-roof glazing, skylights that open, lantern lights and dome lights. Roof lights are fitted to both pitched and flat roofs and consist of glazing which is set in a frame and made watertight with the main roof structure (*Figure 5.6(a)*). The glazing will be in the form of sheet glass (not particularly suitable); cast plate glass or wired cast plate glass that is 6 mm thick (strong and suitable); or plastics sheets or domes (very durable). The glazing is first fitted into a structural frame and then set and bedded into prepared grooves or rebates with a mastic bedding compound and suitable metal fixing clips. A roof light is usually constructed with glazing bars supporting members and flashing.

Glazing bars   Glazing bars are required to support the glazing and can be made from softwood or hardwood, which are liable to decay, metal T-sections made in either galvanized iron or aluminium, or patent glazing bars in the form of a metal section encased with a lead covering (*Figure 5.6(b)*). The latter is the best type of bar in many respects and produces a very satisfactory and durable member.

Supporting members   Supporting members give support to the glazing bars in pitched roofs and are in the form of purlins and plates, which may be made of either timber or steel. Flat roofs require the provision of an upstand or kerbs (made of either timber or concrete) which has a watertight joint with the main roof.

Flashings   Flashings are required, and are fitted around the edges of glazing units. They are usually made of sheet lead which is well secured and either dressed or bedded in to the frame. In certain cases the whole of a roof surface may be glazed but the construction is similar to that of a roof light.

Defective roof lights and glazing

Roof lights and glazing are situated in inaccessible positions and exposed to the weather. They are often forgotten items until rain penetration occurs. Their shortcomings are as follows:

Timber forms are liable to decay and to weather, and metal forms are liable to corrode. Regular maintenance is therefore a necessity, especially in positions that are extremely exposed.

Lead coverings and flashings are subject to movement and the fixing nails often either lift due to metal expansion, or corrode, thus allowing the metal to fall away.

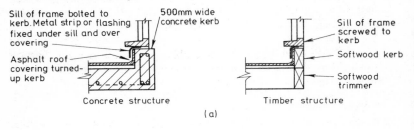

Sill of frame bolted to kerb. Metal strip or flashing fixed under sill and over covering

500mm wide concrete kerb

Sill of frame screwed to kerb

Asphalt roof covering turned-up kerb

Softwood kerb

Softwood trimmer

Concrete structure

Timber structure

(a)

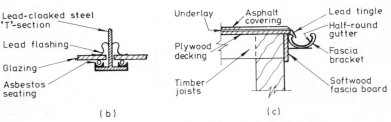

Lead-cloaked steel 'T'-section

Lead flashing

Glazing

Asbestos seating

Underlay

Asphalt covering

Lead tingle

Half-round gutter

Plywood decking

Fascia bracket

Timber joists

Softwood fascia board

(b)

(c)

Figure 5.6

Internal condensation, which at times may be excessive, may cause either decay or corrosion of parts of the frame.

All forms of opening lights require ironmongery, which is liable to corrode. This must be checked; if there is corrosion, it may be a source of danger if not corrected.

All forms of kerbs and upstands must be in a weatherproof condition.

Any faults will lead to leakages and water penetration. All fixings and bedding materials must be well maintained.

Glass may crack and allow water to penetrate; bedding putties may also deteriorate and allow moisture to penetrate the glazing bar and cause damage, as above. Patent glazing bars are normally trouble free, because putty is not used; they are, therefore, the best type to use.

Remedial work If the structural frame decays or corrodes it will need to be replaced either in part or completely. It must also be given an adequate protective coating of paint. Frames set into roof structures require protective flashings in order to keep the joint with the main roof watertight. If soakers, flashings and gutters are being renewed, part of the roof covering will have to be removed first. It should then be replaced and made good after the metal items have been fixed.

Roof glazing bars that have deteriorated will have to be replaced with sound bars, which are then given adequate coats of paint. Roof glazing can easily be removed and replaced, but care should be taken to provide adequate mastic bedding compounds; then the glazing is face sealed and left watertight. Opening lights are often a source of trouble. If they are found in any form of decay it is best to replace them with new lights and to use sound ironmongery of the non-corrosive type.

Adequate access to roof lights is also a necessary consideration to be borne in mind. It helps considerably to encourage the regular maintenance which is essential after remedial work has been completed.

Rainwater drainage

Rainwater must be collected and directed into gutters or outlets without hindrance or delay. All gutters require regular maintenance to avoid deterioration. The usual types of gutter and pipe are considered below.

Eaves gutters These can be half-round, ogee or box sections, in various materials such as cast iron, pressed steel, wood, asbestos, aluminium or plastics. They are supported by brackets secured to the fascia in the case of half-round sections, while the others are secured directly to a fascia board or wall plate (*Figure 5.6(c)*). Jointing is made by a bolt and linseed oil putty, red lead putty or mastic putty, the latter being the more durable. In the case of plastics guttering, joints are made with a pre-formed seal.

Parapet gutters These are placed behind parapet walls or kerbs and at the foot of sloping roofs (*Figure 5.2(a)*). They are made of timber and are lined with sheet copper or lead and asphalt. The outlets from the

131

gutter need to be carefully designed to permit free access and to prevent blockages by leaves, etc.

Rainwater pipes These are either round or square in section and are made in cast iron, aluminium, plastics or lead. They must be fixed securely to the wall and well jointed.

Defective rainwater drainage and its maintenance

Eaves gutters These require adequate protection in the form of paint or bitumen which must be applied to the base material. The re-application of protective paint at a later date is difficult as it is first necessary to remove all traces of moisture and silt before commencing to paint. This is often somewhat difficult and so the protective coating is not always as effective as it might be.

Cast iron gutters. Gutters made in cast iron may corrode, become perforated or crack as the result of normal deterioration and the action of water freezing to ice. Jointing materials often fail and require rejointing; fixing brackets may deteriorate by corrosion and will need to be replaced. Gutters may have insufficient falls and as a result they may silt up. This may be rectified by re-fixing the gutters to correct falls.

Plastics eaves gutters. This is the type that is in current use. They are non-corrodible and need no maintenance other than to keep them clear of silt. Jointing insert seals may deteriorate over a period of time and require replacing.

Asbestos gutters. These are usually used with asbestos covered roofs. They are normally durable and trouble free, but they may crack. In this case they will need to be renewed and jointed with a mastic jointing compound.

Wood gutters. These may be encountered in older types of properties. They may be made of either plain timber fitted on timber bearers, or lined with lead. Timber is liable to decay and requires regular maintenance in the form of paint or bitumen coatings. Lead lined gutters require similar treatment; the lining provides the watertight condition and if it fails, deterioration will follow.

Parapet gutters These can be lined with lead, copper or asphalt. They must be well constructed and jointed, laid to the correct falls and kept free from silt and vegetation (*Figure 5.2(a)*). Metal surfaces may corrode and deteriorate and it is therefore necessary to check all joints, angles, etc., for faults, particularly as perforation of metal may occur owing to attack by the chemicals in the waste products of moss and lichen growths. Thermal expansion may also occur. This may eventually cause the lifting and cracking of the metal linings. Asphalt reacts in a similar manner to that described on page 128. Gutter leakages may result in the decay of the timber structures beneath, which will have to be replaced. Outlets must be kept clear of all potential sources of blockage, particularly fallen leaves; a wire guard will be of assistance.

Rainwater pipes   These are the pipes that convey the large volumes of roof water to storm drains at ground level. They must be constructed of sound materials and must also be well maintained in a watertight condition. Regular maintenance is essential as small defects may develop and cause other defects in adjacent structures and materials.

Deterioration and failure may be caused by:

The fracture of the rainwater pipe (especially in the case of cast iron and asbestos pipes) may be caused by impact or water freezing to ice. This results in splits in the pipe or collar.

Corrosion of metal pipes (particularly cast iron pipes) as a result of a lack of protective paint.

Pipes becoming filled and blocked with silt and leaves at the base, bends, and in rainwater heads and outlets. This causes water to overflow or to leak from joints, which will then cause saturated walls.

Cast or drawn lead pipes are normally damaged by being compressed or dented. This may result in blockages within the pipe.

Regular maintenance in the form of painting, jointing, and the clearance of silt and blockages is essential. In addition, it is necessary to maintain free and adequate outlets from gutters and free discharge to drainage systems at ground level.

Pipes can easily be removed and replaced as required, and repairs are normally effected by replacing damaged pipes with new ones. When fitting pipes it is best to keep them clear of the wall for subsequent maintenance purposes. This can be done by using bobbins, standaway lugs or holder bars. It is often found that metal gutters or pipes can be economically superseded by p.v.c. gutters or pipes, as p.v.c. is more durable and gives a longer life, virtually free from deterioration.

Other roof features

Insulation layer

An insulation layer is a requirement that is incorporated into the modern roof structure but it may be absent in older structures. In order to maintain the required thermal conditions, existing insulation layers must be maintained. If none exist then one should be incorporated either by providing a layer of glass fibre or expanded polystyrene, or laying cork or vermiculite granules upon the ceiling between the joists.

Vapour barrier

A vapour barrier may be required in order to control excessive condensation. Placed beneath the insulation, it will maintain dry conditions and keep moisture away from underneath the impervious layer in flat roofs. It is essential to maintain this layer and if one is absent it could be incorporated as repairs are carried out.

Chimney stacks

Chimney stacks are often a neglected part of the building, and they are situated in very exposed positions. Inspection often reveals the following:

Failure of mortar joints and deterioration of the bricks.
Surface deterioration only.
A serious failure with the whole structure in a state of collapse and only remaining in one piece by virtue of the weight of the bricks. In addition, the bricks and joints will have perished and weathered.
Flashings around the base of the stack and the joint with the roof may not be watertight; this is quite common (*Figure 5.5(c)*).

In addition, the chimney pots themselves may not be safe. The causes of these defects are general weathering, atmospheric pollution, impurities and condensation within the chimney flue and sulphate attack of the brickwork. The necessary courses of action for repair could be one or more of the following:

Take down and rebuild the stack. This can be either the complete stack from roof level, or the top courses.
Rake out defective brick joints and point either the whole or part as may be required.
Renew or reset chimney pots. In either case a sound base is required for the pot to be reset upon. Finally flaunch around with fine concrete.
In the case of sulphate attack it will be necessary to rebuild the affected stack using bricks of low sulphate content and a gauged mortar. It will help to improve the situation if the flues are lined.

If the stack is affected by thermal expansion caused by excess heat in the flue (especially if either half-brick thick walls are used or they are unlined) then rebuilding will help to solve the problem, using one-brick thick walls and lining the flue, either with a flexible flue liner or rebated clay liner.

Fit and make watertight metal flashings at the base. Bevelled mortar fillets around the base are not good practice and it is better to replace them by lead soakers and cover flashings (*Figure 5.3(c)*).

Bibliography

Building Research Establishment Digests, HMSO:

Series 1, No. 116, 'Roof Drainage'
Series 2, No. 8, 'Built-up Felt Roofing'
Series 2, No. 51, 'Development in Roofing'
Series 2, No. 99, 'Wind Loading'
Series 2, No. 101, 'Wind Loading'
Series 2, No. 117, 'Condensation in the Design of Factory Roofs'

B.R.E. Research Paper No. 23, 'Condensation in Asbestos Roofs'

CHAPTER 6

FLOORS

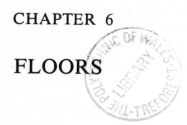

Floors are that part of a building upon which the activities are carried on for which the building was built. These activities differ considerably from domestic, office and commercial, to light and heavy industrial operations and public and social uses. Each floor therefore requires a type of surface suitable for its particular use. Choice of floor finish depends upon the type of building, and the purpose and use of the floor, together with its area and setting.

It is necessary to consider the construction of the structural base and the preparation to receive the finished surface. The success and performance depends upon each and all of these points. Structural bases are of different forms for various types of floors, and the construction of each is of prime importance. The base requires adequate strength, soundness and stability, and must be capable of resisting the many detrimental conditions that may arise.

GROUND FLOORS

Solid ground floors

The base of solid ground floors is normally of concrete laid upon a hard-core bed, carefully laid and levelled (*Figures 6.1(a)* and (*b*)). Such floors are subject to:

Rising moisture, causing damp conditions and invariably affecting the floor finishes. This will be controlled by using a suitable damp-proof membrane of polythene sheet laid beneath the concrete bed (*Figure 6.1(c)*).

Chemical action. This is the effect of sulphate salts on the Portland cement, such as those that rise from the ground clays or ashes (*Figure 6.1(d)*). A polythene membrane ought to prevent this contact.

Soluble salts cause efflorescence or crystallization of salts near to the floor surface.

Movement, causing cracks which allow deterioration (*Figure 6.1(e)*).

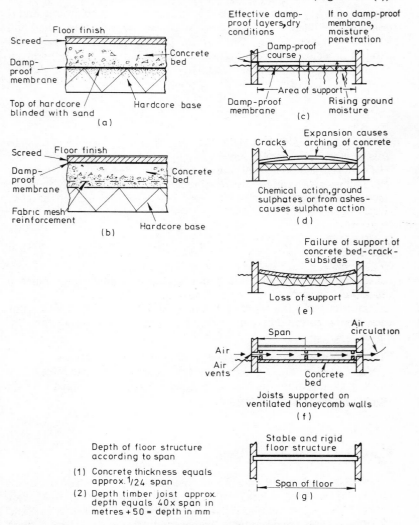

Figure 6.1   (a) Structural base—solid floor; (b) Reinforced base; (c) Rising moisture; (d) Chemical action; (e) Failure of support; (f) Ventilated ground floors; (g) Upper floors

In order to prevent these faults the floor should be constructed with an adequate hardcore bed and a concrete base with a damp-proof membrane.

Hardcore bed   The hardcore bed is laid upon excavated ground and is composed of clean broken brick or quarry waste, well compacted and levelled in thickness of 100–150 mm. The top must be covered with sand in order to provide a surface to receive a polythene damp-proof membrane. The hardcore should be free of sulphates and other harmful substances. For this reason old crushed brickwork should never be used.

Concrete base   This requires a thickness of 100–150 mm according to area and use, and should have a strength suitable for most purposes. The concrete should be well compacted and levelled, with a taper finish. The inclusion of fabric mesh reinforcement will considerably improve the tensile strength of the base and prevent possible movement cracks.

Damp-proof membrane   This may be applied above or below the concrete bed, and can consist of:

A polythene sheet of 1000 gauge, or bitumen paper laid upon the hardcore.

Bitumastic solution applied hot or cold, latex emulsion, asphalt or epoxy pitch compound, any of which may be applied to the concrete surface.

The membrane must have 100 per cent cover without flaws.

Many modern floors incorporate the above requirements but many existing ground floors are deficient, and remedial work must provide what is required in each case.

Suspended timber ground floors

Suspended timber ground floors are composed of softwood or hardwood boarded floors supported by softwood joists that span between and upon supporting walls (*Figure 6.1(f)*). Timber in these situations is liable to decay. For this reason timber and this type of floor are dealt with more fully towards the end of this chapter.

UPPER FLOORS

Upper floors can be constructed of concrete slabs or beams. They may be cast *in situ* or be precast, and span between structural walls or beams. Their performance relies upon their initial design being correct, the depth or thickness being in relation to the span and the load supported by the floor (*Figure 6.1(g)*). If the design is not correct it may lead to movement and vibration during use.

Preparation of structural base

In order to apply finishes to the base it is necessary to prepare it with a suitable surface. This is done by the application of a screed. This is applied to concrete surfaces in order to provide a level, hard and smooth surface ready to receive various floor finishes. Some finishes require a high quality surface, while with others this is not so important. Screeds need to be of adequate thickness according to type and must resist the liability to crack or craze, and provide a surface suitable for satisfactory bonding of surface finishes.

Types of screeds

Monolithic screed   This is a 1:3 cement and sand mix, laid upon the concrete base whilst still green, i.e. within three hours of being laid. It will therefore bond and become an integral part of the concrete.

Superimposed screed   This is a 1:3 cement and sand mix laid upon the concrete after the concrete has dried; this may be some considerable time later. Precautions are needed in order to obtain an adequate bond between the wet screed and the dry base. This can be achieved either by using a bonding agent or by the wetting and the application of wet cement slurry to the base.

Floating screeds   Three types are available.

(1) *Synthetic anhydrite screed*. This is a fine white powder by-product of hydrofluoric acid manufacture. It acts as a cement and is mixed with a fine aggregate, an activating agent and water. It is laid in 25 mm thick layers as a floating screed upon oiled paper or polythene sheet. The screed dries quickly and forms layers having flexible strength

139

with negligible shrinkage, and because it floats is isolated from any effects of the main base.

(2) *Latex based screed.* This is composed of synthetic latex liquid and cementitious powder mixed with fine aggregates to form a resilient screed which can be laid in thin layers, having good compressive and tensile strength. It dries quickly and hardens early, and is also resistant to mild acidity and alkalinity.

(3) *Epoxy resin screed.* This is composed of compounded epoxy resin liquid with a chemical hardener and a powdered component of graded quartzite sands or silica flour. This screed has a high compressive strength and good chemical resistance.

Screeds may deteriorate and can be damaged in several ways which may cause loss of bond or affect the finished covering. Damage to the surface usually occurs after the screed has been laid and before the finish is applied, either by workmen or by weather conditions. Over-trowelling by the laying operatives will cause weak friable surfaces which are liable to crack and craze. Poor quality screeds have weak strength, which causes dusting of the surface, and they are easy to damage. Loss of adhesion and bond with the main base will cause cracking and possible lifting of the screed. Rising moisture in the screed will affect the bond of the floor finish. High spots cause wear of the floor finish, so that a smooth, flat and hard surface will help to reduce wear.

Levelling compounds may be used to level out any variations in the screed surface and so provide good flat surfaces. They may be:

Casein based compounds
Polymer based compounds
Latex cement compounds.

Screeds in which heating cables are embedded will need to be strongly bonded to the base, care being taken to reduce drying shrinkage, or in the case of floating screeds to be laid in sufficient thickness, i.e. a minimum of 40 mm.

Suspended timber upper floors

Timber joists or beams span between structural walls with the depth of the joist being relative to the span and load supported. The joists require cross-bracing in order to stiffen the centre line of the joists and prevent undue vibrations. Timber in upper floors may also be attacked by deterioration and decay, and this subject will be dealt with towards the end of this chapter.

FLOOR FINISHES

There are a wide variety of floor finishes available, each suitable for particular uses. It is very necessary to make a careful selection of suitable material for the position in the structure and the use to which it will be put.

Selection of finish

Resistance to wear

The type of traffic that a particular surface is required for is an important consideration when selecting the type of finish—e.g. whether normal footwear in a commercial situation is to be expected, or heavy footwear in an industrial situation. Therefore resistance to the type of wear governs the type of finish to be used and the maintenance likely to be required.

Appearance

The appearance of the finished floor surface depends upon the initial choice of material and the maintenance given afterwards. The frequency of cleaning and polishing the surface will govern the good or bad appearance of the surface. The type of polish and seals used depend upon the amount and type of traffic. It is also necessary to have high maintenance standards in order to retain the good appearance.

Floors often receive damage during the construction period; dirt, grit and similar debris are walked into the finished surface causing scratches and general deterioration. For this reason the laying of the floor finish should be delayed as long as possible, and then if necessary it should be protected by sheeting until the job has been completed.

Floor finishes may be classified as follows:

Jointless floorings, having a continuous surface without joints
Sheet flooring laid in sheets with minimum joints.
Tiles and blocks with numerous and regular joints.

Within each group there are a number of alternative materials, several of which are discussed below. Some are modern but others are of the older type which the surveyor will meet up with in maintenance work.

Jointless flooring

Asphalt Mastic asphalt flooring, composed of natural rock asphalt with limestone aggregates, is available in varying colours of red, brown and black. Asphalt provides a waterproof base, dustless, jointless, impervious to moisture movement and easy to clean. Several grades are produced for floor finishes, such as acid resisting, industrial grade and one grade for normal use.

The durability of asphalt is normally good and it is able to take traffic and loads. However, it will soften with prolonged contact with grease, fats and oils; it may also be affected by acids, alkalis, alcoholic liquids, syrups and sugar solutions, and tend to become slippery when wet. Asphalt coverings need to be kept separated from the base to overcome the effect of movement, using a membrane of black sheathing felt or something similar, especially on timber, porous or open textured bases or similar movable bases. If affected by moisture beneath, then asphalt may bubble up in certain parts (*Figures 6.2(a)* and (*b*)).

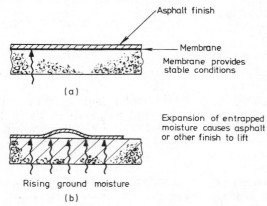

Figure 6.2   (a) Preparation; (b) Defects to impervious floor covering

Asphalt is easy to repair and joint. An application of heat will soften it for easy removal, and new layers are easy to joint with complete annealing. Asphalt should be cleaned by washing with soap and warm water, and then with clean water, followed by polish of aqueous emulsion type.

Pitch mastic floor finish   This material is very similar to mastic asphalt in effects and conditions.

Cement bitumen   This is composed of cement, pigment and a hard aggregate gauged with bitumen emulsion. It is obtained in a variety of colours. When laid, a priming coat of bitumen is applied to the base, to which a layer of cement bitumen is laid cold and trowelled level and smooth and damped down to cure.

This type of floor provides good resistance to abrasion, will not dust and is resistant to moisture; there is a tendency for oils, greases and fats to soften the bitumen unless it is protected by synthetic resins. For maintenance, it should be washed with warm water and soap and then clean water, followed by a seal and emulsion polish.

Cement wood   This is composed of Portland cement, limestone, sand aggregates and sawdust with added pigments for colour. When laid and dried, apply a surface treatment of linseed oil or wax, or seal and polish with emulsion polish. It will not dust, but may be affected by chemical solutions.

It should be washed with warm water and soap, then sealed and polished with emulsion polish.

Fleximer and rubber latex cement flooring   This is composed of latex or resinous binder, a setting agent of hydraulic cement, pigment for colouring, aggregate or filler of fine chippings of granite, or granules of cork, wood, spar or marble. It provides a good hard flexible floor which will not dust or chip. It is resistant to oils and grease and has wood wearing qualities. It requires regular cleaning and polishing.

Magnesium oxychloride   Magnesite composition floors are composed of magnesite, a filler, and solution of chloride. Fillers may be wood-flour, sawdust, ground silica powdered limestone, or powdered asbestos. They provide a good hard surface which may be oiled or waxed. It may be affected by chemical solutions, damp conditions, and the composition itself may cause detrimental effects on metal work. Regular cleaning or scrubbing with warm water are necessary.

Polymer floor   This is composed of polyester resin and special Portland cement with water. It provides a tough, smooth and non-slip surface, which is laid *in situ* upon a new or an old, prepared and sound base surface, in thickness of 5 mm.

Polymer floors will resist damp conditions or oil contamination and offer resistance to abrasion, impact and chemicals.

Granolithic paving   This may be laid as a monolithic or as a separate layer, and is composed of Portland cement and fine rock chipping

143

aggregate in a 1:3 mix, with the addition of an accelerator in the form of calcium chloride. Granolithic is laid in layers 25–50 mm thick and requires to be well bonded to the base concrete; its drying needs to be controlled with adequate curing. If the bond is inadequate or uncontrolled drying takes place, then cracking and lifting of the paving will occur.

A surface abrasive of carborundum powder sprinkled upon the surface and lightly trowelled in, gives harder wearing and a non-slip surface. Surface treatment of hardened surfaces may be carried out by applying sodium silicate in two or three applications and will harden the surface for better wear and reduce possible dusting.

Terrazzo   This is composed of Portland cement and crushed marble chippings of 1:2 mix in layers 50 mm thick. Terrazzo provides a surface of high resistance to abrasion, is easy to clean and is unaffected by water. Surfaces may crack or craze due to differential shrinkage in the terrazzo and the screed base; this may be prevented by:

Limiting the area of paving by dividing the area with metal strips.
Controlling the water–cement ratio when mixing.
Ensuring the aggregate is of correct size; dust and fine particles must not be used.
Controlling drying during the initial drying period and curing stage.

Periodic washing with water is necessary, with occasional use of fine abrasives followed by washing. Soap must not be used.

Sheet flooring

Sheet flooring needs to be laid on a well prepared base of good level surface; levelling compounds may be used to level out any defective areas before any of the following types are laid.

Linoleum   Linoleum is composed of oxidized linseed oil fluxed with resin and gums, pigments, mineral fillers of powdered cork and wood flour; these are pressed upon a canvas or bituminous felt paper backing. Linoleum is laid upon a screed surface or boarded surface with an underlay of hardboard, plywood or bituminous felt paper.

Cork carpet   This is composed of compressed cork formed on a canvas backing and laid upon a similar surface to linoleum. It provides a good sound insulating layer, but the surface, being soft, may easily be damaged with wear, dust and dirt; it therefore requires regular cleaning and surface treatment.

P.V.C. (polyvinyl chloride)   This is supplied in sheet form in thin thicknesses that require a perfect, flat and smooth surface on which to be laid; any faults in the screed will show on the finished p.v.c. surface. It provides a very hard-wearing surface and joints may be welded to give a continuous area. It is flexible and impervious to water, oils, greases, petrol, alcohols and chemicals.

It should be washed and cleaned with soap and water, then sealed and liquid emulsion polish applied.

Rubber   This is in sheet form, composed of natural rubber and filler compounds, and laid similarly to p.v.c. It is affected by oils, fats and grease, causing swelling and softening. Rubber surfaces become slippery when wet. Cleaning with damp cloths is necessary, then polishing with emulsion type polishes.

Tile and block flooring

Tile and block finishes require a solid base in all cases, a flat surface for heavier tiles and a smooth, flat and level surface for thinner tiles.

Thermoplastic tiles   These are formed of asbestos or mineral fibres with thermoplastic binder and pigments for colouring. They are 225 × 225 mm with a thickness of 3 or 4 mm and are laid in bitumastic adhesive which is itself a waterproof layer. The tiles are available in various grades such as acid resistant, greaseproof, oil resistant, and for industrial floors.

P.V.C. (vinyl tiles)   These are similar to sheet forms of either asbestos based tiles or flexible tiles; they provide a very good wearing surface, easy to clean and maintain. They are bonded to the base surface with mastic adhesive.

Cork tiles   Cork tiles are of granulated and shaved cork, compressed hydraulically under heat into tiles. The cork particles can be bonded together with either natural gums and resins of the bark, or synthetic resins. They are manufactured in sizes of 300 × 300 mm and 6–12 mm thick and are laid upon screeds with a bitumen adhesive. They have a good wearing quality, do not dust, and may be treated with a surface sealing coat, and emulsion polish. They may be affected by grease.

Cork tiles should be washed frequently so as to prevent dirt and dust being embedded in depth. After washing they should be sealed and polished with a liquid emulsion.

Linoleum and rubber tiles These are similar to the respective sheet forms but are in tiles.

Wood fibre tiles These are a composition of wood fibre chippings bonded with synthetic resins of the urea and phenolic type, pressed and cured, and then seasoned. They are laid with hot or cold mastics of bitumen or latex, and the surface is then sanded; this is followed by a sealer or filler coat which is waxed and polished.

Brick pavings Floor bricks are 50 mm thick and made of vitreous or semivitreous well burnt clay in several colours, and sizes 220 × 110 mm. The bricks are hard-wearing, moisture resistant, acid resisting and durable. They are laid, bedded and jointed in cement mortar upon a concrete base. They are normally used for external pavings and for industrial uses. If repairs are needed they are easily replaced.

Clay quarry tiles Clay tiles are of various qualities, some hard others less durable, each having a vitreous skin that provides the hard-wearing qualities, and which if worn away may allow wear and disintegration to occur. They are of 150 × 150 mm and 225 × 225 mm sizes, and with plain, ribbed or shot faced finishes; they are laid upon a concrete base bedded and pointed in cement mortar. Clay tiles are resistant to acids, oils, heat and water. Shrinkage of the concrete base may result in tiles lifting from the base; other failures may be due to loss of adhesion.

Concrete tiles These are made with various face finishes and are formed with coloured matrix, and marble or other such aggregates. They are similar to terrazzo tiles and normally inferior to them.

Ceramic mosaics Small squares of ceramic are laid upon a screeded base with cement or mastic adhesive; they are decorative but not hard-wearing.

Marble   Natural marble in tile or slab form is cut to thicknesses of 18, 25 or 30 mm, the top surface being polished or finished with gritted or sanded surface. It forms a very decorative and durable surface in a wide range of colours.

Marbles are laid, bedded and jointed in cement mortar upon a concrete base; they have good resistance to abrasion, oils and fats, and alkalis, and are impervious to water. They should be washed with soap and water; powders should not be used.

Terrazzo tiles   These are pavings in 225 mm or 300 mm squares and 20–25 mm thick. They are formed with coloured marble pieces set in and upon a concrete backing. They are bedded upon a concrete base or screed with cement mortar and form a hard-wearing and durable surface. They should be washed regularly.

Slate   Natural slate can be cut to various sizes and thicknesses with ground or polished surfaces, then laid upon a screed and bedded and jointed in cement mortar. Slate is normally hard-wearing and durable; it may be washed, waxed or treated with a sealer which helps to preserve colour and surface. Oils and greases leave stains upon the surface. Regular cleaning and washing are necessary.

Natural stone   Various sandstones, limestones or granite may be used as pavings in 50 mm thickness and bedded and jointed in cement mortar upon a concrete base. The durability of stone varies according to quality; normally it has good resistance to wear, chipping and movement, and to oils but not acids. Rising moisture will cause efflorescence and staining.

Cast stone is a mixture of ground stone with white cement to form the face, and coarse aggregate concrete as the mass; the whole is hydraulically pressed into moulds, then cured. These stones are similar to natural stone.

Regular cleaning and washing are necessary to keep the stone in a satisfactory condition; an application of silicone solution will harden the surface for better wear.

Metal tiles   These may be steel plates of 10 gauge steel stamped into shapes to form the surface of concrete floors. They are pressed into the surface of newly laid concrete and form the finished surface of industrial floors. They are hard-wearing, resisting all forms of wear, impact and abrasion.

An alternative are metal paving tiles of cast iron, 300 mm square and 25 mm thick, with plain, studded or ribbed surface, laid upon a concrete base. The tiles are forced down into a bed of cement mortar which also fills the joints. Metal tiles are impervious to oils, grease and weak acids, they withstand various temperatures, vibrations and heavy impact. The main use is in works connected with heavy industries.

Remedial work

In all cases of remedial work the selection of a suitable material for the finish is important. Correct choice gives better life, poor choice gives a limited life before deterioration.

A deteriorated surface will need to be either repaired or replaced; if the deterioration only covers a small area, then repairs may be carried out, but often it may be better to replace the whole area. This can prove to be more satisfactory from the aesthetic point of view and can also be more economical. When it is necessary to replace a surface finish then consideration should be given to the floor use, i.e. the type and intensity of wear. It is possible that an alternative material from that previously used will give a better surface and be more economical. Make sure that any treatment or repair to the base is carried out in the first place, then build up for and provide a suitable surface to receive the finish. At all times check for possible moisture penetration, and make provisions for its exclusion from between the floor base and the actual floor finish.

Maintenance

In order to maintain the good qualities and appearance of the floor surface, care and maintenance are essential. New floor surfaces require to be maintained from the time they are laid; if materials are well selected and correctly laid in all respects it will eliminate trouble when in use.

It should be borne in mind that the finished surface of a material is always the more durable and resistant to many effects; if this surface is allowed to deteriorate then the layer beneath will generally deteriorate more quickly. It is therefore important that the initial durable surface is well maintained. Much will depend upon the type of traffic, whether it is light or heavy, the degree and concentration of wear, and the actual material.

Wear is caused by dirt, dust or grit being walked into the material surface, causing indentations and scratches which will generally destroy surfaces to varying depths, or by friction over the surface.

Maintenance requirements

The initial finished surface and final treatment are most important, and the nature and effect of aftercare depends much on the initial preparations. The success of maintenance will depend a lot on the frequency of cleaning and treatment, which comprises sweeping, cleaning and washing, surface sealing and polishing, plus any periodic maintenance that may be required. The sealed and polished surface should be well maintained, otherwise the surface treatment deteriorates and wear will be upon the actual material. If surface protection can be maintained the wear is of the seal and polish only. General cleanliness is required for safety and health reasons; slippery surfaces cause hazards to the user and must be prevented.

General maintenance   In considering maintenance programmes for floor surfaces it will be found that material surfaces fit into groups:

Hard surfaces, such as concrete, clay tiles, terrazzo or marble; these have good, hard and resilient safe surfaces which require regular sweeping and washing with warm water, followed by buffing.

Composition surfaces, such as cementwood, asphalt or pitchmastic and other compositions; these require regular sweeping and washing with warm water and soap, followed by coating with linseed oil or wax and then buffing.

Plastics surfaces, such as thermoplastics, p.v.c. linoleum, fleximer, etc.; these require regular sweeping and washing with soapy water, followed by coating with emulsion polish and then buffing. Rubber surfaces need to be cleaned with a wet cloth and then emulsion polish added.

Timber surfaces, being of porous surfaces in various forms, require daily cleaning by sweeping; the use of a sweeping powder helps to absorb and collect dirt. The occasional application of emulsion polish which can be regularly buffed helps to protect the surface.

Cork surfaces. These encourage a dirty appearance and require regular cleaning and surface sealing, followed by emulsion polish. An occasional light sanding of the surface may be found necessary, to be followed by a sealing coat and then emulsion polish.

Floor finishes last many years provided they are given regular care and maintenance. Good initial preparation assists good maintenance, and the use of correct sealing and polishing coat is essential.

Floor seals

Sealing coats penetrate the surface layers and will reinforce the material fibres and produce even wear. Regular maintenance of the surface will then be easier.

Before sealing it is necessary to ensure that a moderately good surface exists that will take the treatment. It is necessary to eliminate all traces of wax, grease and oil; it may require sanding in order to provide a suitable surface. The floor seal should then make a good hard surface upon which the polish may be applied.

Oleo-resinous seal　This is a mixture of essential oils, resins, solvent and driers, being a traditional seal which is reasonably easy to apply.

Plastics type seal　This is a synthetic type that dries by evaporation of the solvent and chemical action. It is more modern and is more durable. There are two varieties:

Urea formaldehyde seal, which provides deep penetration.
Polyurethane seal, a hard surface seal.

They are suitable for applying to wood, wood compositions, cork, magnesite, etc.; they should not be applied to concrete surfaces and are harmful to asphalt, p.v.c., thermoplastics and rubber, due to the action of the solvent. They are not recommended for use on terrazzo, marble, quarry tiles or stone, where they are unable to achieve satisfactory penetration.

Water-based seal　The water-based seal is the new modern seal of acrylic polymer resins, and plasticizer, suitable for most material surfaces but not timber type materials.

Silicate dressings　Silicate dressings are applied to concrete surfaces for the purpose of hardening and preventing dusting of the surface; they can be applied to concrete, stone and other such materials, usually in two or three dressings.

Polishes

Polish acts as a buffer coat which takes all the wear and protects the actual floor surface. It is based mainly on:

Natural waxes: beeswax or carnauba wax.

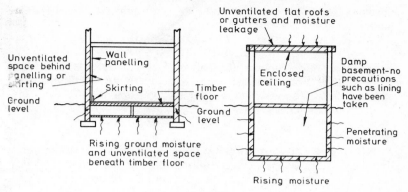

Figure 6.3

the moisture content of the timber, its rate of moisture absorption and the atmospheric effects of rain, sun and drying winds. Other causes of deterioration and failure are fungal decay, insect attack, general weathering, wear and tear (e.g. abrasion) and fire.

Fungal decay

Fungal decay occurs in most timbers, particularly sapwood and timber in damp and unventilated situations. There are several types.

Dry rot (Merulius lacrymans)   This is the most serious form of decay and is particularly rapid in its development. It attacks both the cellulose content and the lignin structure. The timber becomes brown in colour, dry and powdery and results in the cuboidal splitting of the timber (*Figure 6.4*).

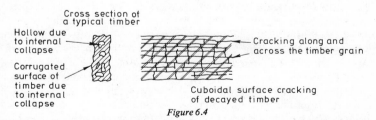

Figure 6.4

Cellar fungus (Conidiophora cerebella)   This is a wet rot which feeds on damp timbers. It requires considerably more moisture than dry rot, and is found in cellars and damp positions. The appearance is of dark brown strands over the timber surface, and thin olive-green fruiting bodies.

Pore fungus (*Poria vaporaria*)   This is a wet rot that feeds upon damp timbers. It is able to stand extreme temperature conditions. The appearance is of snow-white fan-shaped rootlets and fluffy areas forming upon the timber surface.

Brown wet rot   This is normally found in timbers that remain continuously saturated, particularly out-of-doors in wet climates (*Figure 6.5*). It is slow in its development and is light brown in colour.

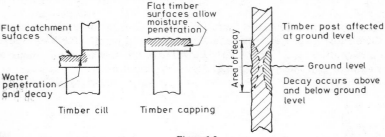

Figure 6.5

Fungi require food for development. This is obtained from the cell structures in the form of cellulose and lignin contents. They also require moisture, a suitable temperature, oxygen and still air conditions if they are to develop and survive.

They start life in the form of a minute spore which remains dormant until conditions are suitable for development. They grow in the form of a system of hair-like roots which travel throughout the cellular structure of the timber. They consume the cellulose contents of the cells, breaking them down to carbon dioxide and water. During development the root systems grow in size up to about 8 mm in diameter, and dry rot forms into layers of mycelia. Fungi develop spore-bearing fruiting bodies called sporophores. These produce millions of fine spores which can be carried about by air currents over a wide area. They can lie dormant ready for further development when conditions are suitable.

Under suitable conditions the decay will develop and spread unchecked. It can grow to alarming and serious proportions, particularly dry rot, which often causes the collapse of timber structures. Conditions that are essential for the development of fungal growth are dampness, poor ventilation and adequate temperatures. Therefore, in order to prevent an attack, one or more of these conditions must be removed or

154

prevented. However, good ventilation, adequate temperatures and dry conditions are obviously essential requirements in almost all buildings.

Consequently, it is necessary to be able to detect the presence of fungal decay, and a few points that will assist in identification are the appearance, colour and surface condition of the timber, e.g. irregular and discoloured surfaces. The surfaces should be tested with a knife for soundness in depth, and by tapping for hollowness. In addition, check with a moisture meter for dampness, smell for decay and look for fruiting bodies and spores. Early detection can prevent widespread damage, and further reading on the subject from titles listed in the Bibliography at the end of this chapter is recommended.

Sap stains   Another form of decay not included in the previous group is sap stain. This is a blue discolouration of freshly cut softwoods. It occurs when unseasoned timbers are close-stacked in unventilated conditions such as during shipping. It is a mould which develops under moist and warm conditions. However, with the continuation and completion of seasoning, further development stops and it is then inactive. It simply gives rise to discolouration and causes no structural defect.

Beetle attack

Beetles of various types breed and live within the cellular structure of timber and cause destruction by eating the cellulose and lignin contents. The more common timber beetles are described below.

Furniture Beetle. This is a small beetle that is common and very widespread. It attacks seasoned softwood and hardwood, normally in dry conditions. The bore holes are about 2–3 mm in diameter, and although smaller than some, nevertheless cause extensive damage to both structural and finishing timbers (*Figure 6.6(a)*).

Death Watch Beetle. This is a larger beetle that normally attacks hardwood and causes considerable damage to structural timbers, especially those in open church roofs and similar properties (*Figure 6.6(b)*). Destruction can go undetected for considerable periods. The bore holes are 4–5 mm in diameter, and cause extensive damage, especially where the timber is affected by slight decay.

Powder Post Beetle (Lyctus Beetle). This is a larger beetle than the furniture beetle but is much less common. It attacks mainly the sapwood of freshly seasoned structural timber (*Figure 6.6(c)*). The bore holes are about 3–4 mm in diameter.

House Longhorn Beetle. This is the largest of this group. It is a very destructive pest but is found only in south east England and on the Continent (*Figure 6.6(d)*). The bore holes are about 6–8 mm in diameter, and consequently considerable damage occurs, mainly in the softwood of roof timbers under dry conditions. Building Regulations specify the areas of attack and state that all timber in these areas should be protected with timber preservatives.

Pinhole borer. This is a very small beetle which attacks timber in forest areas, especially timber in log form. It is normally exterminated

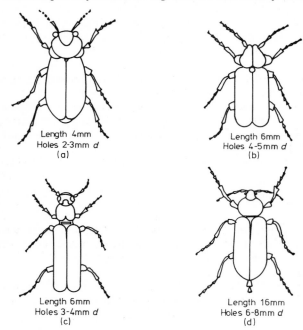

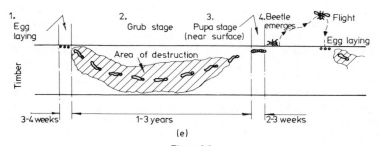

Figure 6.6

during kiln drying processes, but the timber remains with small black pinholes that are no longer active and their effect on the appearance of the timber is not welcome.

Knowledge of the life cycle will help in the understanding of the beetle problem (*Figure 6.6(e)*). It can be summarized in the following stages:

(1) *Egg laying.* The eggs are laid in surface crevices and they hatch in 3–4 weeks.

(2) *Grub stage.* The eggs hatch into grubs which commence to eat into the cellulose and lignin structure. This period continues for about 1–3 years during which time the timber is being devoured.

(3) *Pupa stage.* The grub works towards the timber surface where it changes into a pupa or chrysalis just beneath the timber surface. It remains in this stage for 2–3 weeks.

(4) *Beetle stage.* The pupa changes into a beetle and emerges from the timber to mate and lay further eggs. This stage lasts for 3–10 days, after which the beetle dies. When the eggs hatch the cycle continues.

Destruction of timber occurs during the grub stage as the timber is eaten for food, thus causing either partial or complete destruction. Pupae form in the spring and the beetles emerge during early summer, so it is during this period that beetles are active near the surface; it is also the time that treatment should be carried out to destroy both the grubs and the beetles. It is essential that detection and recognition of any attack is made early before the situation becomes serious. Further reading from the titles mentioned in the Bibliography at the end of this chapter is recommended.

Weathering

General atmospheric conditions will have the greatest effect on the durability of timber in external situations. Timber absorbs moisture in wet situations and becomes saturated, which results in the swelling of the timber. This is followed by surface drying that causes shrinkage and eventual opening of the timber grain. Sunlight and winds assist in drying off surface moisture. The action of the opening and closing of the timber grain during the dry periods will enable moisture to penetrate to greater depths and will also cause the open grain to become brittle and break away. This results in the slow disintegration of the unprotected timber surfaces, and the inner timber, which is wet, is also liable to decay (*Figure 6.7(a)*). The timber then appears to be in a weathered condition.

Wear and tear

The general wear and tear of timber occurs during the normal every-day life of the building, and occasionally as a result of misuse. Abrasion is the wearing away of the timber as a result of the rubbing together of material surfaces. It can be caused in a number of ways, particularly by the following actions:

Footwear, which is the action of feet treading over the surface.
Moving machinery.
Different types of traffic travelling over it and sudden impact which may cause severe local damage.

The amount of abrasion depends on the type and hardness of timber, some being more resistant than others. The amount of concentration of the applied wearing force varies according to the situation and the use to which the floor is subjected.

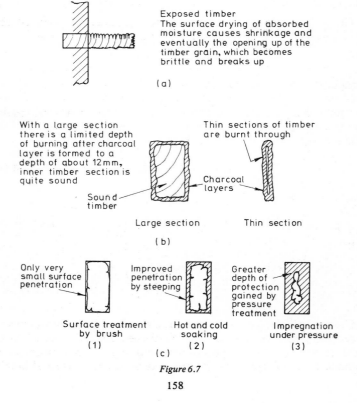

Exposed timber
The surface drying of absorbed moisture causes shrinkage and eventually the opening up of the timber grain, which becomes brittle and breaks up

(a)

With a large section there is a limited depth of burning after charcoal layer is formed to a depth of about 12mm, inner timber section is quite sound

Thin sections of timber are burnt through

Sound timber

Charcoal layers

Large section

Thin section

(b)

Only very small surface penetration

Improved penetration by steeping

Greater depth of protection gained by pressure treatment

Surface treatment by brush
(1)

Hot and cold soaking
(2)

Impregnation under pressure
(3)

(c)

Figure 6.7

158

It is essential to carefully select suitable timbers for the particular situation and use, and protective treatments may be given in order to strengthen the surface fibres and to give them a greater resistance to wear.

Fire

When a building catches fire the timber structure is often severely damaged, frequently beyond repair. This is because timber is a combustible material and permits the spread of flames over its surface. The rise in temperature that accompanies fires is often sufficient to cause the ignition of timber. As the surface of the timber burns a layer of charcoal forms upon its surface and when this layer reaches a thickness of approximately 12 mm it acts as an insulation layer and prevents further burning (*Figure 6.7(b)*). The main effects of fire on timber are the burning of it either completely or to a limited depth if the charcoal layer is sufficient to act as an insulator, and the spread of the fire.

Various treatments can be given in order to reduce the combustibility and improve resistance of timber. These are described below.

Treatment against deterioration

The following treatments will help to combat the various causes of timber deterioration and to improve its durability.

Fungal attack   The application of the following preservatives will prevent the spread of decay:

Coal-tar oils or creosote, which are strong smelling preservatives that leave an oily surface which cannot be painted for some considerable time. Timber treated in this manner must be kept away from foodstuffs.

Water-borne solutions, e.g. a chemical solution containing copper sulphate or sodium fluoride, which will penetrate into the timber.

Solvent-borne solutions, e.g. solutions of similar chemicals to those above that are mixed with a spirit of petroleum to give a greater depth of penetration.

The preservative treatment will coat the timber surface and, more important, the inner cellular structure, with the chemicals. The water and spirit content facilitates penetration and they then evaporate, the chemicals being left behind. These preservatives kill and repel fungi.

Damp conditions   In damp conditions timber needs to be protected against moisture penetration in order to prevent decay. This may be achieved by the application of:

Water-borne solutions to coat the cellular structure.

Creosote, which when applied under pressure may either fill or partly fill the cellular structure with creosote oils.

Protective coats of paint. This must be applied in completely dry conditions and the timber must be completely sealed.

Building fires   Treatments can be applied to timber in order to reduce the possibility of combustion. They take the form of applications of:

A charcoal layer which provides insulation against burning to any great depth.

Water-soluble ammonium salts or boric acid solutions which are impregnated into the cellular structure of the timber. They have the effect of preventing ignition and repelling flame.

Fire-retarding paint which contains either phosphate resins or sodium or potassium silicate. It is applied as a normal paint and it can also be used for decoration. When it comes into contact with flames it causes a chemical section that produces a charcoal layer over the surface which acts as an insulation layer. In each case the treatments reduce the spread of flame.

Methods of application

The protective treatments mentioned above can be applied by:

Surface application by brush to the timber surfaces (*Figure 6.7(c)(1)*). This gives limited protection only and is not considered particularly suitable.

Steeping or soaking the timber in the preservative (*Figure 6.7(c) (2)*). This may be done in either cold solution or by the hot and cold method, which is recommended. In the latter method the timber is placed in tanks which are filled with solution. This is then brought to the boil, and boiled to remove the moisture from the timber cells. The tank and contents are then left to cool and the vacuum formed in the cells is gradually replaced by the incoming solution. The excess preservatives are drained away and the timber is allowed to dry. A good depth of penetration is obtained by this method.

The pressure impregnation method (*Figure 6.7(c) (3)*). The timber is loaded into kilns which are then made airtight by withdrawing air with a suction pump to leave a vacuum. Preservative solution is then added to the kiln and pressure is applied. This causes the cells to fill with solution. Excess preservative is then drained away and the timber is allowed to dry. This method provides the maximum penetration and gives excellent protection.

Before fixing timber, any cut-off ends will also need to be treated so as to complete the sealing.

General remedial work on-site

There are a number of points for observation on site, and various treatments and remedial work that can be carried out.

External work

Timber exposed to the atmosphere in a number of situations is subject to deterioration. It is essential that it is given a close inspection fairly frequently in order to determine the actual condition of the timber units or member, especially in areas where moisture is likely to collect and remain for longer periods.

Areas for particular attention are:

Horizontal surfaces, rails, cross members and cover boards which provide catchment surfaces for moisture.

The base of structures where moisture is held and absorbed upwards.

Joints, which often open, allowing moisture to penetrate between the members.

Coatings of protective paints, which should be checked because they deteriorate, especially if moisture has collected in the timber from behind.

Fixings.

In all cases, decay, particularly wet rot, should be checked at door and window units. The close inspection of the following areas is essential if wet rot is to be detected (*Figure 6.8(a)*): sills and jambs (particularly the bottom of each vertical member, wherever possible); the tops of horizontal rails (particularly where they are grooved which might encourage moisture to collect); the parts of frames that abut the structural wall, which are susceptible to decay because they are unprotected and out of sight; and glazing rebates where glazing mastic or putty has broken away, thus allowing moisture to collect beneath. Another item to be periodically checked is the correct opening and closing of windows and doors, as moisture can cause movement of the timber to disturb this, and can also cause ironwork to corrode.

Exposed positions for timber include some that are both inaccessible and subject to atmospheric conditions, such as roofs, towers, balustrades, and also fences and gates, etc., which are also exposed to

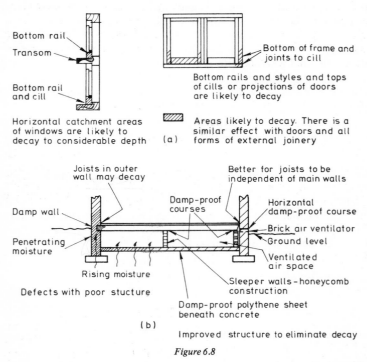

Figure 6.8

ground moisture. Many of these structural forms are often neglected, with the result that any protective treatment which has been applied is liable to deteriorate and allow moisture to be absorbed, thus causing decay. In addition, the wetting and drying periods may result in surface weathering as well as decay.

Remedial work   In all cases it is essential to cut out and remove decayed timber, and occasionally it will be necessary to make decisions as to the extent of repair needed, such as to remove the complete structural unit, renew a member of the frame unit, e.g. a sill or jamb, or repair a portion of a member, e.g. splice the bottom portion of a jamb.

The choice may well be the one which is the most economic when comparing initial cost with those of maintenance over a period of years. In cases of renewal it is first necessary to establish the cause, then to make provisions to prevent recurrence and/or upon completion to provide good protection. Timber requires protective treatment before fixing, especially if it is a part that will be covered and will not be able to receive further treatment. A final protective coating of paint will be applied on completion of the remedial work. In the case of deteriorated fences, it may be wise to replace decayed timber posts with suitable precast concrete posts in order to eliminate any further occurrence of decay.

Internal work

Internal situations are normally more stable, as the timber is exposed to comparatively dry atmospheres, although it may be subjected to the effects of rising moisture, condensation, poor ventilation and wear and tear. In these circumstances timbers will need to be checked for fungal and beetle attack and shrinkage and swelling movements, which are common types of defects.

Timber floors

Ground floors

Ground floor timber and timber in similar situations will require close inspection for signs of dry rot or cellar fungus, as early detection can help to prevent an attack from spreading and becoming serious. Brown or wet rots may be found at the ends of timber joists fitted into damp walls.

The extent of decay may be difficult to determine. Although the surface condition can be seen, this does not reveal the condition underneath, and the surface boarding must be removed so that observations can be made. It may be that there is either:

Full decay of the majority of the floor timbers, which would require a completely new floor and supporting joists, or

Partial decay, which would require a full inspection to decide the extent and area of the boarding and its supporting joists that are affected.

In addition, the amount of ventilation, the space beneath the floor and the moisture conditions should also be checked.

Remedial work   The following courses of action should be carried out:

(1) Remove all decayed and rot-infected timber and burn it on site; clear out all rubble, dirt and debris from ventilated areas and the ventilators themselves.

(2) Sterilize the ground and structural brickwork with a suitable preservative by spraying or impregnation.

(3) Make sure that the space beneath the floor is properly ventilated. Lay an approximately 100 mm thick layer of site concrete over the ground beneath and include a polythene damp-proof membrane and adequate air bricks and ventilating holes (*Figure 6.8(b)*).

(4) Check that the cross-walls and sleeper walls are both correctly constructed and adequately ventilated.

(5) Eliminate any dampness, leakages from rainwater pipes, troughings, etc., and rising dampness. This will require the placing of damp-proof barriers in each wall and beneath each timber joist.

(6) Treat all timbers of the existing floor with preservative and pre-treat all new timber.

(7) Make sure that the standard and quality of the timber used is good. Decayed ground floors can either be repaired or totally replaced with a new timber floor as already stated. However, another alternative is to remove all traces of timber and replace with a concrete floor covered with p.v.c. tiles or other suitable finish.

Upper floors

Upper floors also require a close inspection for signs of beetle attack and decay, and it is important to be able to determine the difference between new and old workings. It may be found difficult to determine the extent of an attack because grubs may have been working within the timber for 2–3 years before emerging and the surface appearance does not reveal the extent of the damage. An accurate assessment can therefore only be made by an experienced person.

Remedial work   As for ground floors, immediate action must be taken to remove the pest and the following steps should be taken:

(1) Burn every trace of the affected timber on site, as before.

(2) Great care should be taken in removing all debris and frass (bore dust). The use of a vacuum cleaner will help.

(3) If the joists are only slightly affected, then treatment may be sufficient, but if they are more seriously affected the timber must be

removed and renewed. This may then require the removal and replacement of other parts of the structure, and redecorating, e.g. a ground floor ceiling secured to the floor timbers above.

General conclusions

Whenever timber is being replaced a number of precautions must be taken. Firstly, make sure that the correct timber is selected, that it is given an adequate protective treatment and well designed joints and fixings. On-site checking should be done to eliminate bad materials and poor construction work.

Bibliography

Forest Products Research Leaflets:

No. 6, 'Dry Rot in Buildings'
No. 4, 'The Death Watch Beetle'
No. 8, 'The Common Furniture Beetle'
No. 3, '*Lyctus*, Powder Post Beetle'
No. 14, 'House Longhorn Beetle'
No. 11, 'Hot and Cold Tank Method of Impregnating Timber'
No. 12, 'Sap Stains in Timber'
No. 50, 'Ambrosia Pinhole Beetles'
No. 39, 'Timber Decay and its Control'

Building Research Establishment Digest, No. 73, 'Prevention of Decay in Joinery', HMSO
M.P.B.W. Advisory Leaflets:

No. 10, 'Dry Rot'
No. 42, 'Woodworms'

The Enemies of Timber, Cuprinol Ltd.

CHAPTER 7

FLUES, FIREPLACES AND FIRE PROTECTION

CHIMNEY FLUES

Heating is an essential factor in the design and functioning of buildings. There are many methods of heating but modern methods are much more efficient than the older conventional ones. The particular heating methods employed will roughly depend on whether the situation is a domestic one, in which case a small unit would be used, or commercial or industrial, in which case a large unit would be used. This chapter is mainly concerned with the domestic situations, but the principles are essentially the same and in either event, the unit used will be solid fuel, gas or oil fired, all of which are capable of producing a lot of heat. The correct choice of unit is very important and it must be correctly installed and regularly maintained. In addition, correct air control and ventilation are also important if the unit is to operate satisfactorily.

When a new heating unit is installed it is essential to provide an efficient flue which terminates at the stack cap. It must include a suitable flue lining and insulation, both of which will improve the efficiency of the heating unit.

Main faults

The function of the chimney is to induce a flow of air, necessary for the combustion of fuel, and also to enable the unwanted gaseous products to be carried into the atmosphere. The main faults of chimneys are due to condensation and smokiness.

Condensation Condensation problems in chimney flues are created

166

by poor flue design. Carbon dioxide and water, the products of combustion, may condense and cause problems if allowed to penetrate into the brick sides of the flue. Suitable flue liners will reduce the risk of condensation attack and the space between the flue liner and the brickwork can be filled with a suitable insulating material which will reduce heat loss and help to reduce condensation (*Figure 7.1*).

Smokiness   This refers to the escape of smoke and gases from the appliance that are unable to perform their normal function of rising directly and being emitted from the chimney pot. It is not normally due

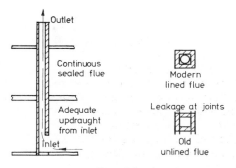

Figure 7.1

to a faulty appliance but more likely to poor flue design and construction, while unfavourable site conditions can also affect the performance of the fire or appliance, and may cause the escape of smoke and fumes into the internal atmosphere. This situation may be due to one of the following reasons:

Insufficient draught through the flue making it impossible to carry away all the smoke and fumes, some of which may escape into the rooms without any signs of it being blown by the wind. Strong winds can have the effect of either improving or worsening the situation.

No updraught at all, usually a constant situation with no signs of blowing back and the wind conditions having no effect.

Steady downdraught, resulting in a steady blow-back of smoke or gases, usually when the wind blows from a certain direction. It can also vary with the strength of the wind.

Intermittent downdraught occurs when difficult site conditions cause intermittent blowing back when the wind is in a certain direction.

Remedial work

Condensation   Condensation, as described above, is due to flue gases condensing and penetrating into the brickwork. All defects connected with it may be remedied by one of the following methods:

Use of a flue liner. The modern flue has been improved by lining it with a flue liner (*Figure 7.2(a)*). Unlined flues will always be a source of trouble as they may leak and be damaged by condensation. A flue that is lined and well constructed will eliminate any possible obstructions, leakages and condensation problems. Flue liners can be made of salt-glazed pipes, fire clay or refractory cement concrete pipes and asbestos

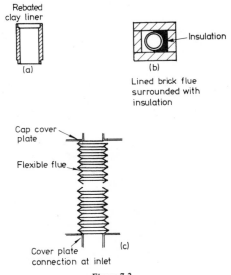

Figure 7.2

cement pipes. The older type are butt jointed but the modern ones are rebated and jointed. The space between the liner and the brick sides is best filled with an insulation of exfoliated vermiculite (*Figure 7.2(b)*). This will require protection at the top in the form of a suitably designed cap in order to keep the insulation fill dry.

Lining an existing chimney flue. This may be carried out in three ways. First, in straight chimneys asbestos flue pipes can be used. They must be rebate jointed, treated inside with an acid resisting compound and surrounded with a lightweight insulation fill.

Second, flexible metal liners can be used. They are used primarily for gas- or oil-fired boilers, but they can be used with some success on other appliances. They may be made of stainless steel or aluminium, they are flexible by virtue of their corrugated structure, and they come in continuous lengths as required (*Figure 7.2(c)*). The top is fitted with an asbestos flue terminal and the space between the lining and the brickwork is filled with a lightweight insulating material such as exfoliated vermiculite. Flexible liners require careful handling as they can be easily damaged when they are being pushed down inside the flue.

The third method involves the reconstruction of the flue by means of inserting concrete around a flexible rubber tube that has been inserted in the flue and inflated. When the concrete has hardened the tube is deflated and withdrawn, leaving a smooth continuous flue of the correct diameter.

Chimney pots. A chimney pot is the terminal end of a continuous flue and one is always fitted to each flue. The top of each flue and the chimney pot are contained in the chimney stack above roof level and are therefore considerably exposed to the atmosphere. The exposed portion of the stack and chimney pot are subjected to the cooling effect of the atmosphere, which results in cold flues (*Figure 7.3(a)*). This will tend to cool down hot smoke and flue gases, which in turn results in condensation and accumulation of soot, particularly in the pot, which is usually about 20 mm thick; the result will be smokiness at the base of the flue (*Figure 7.3(b)*). Soot deposits can normally be removed by a sweep's brush but tarry deposits adhere and harden on the flue and pot surfaces. They are difficult to remove and sometimes a scraper or chisel may be necessary.

Remedial action to prevent this problem from recurring may be chosen from the following:

Keep the stack as short as possible above the roof.
Increase the brick thickness to 225 mm, which gives better insulation than one that is 112 mm thick.
Reduce the projection of the pot above the stack top to about 150 mm and avoid corners and ledges beneath the pot. It is best to taper the brickwork to the pot.

Insufficient draught or air starvation   Heating appliances require an adequate flow of air into the room so that a sufficient quantity is available to flow through the burning fuel (to cause complete combustion), through the appliance or firegrate opening, through the throat, up the flue and finally to be emitted from the chimney pot. Some appliances require more air than others and it is therefore essential to control the air flow and to allow the required amount through the system. The existing conditions may be found to be unsatisfactory, with an inadequate air flow preventing the appliance from functioning properly. The necessary remedial work may be chosen from one of the following:

Replacement of appliance. This could be the first consideration, because some of the more modern appliances (such as the free-standing convector type of fire) require a smaller amount of air. The limited

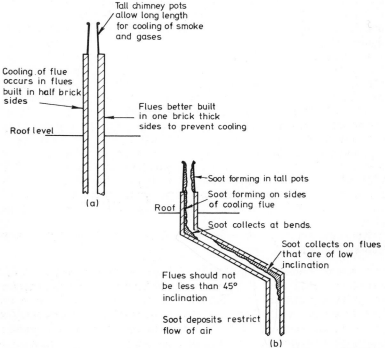

Figure 7.3   (a) Tall, exposed flues and pots allow cooling of hot gases; (b) Restricted flow due to soot deposits

amount of air available would then be sufficient. It may be necessary in certain cases, however, to adjust the velocity of air flow up the flue as the required amount of air for the appliance is less than the amount available. This is often a result of the throat being too large, and it should be reduced to about 125 mm by using a specially prepared throat constrictor (*Figure 7.4(a)*). The actual amount of air flow may vary, depending on whether the flue is warm or cold. It functions best when warm and initially, when cold, is apt to smoke.

Over-large fireplace opening. The flow of air and gases through the flue is limited by the size and construction of the flue. A badly formed throat that is too large will restrict the flow. It will require re-designing and the use of a throat plate will be necessary in order to obtain a suitable size of opening (*Figure 7.4(b)*).

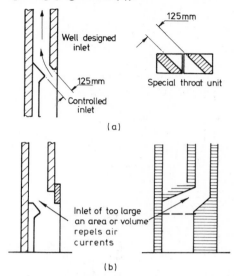

Figure 7.4 (a) Restricted inlet throats; (b) Inlets of poor design—prevent movement of air currents

Partial blockage of the flue. This may be the result of bad workmanship, mortar droppings or loose bricks causing blockages at bends. These can sometimes be removed by brush and rods, or by the use of a scraper. However, in serious cases it may be necessary to remove part of the stack and break into the flue to remove the stoppage.

Unsuitable flue size. In older properties the size of the flue varies considerably and in general they are too large. Open fires require a flue of not less than 190 mm diameter and not more than 225 mm diameter. Those of small independent boilers vary with size but are approximately 100–150 mm diameter, depending upon the type of appliance. The correct size must be fitted, as too large a flue causes smokiness and the larger the flue the longer it takes to get warm.

No draught at all This is the result of a complete blockage, which may be a collection of soot deposits sufficient to impede the flow of smoke and gases; collections will normally be found in the chimney pot and in the area of bends in the flue (*Figure 7.3(b)*). They can be cleared by regular cleaning. Stoppages may also be caused by fallen bricks or parts of bricks from decayed flues or during building operations. A simple test to identify the stoppage is to insert a lighted paper at the flue inlet, then observe rising smoke or draught.

It should be borne in mind that flues get cold after periods of non-use and must be warmed again before they can function properly.

Steady downdraught Buildings can cause an undulating effect to winds blowing over the roofs, resulting in a zone of high pressure or compression on the windward side of the roof, and a zone of low pressure or suction on the leeward side. The zone of compression tends to suppress rising air currents and the suction zone tends to assist rising air currents (*Figure 7.5(a)*). Consequently chimney flues on the leeward

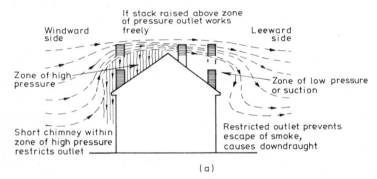

(a)

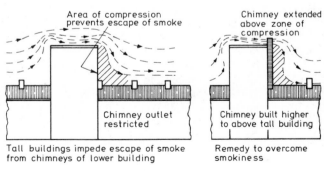

(b)

Figure 7.5   (a) Downdraught by high pressure; (b) Effect of tall buildings

side function, whereas those on the windward side, if not of sufficient height, may be compressed and the draught of air through the appliance and flue may cease, the pressure at the bottom being much less than that at the top. If on the other hand the chimney is higher, so as to pass through this zone, it will function although it is on the windward side. Chimney pots that are lower than the ridge level may be affected, while those above that level will normally be free of trouble. The effect upon a flue in this way will change according to the wind direction. A simple test is to open doors and windows and see if any difference is noted.

To remedy the defect it will be necessary to raise the level of the chimney outlets to clear the level of the ridge and be above the zone of pressure.

Downdraughts may be also due to inlets or outlets of air in the room, doors and windows again being in zones of low pressure. Those in the low pressure or suction zone may cause suction of gases or smoke from the appliance. To remedy this defect it will be necessary to restrict the throat inlet of the appliance and so induce updraughts, or to change to a more suitable appliance.

Intermittent downdraught This is caused by site conditions and the situation of buildings relative to one another. *Figure 7.5(b)* shows how tall buildings adjacent to lower property can have an effect on the lower flue, according to the direction of the wind. The remedy is to take the flues up to a higher level, dictated by the higher property; a possible better alternative is to change the form of heating system.

Baffling of flue gases This defect is caused by the incorrect fitting of flue pipes from independent appliances into a brick flue. The incorrect fitting may occur in the original construction or when a replacement appliance is being fitted into an existing flue. In all cases the flue pipes are allowed to project too far into the flue, or in such a manner that the free flow of smoke and gases is hindered. To prevent this, entry pipes should be at an angle of 135° (*Figure 7.6*) and finish flush with the inside of the flue, so avoiding a sharp change of direction. The position of a soot door is important; if it is directly opposite the inlet pipe it will tend to cool hot smoke and gases that will impede the updraught. These doors should always be situated below the entry of the flue pipe and preferably be of the double-door type to increase the insulation value.

Air leaks Flues are required to be continuous and sealed lengths with an inlet at the base and an outlet at the pot; all joints between these two points must be sealed and airtight. Leakages that occur will allow cold air in, which will cool the hot gases and so reduce the upward draught. Any air leak may be cured by fitting a flue liner as previously described. When a smoke pipe from an independent boiler passes through brickwork into the flue, the space around the pipe needs to be filled and packed with asbestos rope.

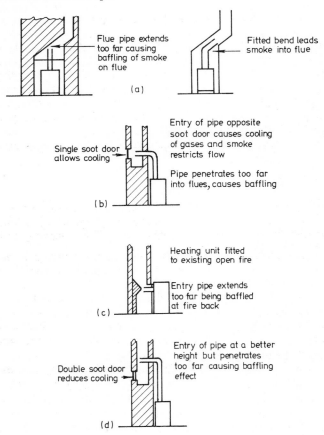

Figure 7.6

Fitting new appliances to existing flues

When a new appliance is to be fitted into an existing flue it is necessary to check that the flue and its opening are suitable for the new unit. Make sure that the throat is correctly designed and that a continuous airtight flue exists. If there is the least doubt, it is far better to fit a flue liner and make sure that the cap or chimney terminal and the stack are safe and sound. A change of heating systems, as in the case of gas replacing solid fuel, will provide additional high temperatures in the flue. In these cases it will be necessary to fit a suitable flue liner with adequate insulation.

BUILDING FIRES AND FIRE PROTECTION

Buildings are subject to property fires, which may be small with little damage, or extensive with complete destruction. Damage can also vary considerably according to the material and the severity of the fire, varying from discolouration by smoke to actual destruction by burning. Modern buildings are constructed in a manner to prevent the spread of fire and with fire resistant materials, and so fires are less likely. Older types of buildings, however, are often a fire hazard, but may receive various treatments and changes in design in order to give protection.

Causes of fire

Although it is not always possible to ascertain the reason for a particular fire, it can be said that fires are caused by heat which is gradually built up to a temperature of ignition from one of the following sources:

Electrical faults, which normally cause short circuits that spark or cause wiring to overheat. In each case the surrounding materials can be raised to ignition temperature.

Open fires with radiant heat, falling branches or coals from which may cause adjacent flammable materials to ignite.

Heating systems, which may be gas, electrical or oil-fired, together with a system of distributing hot water or air, are a danger to adjacent flammable materials.

Accidents, which lead to direct contact with a flame, causing fire spread.

Fire spread

Normally, radiation from the heat source causes the surrounding temperature to rise until it is at sufficient level to cause ignition. The temperature will differ according to the type of material but is around 200°C. Ignition is followed by flaming, which will cause rapid spread of flame. Flaming continues into actual burning, after which it will die down and remain as a smouldering mass.

The flaming period is the spreading of the fire, the burning period is the destruction period, and the smouldering period is the time when there is a danger of renewed flaming.

Influencing factors

The intensity of the fire, its spreading action and its effect are dependent on the following factors.

Materials Much will depend on the quality, nature and amount of combustible materials that exist. They may be structural or decorative, or in the form of equipment or contents. The actual structure and nature of these materials differ in their combustibility and tendency to spread fire.

Air movement The effect of variable draught which arises through window and door openings, stairways and lift shafts can be considerable. Draughts will assist the burning of materials, and encourage fire intensity and flame spread.

Ash A considerable amount of ash forms as the result of burning. It will form layers, and assist to reduce burning on some materials such as timber, where it forms an insulation layer over the surface and protects the timber beneath from further burning. Ash will, however, maintain accumulated heat for long periods and therefore constitutes a danger of possible renewed flames.

Transfer of heat

Heat, from whatever source, is easily transferred in several ways, and the continuance and spreading of a fire facilitated.

Radiation. The direct effect of heat will cause the rising of temperatures in its path. Sparks will then cause ignition and flaming.

Conduction. Heat can be conducted through a material, especially metals, to contact other flammable materials.

Convection causes the movements of hot air and gases around the space of a room, which will cause indirect contact with exposed faces of flammable materials.

Flying brands. The burning fragments that may be thrown out of a fire can be sufficient to ignite any heated material with which they come into contact.

The effect of all these factors varies considerably according to the circumstances, situations and type of materials in use. Material surfaces will rise in temperature, ignition will occur and flames will reach other flammable materials that are in contact with or on the reverse side of a structure.

Radiation may cause dangerous conditions to materials that are near and to those some distance away. Materials of neighbouring properties will, according to the distance and the intensity of the fire, be raised in temperature, ignite with a flash, and spread flames over a large surface area. For example:

At 100°C heated timber causes a flow of resin over the heated surface.

At 150°C there is a considerable flow of resin.

At 200°C severe charring occurs over exposed surfaces, radiation not being high enough to cause ignition, but a spark or flying brand would result in flaming.

Control of fire spread

If a fire does occur it is necessary to contain it within as small an area as possible. In order to accomplish this it is necessary to make certain constructional provisions such as forming vertical compartment walls across the total height and width of the building and formally separating floors, each constructed with fire resisting materials. These walls and floors are planned to limit the spread of the fire by containing it within these fire stops or divisions (*Figure 7.7*). Openings in these fire divisions must be controlled and fitted with fire resistant units so as to retain the resistant division. External window openings between or opposite other

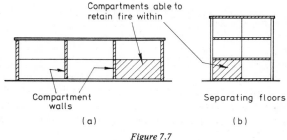

Figure 7.7

such buildings should be considered, as they are an element that will allow the penetration of heat by radiation from a fire in other buildings. For this reason such openings should be kept to a minimum.

Effects of fire-fighting

In order to combat building fires water is poured on to material surfaces and flaming units. The effect of fire-fighting is to prevent further flame spread and ignition, contain the fire, cool other surfaces about the area of the fire and deaden the actual fire.

During the fire, materials absorb heat and expand, which may cause damage. Water causes sudden cooling and contraction, which again causes damage to some materials. Water damage can be as destructive as damage caused by fire, and will affect material structures and surfaces, especially those that have been heated and then doused with water. Water may cause flooding in basements, under floors and in other undesirable parts, e.g. on top of damp-proof membranes and courses which may result in the prolonged after effects of dampness. Floors within buildings can become overloaded with water that has been pumped into the building, as well as with fallen debris.

Treatment to increase fire resistance

Materials may be classified as either flammable or non-flammable, and while each will be affected by rising temperatures, one will burn and the other will expand and contract. Treatments may be applied to materials in order to minimise or prevent flaming and fires (*Figure 7.8*). Treatments may be applied by:

Impregnation of fire resistant chemicals in a soluble form, to prevent burning.

Surface treatment in the form of paint coatings, to cause the formation of a charcoal layer which will prevent burning.

Protective covering of materials by other non-affected materials such as encasing steel, to give varying degrees of protection.

Effects of fire

The various effects mentioned above indicate what is required when considering remedial work. Whenever possible the use of suitable non-flammable or a treated material, or a better form of structure, should be considered.

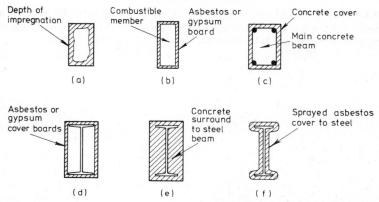

Figure 7.8   (a) Chemical treatment of timber; (b) Material surrounded with non-combustible material; (c) Concrete cover to reinforcement; (d) Non-combustible cover to steel; (e) Concrete surround to steel; (f) Sprayed-on cover

Defects may occur due to:

The burning of material structure or surface.

Expansion in the material unit causing movement, with possible fracture of that or other parts of the structure.

Cracking of materials, causing surface or structural failure with possible collapse.

Materials may fall and explode causing further damage.

Materials may become mis-shapen, twist or curl with loss of strength.

Taking these points into account, individual materials may now be considered.

Structural steel

Steel can suffer damage by expansion, deformation, reduction in strength and burning.

Expansion. Steel will absorb heat, the amount depending upon the proximity of the fire. Expansion will then take place. In those areas affected by heat, movement will occur, but other cooler areas will restrain this movement with the resulting distortion of the unit member. Movement is outward from the source of heat and will affect connecting joints either by shearing or loosening the connecting device.

Deformation. When steel is encased in concrete or other fire resistant material the temperature rise will be delayed for a period, but then the temperature of the encased steel will rise quickly causing movement with expansion. Eventually it will reach a stage when it becomes soft

179

enough to allow distortion to take place. Distortion or deflection while under load will increase with increase in temperature until even the dead weight of the beam itself will cause deflection. At 400°C creep or movement will be evident, which unless checked will lead to the total collapse or complete distortion of the structure. Cast iron will crack, not bend.

Reduction in strength. At temperatures around 500–550°C mild steel will absorb sufficient heat to cause a change from its more solid crystalline form into a more plastic one. This will cause a permanent loss in strength of 25 per cent or more. Intense heating of steel followed by quenching with cold water will leave it in a brittle form.

Burning. Steel sections can be protected by being encased with concrete, brickwork, gypsum or asbestos. In this manner steel is less exposed to burning temperatures and conditions. If, however, the casing is damaged or missing, then the unprotected steel will be subject to the intense heat. With prolonged heating in these areas there will form a layer of scale and patches of rust-red discolouration. All metal that has been subjected to burning must be considered suspect, due to possible loss of strength. This may be due to change of crystallization or loss of carbon content. In such cases steel should not be retained or re-used.

Remedial work   After a fire, steel members should be assessed as to their condition, using the following criteria:

Steel members that are not distorted or burned and are unaffected by the heat will need to be examined for cracks at rivet and bolt holes. Connecting plates and angles should also be examined to see if they are loose. These members can be re-used when they are put in good order.

Burnt steel should be rejected because of the possible loss in strength, unless it is to be used in positions where strength is not required.

When steel is bent but not burnt it may be re-used, providing that it is not unduly deformed. Sections may be reasonably and economically straightened, or it may be left undisturbed if the bends and appearance are not of importance. Members that soften or buckle under loading and are not burnt may be either replaced with new steel, or encased in concrete, which will provide additional strength; new connections may be required, and if in doubt should be renewed.

Concrete structures

During fires, concrete forms and structures are subject to heat being absorbed, with resulting thermal expansion. High temperatures may affect the strength of the concrete structure, including the steel reinforcing bars as well as the concrete itself. At temperatures between 400 and 800°C there will be a slight reduction in strength; at 800°C and over a marked reduction of strength will occur, perhaps as much as 25 per cent or greater. Changes in the colour of concrete with heat indicate loss of strength and change of condition:

At 200°C colour is grey and condition unaffected.

At 300–600°C colour changes to pink and red; condition remains sound.

At 600–900°C colour changes to a second grey with red particles; this indicates friable concrete with high suction.

At 900–1200°C colour turns buff and then yellow, indicating friable and sintered concrete which is of a soft condition.

The heating of concrete by fire will normally affect the outer layers, generally being confined to a depth of 50–100 mm. This will cause surface cracking followed by surface spalling during the fire. Spalling will uncover and expose steel reinforcing bars which will then be open to further heat and fire.

Mild steel reinforcing bars absorb heat and expand, and will buckle between links or stirrups (*Figures 7.9(a)* and (*b*)). This causes a loss of strength in the steel bars and will also cause the spalling of the concrete cover. Hollow blocks and concrete floors expand when subjected to heat, then contract when quenched with water. This causes the hollow blocks to fall away, with sagging of the floor (*Figure 7.9(c)*).

Remedial work In cases where the concrete beams and floors have sagged and suffered loss of strength it will be necessary to rebuild the complete structure. Some members may be repaired, such as columns, when additional concrete may be added, together with fabric mesh wrapping (*Figure 7.9(d)*). If reinforcement has deteriorated, then new reinforced bars may be added which will need to be attached to the existing ones by wiring or welding. Concrete surfaces which have spalled or eroded may be cleaned down and surface treated with Gunite. In all cases deteriorated or affected concrete must be removed before additional applications are made.

Brickwork

Brickwork that has been subjected to fire can be damaged by heat although the bricks themselves are non-inflammable. Because of this brick walls seldom suffer serious damage, and though with many it will be found that the mortar has been damaged, this is often superficial and can be corrected by repointing.

When cavity and hollow walls are subjected to fire and flames, it will be found that cavities may act as flues and so encourage the continuance of flaming. In this way the walls are exposed to higher temperatures which, if prolonged, will cause the destruction of the mortar. This may necessitate rebuilding.

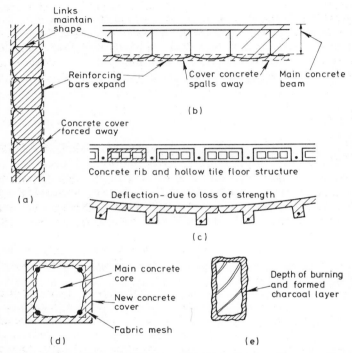

Figure 7.9 (a) Effect of fire on reinforced concrete column; (b) Effect of fire on reinforced concrete beam; (c) Effect of fire on ribbed floor—expansion causing deflection, hollow tiles fall away; (d) Method of repair to concrete column; (e) Effect of fire on timber section

High temperatures may also cause the vitrification of bricks when the additional firing is sufficient to cause the fusion of the brick units. Unequal expansion of brickwork will do no harm in small amounts, but may be more serious in excessive heat; it may cause cracking of walls, either directly or indirectly to adjacent walls due to pressure. Walls, if restrained at the ends, may bulge or collapse. In this case it may be necessary to demolish and rebuild in total or in part.

When water hoses are used during fire-fighting, hot walls are subjected to sudden quenching which causes the temperature to drop quickly. This can cause the brickwork to disintegrate, especially the spalling of brick faces; it can also cause deep cracking of the brick unit or of the wall structure itself.

Remedial work Each wall must be judged on its condition and strength before deciding on the course of action to be taken. It may be necessary to demolish the wall, and then to prepare and rebuild; this gives a sound structure. On the other hand, it may be possible to carry out repairs, rebuilding small areas or strengthening the existing walls, together with some re-pointing. The wall's surface may need to be raked and re-pointed, replacing isolated bricks which are badly damaged.

Stonework

Natural stone will generally be able to withstand the effects of rising temperatures, but deterioration may occur, due to:

The calcination of limestone. When limestone is heated to a high temperature, carbon dioxide is driven off, leaving a residue of calcium oxide (quick-lime). This chemical change starts at 600°C and becomes a more rapid change at 700–800°C. Calcination normally causes surface deterioration only.

Cracking and spalling. Hot stones which are suddenly cooled by quenching water from fire-fighting hoses will spall, with a shattering effect on the stone face.

Disintegration. Heat from fires causes the development of a friable condition of some stone structures, which can result in disintegration.

Strength of stone. The strength of stone is not normally affected to any serious degree by the heat of fires, so they need not be replaced unless they are cracked or the surface is deteriorated. Damaged stone may be repaired or replaced as described on pages 71–72.

Timber

Timber, with its cellular structure and inflammable nature, will burn completely or be subjected to surface flaming. Generally small sections of timber will burn and disintegrate completely; larger sections of timber will burn on the outer surface only. Surface burning of timber causes the formation of a layer of charcoal which acts as an insulation layer. This layer will prevent further burning in depth.

After a fire, timber beams will be found to have burnt on the surface to a depth of approximately 15 mm. The charcoal if scraped away will reveal some unaffected timber immediately beneath (*Figure 7.9(e)*). Timber surfaces are always a source of flame spreading; to control this they can be treated with fire resistant chemicals. These treatments may be:

Impregnation with water-borne solutions which will help to repel flaming and burning.

Treatment of the surface with a paint containing a property that will produce a layer of charcoal when heat comes in contact with it. This layer will insulate and protect the timber.

Burnt timber must generally be replaced; however, larger sections may be scraped clean of charcoal, and if sound and functional left in position. They should, however, be faced with timber boards.

Internal and other finishes

In the course of a fire, most internal finishes are damaged or destroyed by fire, smoke or water.

Timber will require replacement or local repairs. Wall plasters become heated, and at high temperature will be burnt into anhydrous substances in the case of gypsum plasters, and into calcium oxide in the case of lime plasters. They may also be destroyed when the fire fighter quenches the walls with water. In all cases the walls should be cleaned and replastered. Cellular boards will be affected by heat and flaming and will also be damaged by water.

Glass is affected by heat. It may crack and splinter at low temperatures and form into a fused condition at high temperatures. Wired glass is required in fire-doors or partitions as a safety precaution.

Decorations will normally suffer considerably, not only from flaming, but from smoke and water spray. Redecoration will be carried out on completion of the other repairs; smoke damage and stains may be removed by washing down if they are not too severe, otherwise redecoration will be required. Heat alone will cause damage to paint, causing burning and removal of paint surfaces, often at some distance from the seat of the fire. Paint blisters occur quite readily, being the result of moisture or resinous substances extruded from knots and flaws. In all these cases the defective paint will need to be burnt off and the surface redecorated as specified in Chapter 4.

Fire debris

As well as the various defects that occur to the building material units, there is the problem of fire debris. The waste and burnt rubbish left behind should be cleared and the building cleaned before surveying to assess the real damage. Then it may be found necessary to demolish unsafe structures or other parts for rebuilding. This again should be cleared away before rebuilding operations begin. In the case of fire-damaged materials, there is always the possibility of some items that may be salvaged and re-used or sold.

Bibliography

Building Research Establishment Digests, HMSO:

Series 1, No. 18, 'Smokey Chimneys'
Series 1, No. 60, 'Chimney Design'
Series 1, No. 40, 'Heat Transfer and Condensation in Domestic Boilers'

Coal Utilisation Council Manual
Fire Research Publications, National Building Studies:

Research Papers Nos. 12, 4, 5, 6, 'Investigation on Building Fires'

CHAPTER 8

BUILDING SERVICES

Internal plumbing services are formed from many parts of fittings, equipment, and service pipes in order to provide a satisfactory and functioning system of sanitation. It includes hot and cold water systems, domestic central heating systems, sanitary and toilet accommodation, and waste disposal and drainage systems, all of which are found in many types of properties.

Sanitary fittings

Sanitary fittings is the term given to water closets, flushing cisterns (water waste preventers), wash hand basins, sinks, baths and urinals.

Water closets

Water closets are usually fitted as:

High level suites, which are found in older type properties. They have a high level flushing cistern connected by a long flush pipe to the water closet pan (*Figure 8.1(a)*).

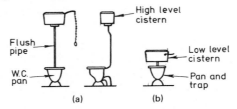

Figure 8.1   (a) High level w.c. suite; (b) Low level w.c. suite

Low level suites, the more modern type, having a cistern in close contact with the w.c. pan (*Figure 8.1(b)*).

When inspecting these fittings it is necessary to consider the type and age, together with the condition.

The flushing cisterns are required to flush the pan with sufficient force to empty the contents from the pan and to discharge them into the soil pipe cistern and then to the drainage system with a self-cleansing velocity. W.C. pans are trapped by a water seal in order to prevent the escape of sewage smells and gases into the room atmosphere, so preserving sanitary conditions.

Water closet pans are of several types, as shown in *Figure 8.2:*

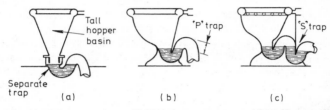

Figure 8.2   (a) Hopper pan and trap; (b) Wash-down type w.c. pan; (c) Double trapped siphonic w.c. pan

The older hopper type pan and trap are occasionally found but are not efficient and should be replaced (*Figure 8.2(a)*).

The single trapped or wash-down type is widely used. They are noisy in their action (*Figure 8.2(b)*).

The double trapped or siphonic type pans are modern, with a more efficient and silent action (*Figure 8.2(c)*).

The pans are fitted to the floor by brass screws into the timber floor boards or bedded and pointed in mortar to a tiled or concrete base. The w.c. pan outlet is then fitted into an earthenware drain at ground level or to the soil pipe stack at other levels (*Figure 8.3*). In both cases it is necessary to specify a sealed joint similar to the one shown in the figure. White or coloured glazed earthenware water closet pans are mainly used because they are hard wearing, but they can deteriorate for the following reasons:

Cracking, crazing or chipped surfaces. These may allow moisture absorption, which can cause leakages and encourage germs.

Cracked bases or outlets due to movement.

Defective joints to the earthenware pipe, soil pipe or with the flush pipe.

The pan bottom may crack if the water seal is allowed to freeze.

187

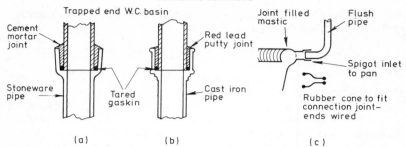

Figure 8.3 (a) Salt glazed stoneware pipe; (b) Cast-iron pipe; (c) Joint w.c. pan/flush pipe

Defective pans should always be replaced with a new pan of a similar type. If a new type is used it may be necessary to alter the various connecting pipes. When inspecting a w.c. pan always flush the pan to reveal leakages. To test the efficiency of the flush, compress some medium absorbent paper into a ball of 25 mm diameter. It should be carried away by one flushing action.

Flushing cisterns (water waste preventers)

Flushing cisterns are of various types and materials, such as:

Cast iron. These are an older type of cistern with a bell-type action, normally used with high level flushing systems. The cast iron will corrode and deteriorate (*Figure 8.4(a)*).

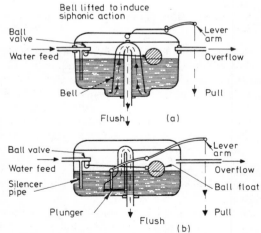

Figure 8.4 (a) Bell type cistern; (b) Piston actuated type

188

Enamelled steel, which will incorporate the piston actuated flush. In these types the enamel protection may be chipped off, causing corrosion of the steel (*Figure 8.4(b)*).

Plastic, with the piston actuated flush. This is a modern and very durable type.

Ceramic, usually fitted in the modern low level suites and incorporating the piston actuated method of flush.

Each type of cistern has a water supply which is connected to the cistern body and controlled by a high pressure inlet valve (*Figure 8.5*), which in turn is controlled by a ball float. The level of water in the

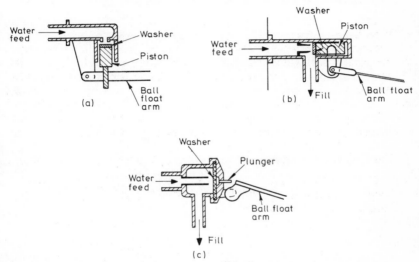

Figure 8.5   (a) 'Croydon' ball valve; (b) 'Portsmouth' ball valve; (c) 'Garston' ball valve

cistern should be maintained at a level 25 mm below the overflow pipes. At this level 9 litre of water should be available; anything less will be insufficient for the operating of the flush.

Each cistern should also have an overflow pipe or warning pipe, which should discharge into the open air so as to be visible for observation. When water is discharged the owner will be aware that the inlet valve or the ball float is faulty and needs attention. The overflow pipe should always be a size larger than the inlet pipe.

Common defects include the following:

Inlet valves are apt to be noisy when filling. This may be overcome by fitting a silencer pipe to the inlet, which takes the water down to the bottom of the cistern and below water level, thus reducing noise.

Inlet valves may have faulty washers that need renewing in order to prevent overfilling.

Ball floats need renewing when they leak and fill with water, which also causes overfilling.

Flush pipes connecting the cistern to the w.c. pan may have faulty connections that will need to be renewed; the joint with the pan is made with a rubber cone connection (*Figure 8.3(c)*).

Deterioration may be caused by corrosion of ferrous metals, the rust affecting the delivery of water and the efficiency of the flush.

Faulty lever action, i.e. worn or loose fittings, may be the cause of inefficiency.

Wash hand basins

Wash hand basins may be of glazed ceramic or enamelled steel. The ceramic basins will crack or chip and then absorb water once the glazed surface is penetrated. This may cause staining and probably allow leakages. Cracks may occur as the result of falling objects, or over-tightening of connecting nuts to taps or waste. The enamel may be chipped off the enamelled steel basin, exposing the steel which will corrode.

Wash hand basins are supported either by brackets, which should be well secured to the wall, or by means of a pedestal. The pedestal should be screwed to the floor and the basin itself secured back to the wall by means of small brackets.

Sinks

Sinks may be of several types and forms.

Glazed earthenware or fireclay, which are available in various sizes and depths from 125 to 250 mm deep. They are supported on cantilever wall brackets which are built into the wall. Sometimes they are supported by brick walls built of white glazed bricks.

Stainless steel is press moulded into the shape of washing-up bowl and combined drainer. These are very popular because they can be moulded in various shapes, i.e. single or double drainers, twin washing-up bowls with double drainers, etc. They are also very hygienic because there are no joints or cracks which can collect food particles.

Plastics and glass fibre are more modern materials that have been used to form combined bowl and drainer units. They are also very durable, having the same advantages as those moulded out of stainless steel, but they are susceptible to damage with unfair use.

190

Enamelled steel can also be used to form combined bowl and drainer units. These need to be cleaned regularly and the enamel may be chipped off, which can lead to deterioration by corrosive action.

All the above combined bowl and drainer units are usually fitted into modern cupboards. These are then referred to as sink units which can be matched up with working tops and cupboards that have plastics surfaces for easy cleaning.

Baths

Baths may be made of cast iron with an enamelled surface, which are very heavy, or enamelled steel, plastics or glass fibre, and react in a similar manner to the sinks described above. The baths are supported on fitted feet which are adjustable in order to position, and provide an adequate fall for drainage to the waste outlet. Baths are known by their length, such as 1.50 m, 1.65 m, 1.80 m long, and this must be checked and the shape described when a replacement is ordered.

Showers

Shower fittings consist of a shower head, mixing valve and shower tray (*Figure 8.6*), and may be formed by either a complete and enclosed

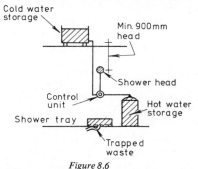

Figure 8.6

shower unit of enamelled steel or plastics structure, or separate fittings comprising a shower tray in glazed fireclay with fitted waste outlet, set upon the floor and enclosed with tiled or plastics covered sides. Shower fittings should be fitted over the bath, which acts as the tray, and protected at the side by a screen or plastics curtain.

In all cases watertight joints are necessary to prevent leakages that may cause deterioration of the structural fabric. A mixing valve, shower head and storage tank are also fitted. A minimum of 8826 N/m² (900 mm head) is required for water pressure and is measured vertically from above the shower head outlet to the storage tank.

Urinals

Urinal fittings can be:

Urinal stalls, comprising a glazed fireclay floor channel with a fitted outlet and trapped waste, threshold and urinal slab; these are set and bedded in cement mortar, all of which require sealed joints.

Urinal bowls, being glazed ceramic ware. They need to be well secured to the wall and fitted with trapped outlets that require sealed joints.

Both systems have a controlled flushing cistern fitted at a high level, and connecting sparge pipes with flushing heads fitted to each stall or bowl.

Wastes

Each fitting must have a trapped waste and pipe to discharge into the soil pipe or drainage system. The waste pipes may be of copper, lead or plastics and should be of adequate size and fall towards the outlet. Single wastes should have a diameter of 30 mm. When several wastes are connected into a main waste this should have a diameter of 38 mm.

The traps are made of brass, copper, lead or plastics and are of several types: 'S', 'P' or 'Q' traps (*Figure 8.7*). Each maintains an

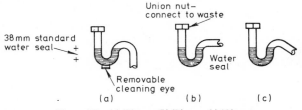

Figure 8.7 *(a) 'S' trap; (b) 'P' trap; (c) 'Q' trap*

efficient water seal with a minimum depth of 38 mm, or in the case of a deep sealed trap a depth of 75 mm. Each trap must contain a cleaning eye or be easily detachable for cleaning purposes.

Water seals These must be maintained at all times to prevent foul smells and gases from the drainage system entering the building, so causing a health risk. If the water seal is not maintained then look for a possible leakage at the joint or cleaning eye washer. In badly designed systems, water discharging into a common waste pipe may cause the siphoning of each water seal as the block of water passes each trap. To prevent this an anti-siphoning pipe should be taken from the top of each trap that is affected in this way (*Figure 8.8*). Deep seal traps may also be used to prevent siphoning (*Figures 8.8* and *8.9*).

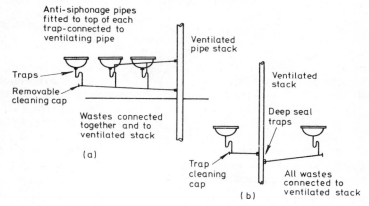

Figure 8.8   (a) Anti-siphonage; (b) Deep seal traps

The wastes may be completely stopped up or partially stopped by the collection of silt, scouring powder, undissolved soap, hair, etc., at the traps, bends and outlets. These may be cleared in one of the following ways:

By removing the cleaning eye in the trap.
By removing the complete trap.
By the use of a force pump or suction pump.
By the use of a force cup.
By the use of a Sanisnake (*Figure 8.10*).

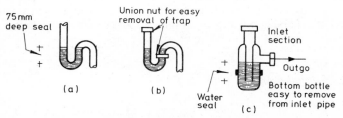

Figure 8.9   (a) Deep seal trap; (b) Two-piece trap; (c) Bottle trap

193

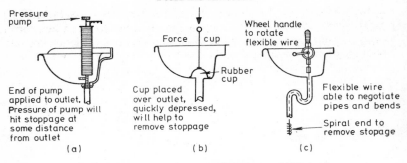

Figure 8.10 (a) Pressure pump; (b) Force cup; (c) Sunisnake

Kitchen wastes tend to become blocked by the casual disposal of waste food. Small food particles such as tea leaves may be allowed to pass into the waste with adequate volumes of water, but larger particles should be collected in bins. Electrically operated waste disposers can be fitted to the sink outlet. In this case the food passes through an enlarged outlet of 88 mm diameter into a grinding chamber, then through the waste pipe to the drainage system. A fused electric plug should always be used as a safety precaution against overloading.

Taps

Taps are classified as:

Pillar taps, those fitted vertically into the sanitary fitting.
Bib taps, those fitted to a back surface with fixing wings.
Stop taps, those fitted in the run of a pipe in order to close off the supply.

General maintenance of taps and similar fittings is assisted by regular cleaning with warm water and soap. Some modern cleaning materials tend to destroy the surface finishes of chrome, gloss or enamel and ought not to be used.

The main defect of taps is their failure to shut off the water completely, which results in a constant drip of water. To remedy this a new washer should be fitted; if this fails then the valve seating is defective, in which case a new tap should be fitted.

Cold water plumbing

Cold water is supplied by means of:

Main water supply, a branch connection being made to the water

194

main and connected by pipes to the cold water storage tank within the building. The connection to the main is made with a ferral connection at the top of the main, from which a looped pipe is taken underground into the building (*Figure 8.11*).

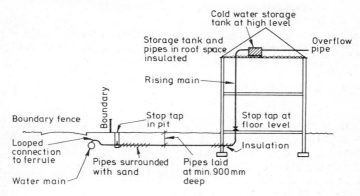

Figure 8.11

Well wall. Underground wells are constructed, and the water is raised by an electrically controlled pump to a storage tank within the building. This method is usually used in rural areas.

External stop valve

The external stop valve is fitted at the boundary of the property in order to cut off the main supply when required. The valve is situated in a brick or concrete pit which is covered by a cast-iron cover and frame at ground level, and must be maintained in a functional condition and free of leakages.

Underground pipes

The underground pipes may be of lead, copper or plastics. Lead is the old traditional material, and is costly and little used today; it will deteriorate with age, and becomes brittle and liable to crack. Copper is the more durable and is widely used. Plastics pipes are now being used for economy, and appear to be satisfactory.

Certain soil conditions are likely to cause corrosion in metals set in the ground, such as wet ashes or clinkers, red marl, wet decomposing matter or wet ironstone, each of which may have a harmful effect on buried pipes, particularly if combined with poor drainage and high sulphate or chloride content of the ground. Pipes then require protection such as a plastic coating, a coating of bitumen paint, or wrapping with bitumen tape, or burying and surrounding in a bed of sand, which also protects the pipes against damage by sharp objects.

Underground pipes are buried at a minimum depth of 750 mm in order to be clear of frost action; where the pipe enters the building at a higher level than this it will need to be insulated against frost damage.

Stop taps

A stop tap is fitted at the point of entry of the cold water supply into the building in order that the supply may be more conveniently turned off, to allow for repairs to the system or when the house is vacated for long periods, particularly during the winter months. Many buildings are found without this valve but one should be added whenever plumbing alterations are made.

Rising main

The rising main within the building needs to be positioned away from possible frost effects. External walls may be cold during frost periods, so pipes may be better situated on internal walls, or protected with insulated wrapping or preformed insulated sections. The rising main connects with the cold water storage tank, which is normally at high level in order to provide maximum water pressure.

Cold water storage tanks

Cold water storage tanks are situated at a high level. They may be within a roof space or upon a roof; in each case insulation against frost action is necessary. The tanks require adequate insulation on all surfaces and should be provided with a top cover; if situated externally upon the roof, then a tank room should be constructed in order to give the required protection. The tanks are traditionally made from galvanized iron, although small capacity tanks may be of plastics fibreglass or asbestos. Galvanized iron tanks are the strongest, but are liable to corrosion by oxidation or electrolytic action (*Figure 8.12(a)*). All tanks are liable to fill with sediment, which may arise from over-boiling of the water in a direct heating system, or from being left uncovered.

Control of water to storage tank   It is necessary to control the supply of water to the storage tank by automatic valves that are called ball valves. They operate by means of a lever arm with a ball float at the end actuating a sliding piston which depresses a washer against the inlet pipe. In all cases the ball valve is regulated to fill the tank to a level of 25 mm below the overflow pipe and so maintain maximum water storage.

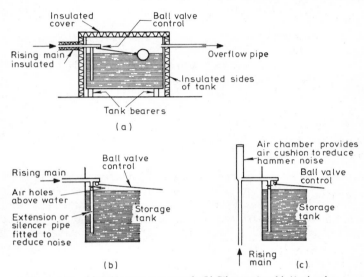

Figure 8.12   (a) Cold water storage tank; (b) Silencer pipe; (c) Air chamber

The ball float may be of copper or plastics. Copper is liable to deteriorate and become perforated. It will then partially fill with water and so become heavier and float at a lower level, which will mean that the ball valve will not be completely closed. The water level will rise and flow out of the overflow pipe. Plastics are an improvement, and more durable.

The overflow pipe or warning pipe is fitted as a precaution against overflowing of the tank, the size of the pipe being larger than that of the inlet. It should discharge externally in a position where it can be seen and should be fitted 25 mm above the water level. The joint between the pipe and tank should also be watertight.

Remedial action   When carrying out a sanitary survey on the storage tank all the joints should be checked to see that they are watertight. The ball valve should be checked to see that it does not leak when in the fall-off position, then pushed down so that the water level rises above the overflow pipe to make sure it functions correctly. When faults are detected they should be corrected as follows:

Washers that are worn or defective should be replaced.

Rust or dirt may interfere with the correct seating of the washer; it should be removed and a new washer used.

A ball float that is water-logged should either have its puncture repaired, or be renewed,

A valve with defective seating should either be re-seated or replaced with a new valve.

A sticking lever arm will be due to a worn piston in the ball valve; it should be replaced with complete new ball valve.

If the inlet at the ball valve is apt to be noisy, it is possible to overcome this by fitting an extension to the inlet pipe, sometimes called a silencer pipe. The pipe takes the water to the bottom of the cistern, which means that it discharges noiselessly below water level. Holes are needed at the top of the pipe above the water line in order to prevent siphoning (*Figure 8.12(b)*).

Another irritating fault at the ball valve is when excessive vibrations occur due to water hammer. When the water supply is at high pressure the water is forced against the walls of the pipes, junctions and bends with a hammer-like blow. The vibrations occur when the ball valve approaches the off position because the hammer causes the piston to vibrate back and forward. The remedy is to install an air chamber, which is a large diameter pipe fitted to the branch at the inlet of the tank (*Figure 8.12(c)*). This enables the air to be compressed, which absorbs the vibrations. Ball floats are vibrated by waves at the water surface. To remedy this, fins can be fitted to the float beneath the surface.

Cold water distribution

Figure 8.13 shows a layout of the cold water supply to the various fittings. Drinking water points at sinks and other places should always be taken from rising mains; all other fittings are supplied from the cold water storage tank by means of a distribution pipe which is referred to as the cold water supply main. This main supply is controlled by a closing-off valve near to the storage tank to close off the supply and isolate the various fittings. Branch pipes are taken from the cold water supply main to the various fittings in such a way as to keep them free from air locks, which can cause noise transmission. All pipes should be protected against damage by frost, corrosion and other forms of physical damage.

Types of pipe   The following types of pipe are used:

Lead pipes are found in most older type properties. Initially lead is a pliable material but becomes brittle with age, leading to fatigue and low resistance to cracking. Lead is also vulnerable to damage by frost action, so lead pipes must be protected by insulating wrapping. In soft water areas there is a danger of plumbo solvency, where the lead is dissolved in the water, creating a poisonous solution which can be very harmful if used as drinking water.

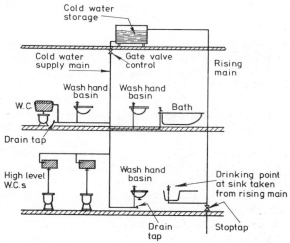

Figure 8.13

Galvanized iron is another old and traditional material that is little used today, except for industrial or land use. These pipes are subject to severe corrosion, and incrustation may form within the pipe to cause choking of small diameter pipes. This reaction will be so severe in acid reacting peat soils that they should never be used in them. If they are buried they require protection in the form of bitumen, or wrapping with bitumen impregnated tape, Denso tape being excellent for this purpose.

Copper pipes are widely used today, being very durable, resistant to corrosion, and able to take both expansion and contraction movements without effect. In soft water areas there may be slight solvent action and in hard water areas there may be slight effects from calcium carbonate deposits.

Plastics pipes made from p.v.c. material are very durable, non-corrosive, pliable and resistant to frost action. Plastics pipes are, however, affected by heat, which causes expansion and loss of rigidity; for this reason they are only used for cold water and waste services.

Types of joint   The type of joint will vary according to the type of pipe used.

Screw type joints; tapped threads to galvanized iron or heavy gauge copper pipes fitted to threaded fittings, with a little joint paste and hemp strands.

Solder joints; wiped solder joints are used to lead pipe connections.

Compression joints are used on light gauge copper and plastics pipes. This is a modern type which is a specially prepared brass or gun metal joint into which pipes are fitted with a copper cone. When the joint nuts are tightened they compress the cone against the pipe, making it watertight.

Capillary joints are modern, specially prepared joints fitted to copper pipes. Each branch of the joint contains a small groove containing solder which when heated will seal the complete joint by capillary action.

In all cases it is necessary to ensure that all types of joints are correctly formed, otherwise leakages may occur and the joints fail. Correct pipe sizes are important; branch pipes are normally 12 mm in diameter and main pipe runs 18 mm in diameter. These may increase in size according to length and capacity of draw-off branch supplies.

It is always necessary to avoid connecting dissimilar metals together, as this may encourage galvanic or electrolytic corrosion. For example, when a copper pipe is connected to a galvanized iron tank, the water will act as the electrolyte, the ensuing action causing deterioration of the zinc coating and iron metal, which acts as the sacrificial anode when connected to the copper by the water. Protection may be given by using a mastic compound to divide the two metals at the connection, but it is far better to avoid dissimilar metal connections altogether.

Other general considerations

Drain taps   These are small fittings at the lower ends of pipe runs; they enable the distributing pipes to be drained (*Figure 8.13*). They contain a spigot end for a hose pipe connection in order that drained water can be taken away.

Concealed pipes   Pipes may be concealed beneath floor boards, in which case the boards will need to be fitted as panels and screwed down. Pipes may be concealed in ducts which should be of adequate size to enable work on the pipes to be carried out. In all cases means of access to the pipes, bends and connections must be provided in order that remedial work may be carried out without delay.

Water softening   Hard water is not a risk to health but it has a number of disadvantages. In hot water pipes and boilers, scale may be deposited and in domestic use, scum; additionally, soap does not lather well in hard water.

There are several ways in which water may be softened. The first is the base exchange process, the second the soda lime process, and finally, inhibitors may be used. Domestic water softeners belong to the first method. The water is passed through a medium called zeolite which converts the calcium, magnesium or potassium salts in the water (which cause the hardness) into sodium salt, which does not. From time to time the zeolite medium requires regenerating by passing strong brine through it, which converts the medium back again to sodium zeolite.

A modern development of this process employs synthetic resins in place of the natural zeolite, so that water of comparable purity to that of distilled water can be obtained for certain industrial processes. This type of process is expensive and unnecessary for domestic water.

Frost action   Water in pipes and fittings is likely to freeze and turn into ice in extreme conditions. Freezing water increases in volume by some 9 per cent, which causes expansion within the limited spaces of pipes and fittings. If they are weak then the extra pressure causes them to crack or burst. Lead pipes are particularly susceptible.

The following precautions can be taken:

A heated atmosphere about the plumbing work should be provided.

Underground pipes should always be laid at a minimum of 750 mm below ground level.

All exposed pipes should be wrapped or lagged with fibre wrappings, glass fibre wrapping or preformed glass fibre sections.

All pipes and storage tanks in roof spaces should be treated as if exposed.

Great care is needed in thawing out frozen pipes, because damage can be caused. The following procedure should be adopted. First close the main stop tap and valves, open all other taps and then start thawing from the nearest open tap and work away from it. In this way there is a means of escape for the thawed water; otherwise, vacuums may be formed which may cause the hot water storage cylinder to collapse due to a lowering of pressure within the vacuum.

If properties are left empty for long periods during the winter then the following action is needed to prevent water damage to the property and safeguard water supplies. Turn off cold water supplies at the lower stop tap, and drain the cold water storage tanks and the hot water storage cylinder and system. This will reduce the possibility of frost damage.

Hot water plumbing

Domestic hot water may be supplied by a direct heating system, an indirect heating system or by individual heating units.

Direct heating system

In a direct heating system the heating boiler is in direct circulation with the hot water storage cylinder by means of a primary circuit (*Figure 8.14*). It is suitable for small systems only and even then it is not suitable

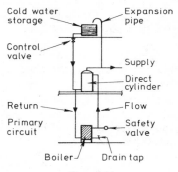

Figure 8.14

if the house is in a temporary hard water area, because there is a tendency for the boiler and the primary circuit to become furred by the continual circulation of fresh water during the process of being heated and drawn off. Furring causes deterioration of efficiency, and small diameter pipes can become partially blocked, which can reduce circulation and perhaps cause dangerous conditions. Fittings become blocked and joints are affected, with possible leakages.

Indirect heating system

The indirect system of heating domestic hot water is preferred in all situations. The heating boiler is in direct circulation with a calorifier

202

situated within the hot water storage cylinder (*Figure 8.15*). The storage water is indirectly heated by the hot water in the calorifier, which constantly re-circulates between that and the boiler; because it is hardly ever replaced there is no furring of pipes and boilers.

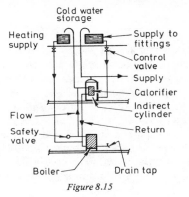

Figure 8.15

Details common to both systems

Flow and return pipes   Often called the circulators, these are normally 50–56 mm for domestic use, but larger for greater sized units; however, too large a diameter reduces efficiency.

Expansion pipes   These are fitted to hot water and heating systems in order to allow for the expansion of water. The pipe, of 18 mm diameter, is fitted from the top of the storage cylinder up to the cold water storage tank, where it is finished with a large bend over the top of the tank so as to disperse above the level of the cold water in the tank. The pipe allows an escape for expanded water, air locks and gases; it must not be in contact with the water in the tank as this would allow siphonic action.

Safety valves   In hard water areas safety valves are fitted where the furring of pipes may cause restrictions and blockages which can result in highly serious conditions and possible explosions. A safety valve fitted to the primary circulation allows the escape of excess pressure.

Hot water storage   This is a copper storage cylinder. (In some cases galvanized iron cylinders may be used; if this is the case, they should be examined at regular intervals for signs of corrosion.) The cylinders need to be of a size to supply sufficient hot water to the number of fittings that may require it. The cold feed pipe from the cold water storage should be of a diameter not less than the draw-off pipes. All hot water cylinders need to be lagged or insulated with a jacket or other suitable means in order to retain heat.

Sludge　Sludge deposits are caused by electrolytic action which may occur at hot pressed fittings that are of a zinc and copper composition. These deposits occur in hot water pipes and collect within primary circulating pipes. They are deposited at the lower point in the circuit, which is the boiler, especially in direct heating systems. In this system, water may overheat and boil, in which case the sludge is displaced and circulated around the system, so causing discolouration of water to a brown tone. With direct heating systems all fittings need to be of cast brass or gun metal in order to reduce possible electrolytic action.

Individual heating units

Hot water may be supplied from individual heating units of varying sizes and capacities.

Solid fuel open fires　These are fitted with a back boiler, with a small back fire controlled by an adjustable damper. The unit is generally used in small capacity directing systems.

Slow burning solid fuel boiler　This requires a concrete base and a suitable flue which is controlled by a damper to adjust air flow. Fire bars may burn and need to be replaced so that its efficiency is not reduced. This unit will, of course, be connected to the direct or indirect system, and depending on capacity is capable of supplying hot water and several hot water radiators (*Figure 8.16*).

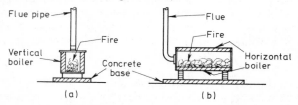

Figure 8.16　(a) Small unit; (b) Larger capacity unit

Oil fired boilers These need to be situated on a concrete base with an insulated flue to cope with high temperatures. The oil storage tank for this type of boiler can be a problem because difficulty in arranging suitable positioning may be experienced.

Gas fired boilers These require a concrete base and a suitably con-structed flue to take high temperatures. The flue lining material should be acid resisting and should be protected by a stack constructed of low

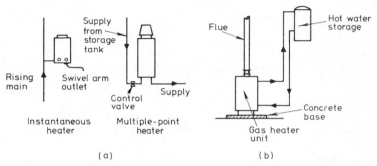

Figure 8.17 (a) Wall mounted heaters, gas or electric type; (b) Floor mounted, larger capacity units

conductivity material so as to minimize cooling. An adequate inlet of air is needed for the efficient working of the unit, especially if North Sea Gas is used. They are capable of supplying hot water and running several hot water radiators (*Figure 8.17*).

Gas fired storage heater This has a gas heating unit combined with a hot water storage cylinder that stores a volume of hot water ready for distribution.

Wall mounted heaters These can be either an instantaneous heater which heats the water at a single point and supplies it from a swivel arm outlet, or can be connected into the supply from a storage tank which will then supply water to several taps. Both of these heaters can also be heated by electricity (*Figure 8.17*).

Electrical water heaters Besides the two types mentioned above the most usual way of heating water by electricity is by an immersion heater which is fitted into a copper cylinder. The heater is thermostatically controlled in order to prevent high temperatures, and normally set at 60°C. In hard water areas there is always the possibility of scale forming on various inner surfaces. Copper tubes and surfaces are tinned for protection but the forming scale can attack and remove this protection; they are then liable to overheating (*Figure 8.18*).

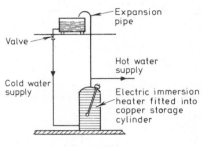

Figure 8.18

Remedial work

The notes in this section give basic information in order that the surveyor may be aware of old and new systems and their fittings.

In remedial or alteration work, systems and fittings may be replaced with similar materials, or it may be advantageous to replace them with more modern fittings and pipework—for example it would be better to replace lead or iron pipes with copper or plastics ones. This would improve the service and be more economical.

Soil and waste systems

Wastes from the sanitary fittings described on pages 192–194 are required to be disposed of through a soil and waste system into the foul drainage system beneath the ground floor level. The waste and soil disposal must be both watertight and airtight in order to prevent leakage of water or gases. It must also be durable and self-cleansing. At one time waste disposal could be divided into external soil and ventilating plumbing, and internal waste plumbing, but buildings erected according to the 1965 Building Regulations must have all soil and waste systems fitted internally. However, since the surveyor will be concerned with all types of property, old and new methods must be described.

Main soil and ventilating systems

Soil and ventilating systems can be classified into three types:

Two-pipe system, which contains a separate system of pipes for the soil waste and one for waste water, each being separately ventilated against siphonic action of the water seals. The system is used for the larger, more complex building (*Figure 8.19*).

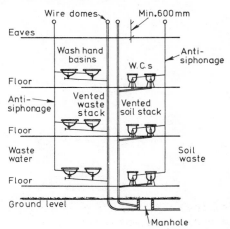

Figure 8.19   Two-pipe soil and waste water system

One-pipe system, which is a combined system of a single pipe for both soil waste and waste water, which is ventilated against siphonic action. This system is widely used for tall buildings and large buildings containing groups of fittings, where several similar fittings may be linked together at each floor level (*Figure 8.20*).

Single-stack system, which is a single ventilated pipe stack to which both soil waste and waste water flow, deep seal traps being used in lieu of anti-siphoning pipes. This system can be used for domestic requirements and flats of limited height (*Figure 8.21*).

Soil and ventilating pipes must now be fitted internally, but are still found fitted on external walls.

Pipes

Soil and ventilating pipes are manufactured from several types of material, each of which is durable and requires to be well jointed together and well secured to the wall structure.

207

Heavy duty cast iron pipes are coated with bituminous paint, jointed with hemp gaskin and fitted with caulked lead wool, molten lead or red lead putty. They are secured to the walls with wrought iron pipe nails.

Plastics or p.v.c. pipes are jointed by a preformed butyl seal which provides a suction type joint. They are secured with holder bats to walls.

Lead. This is used in the form of drawn lead pipe and used as branch pipes in certain older systems. It is jointed together with lead solder joints.

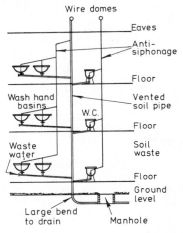

Figure 8.20   One-pipe soil and waste water system

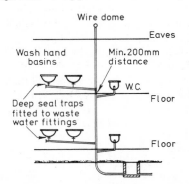

Figure 8.21   Single-stack soil and waste water system

Heavy duty cast iron pipes were used exclusively in the past and are now used for industrial and other important work; plastics pipes are now being used for domestic and similar work in new buildings, replacing other materials during alterations.

All pipes should be fixed in straight alignment, with correct and sound joints securely fixed to wall structures; each stack must be fitted with a wire guard at the top outlet. Soil and ventilated stacks are connected to the salt glazed drainage at ground level, and the joint made with hemp gasket and 1:1 mix cement mortar (*Figure 8.22*). Ventilated

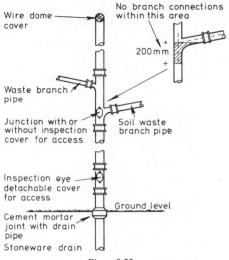

Figure 8.22

waste stacks are connected to a salt glazed back inlet gully at ground level, and jointed with cement mortar; in many cases in existing systems and for small improvements this waste stack may discharge into a trapped gully (*Figure 8.23*).

Stack pipes may be fitted with inspection or cleaning eyes, which may be situated at the base of the stack or at branch connections. They are useful in the case of stoppages, when they afford access for cleaning out. The cover caps are secured by two bolts for easy removal (*Figure 8.22*).

Connections to soil and ventilating stacks

Water closets and urinal fittings on upper floors are connected direct to the soil stack pipe by a branch pipe, the joint being made with red lead putty. Other fittings, such as baths, wash hand basins, showers and sinks, are connected to a ventilated waste stack in some existing systems. These may be discharging into hopper heads and the waste stack discharging over a trapped gully (*Figure 8.24*). This is not a satisfactory method, since the pipes are normally of small diameter and

209

are often found to hold scum and slimy, soapy coatings and have an offensive smell. The scum may clog and impede the flow of waste water, which could freeze during frost action and possibly fracture the pipe. Larger diameter pipes would help reduce this possibility.

In all cases, waste pipes from each fitting must be adequately trapped with a water seal before entering the waste stack. This will prevent the escape of foul gases from the drainage system.

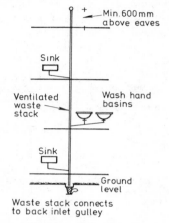

Figure 8.23   Disposal of waste water

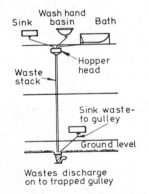

Figure 8.24   Disposal of waste water

Water seal fittings   These traps are fitted to each waste pipe at the fitting outlet; they may be standard seal traps having a water seal of 38 mm deep, or deep seal traps having a water seal of 76 mm deep. They should be self-cleansing and accessible for cleansing by either the removal of detachable cleaning caps or the use of removable traps. It is important that the water seal reseals itself after the use of any fitting. The system needs immediate attention if the seals are accidentally removed in any of the following ways:

Self-siphoning, when the water content is sucked out with the discharging water.

Induced siphoning, when the water content is pulled or sucked out by the discharge from other fittings.

Evaporation of the water content during periods of dry weather, particularly in unoccupied properties.

Anti-siphoning (Figure 8.25) The loss of water seal may be prevented in several ways. In the case of self-siphoning, deep seal traps will

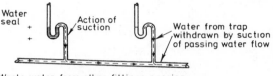

Figure 8.25

counteract the cause. As an alternative, self-sealing traps can be used, which retain water to fill the trap after discharge. Finally, a separate system of anti-siphoning pipes can be fitted from the top of each trap and connected to the vented stack. In this way fresh air is sucked through the pipes instead of the water seal.

Connection of ground floor fittings

It is better for ground floor fittings to make a direct connection to the actual stoneware drainage, i.e. the water closet to connect direct to the stoneware pipe at floor level, and wastes from sink or wash hand basin to discharge into a back inlet gully. On the other hand, wastes from sink or wash hand basins may be found to discharge on to a gully top. This may become fouled and silted up, walls become splashed with slimy deposits, and the whole arrangement become unhygienic.

Defects and testing

Deterioration Deterioration of pipes systems occurs with the loss of watertightness and airtightness, which may be due to the deterioration of the material units or joints.

Smoke test (Figure 8.26)   In order to ascertain its condition the system may be tested. The tops of the ventilating pipes are sealed using an inflated balloon, and then, with all traps possessing their full water seal,

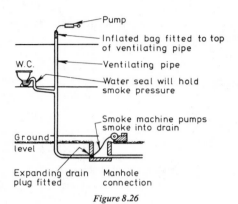

Figure 8.26

smoke is filled in through a stopper plug fitted at the base of the stack pipe or at the connection at the manhole. A low pressure is maintained, and will reveal any faults by smoke being emitted from any defect. The soundness of pipes and joints is thus tested, and with the balloon released, adequate through ventilation is also tested.

Ventilating pipes   It is necessary to check the top of ventilating pipes, which must be a minimum height of 600 mm above the eaves or an opening window. The top must be fitted with a wire guard, to prevent birds nesting in the pipes, which could cause a stoppage in the ventilating system.

Maintenance and inspection   Maintenance needs to be regularly carried out, together with periodic inspection and cleaning to keep pipes clean and sound. Make sure that cleaning caps are well seated after use in order to maintain adequate seals. Check outlet gratings and overflow from fittings, and flushing and discharge from fittings. Maintain regular inspection of protective coatings and replace the coating when necessary or at regular intervals.

Surveying notes In practice varying types of systems and situations will be found, many of which are out-dated although functioning in an efficient manner. Watch out for poor construction, use of incorrect fittings, and wrong joints and connections; these lead to failures.

It will be necessary when making additions or alterations to the system to adapt and include alternative materials and fittings. In all cases efficiency of the service is the essential need.

Drainage systems

Underground drainage systems are provided for the purpose of collecting and conveying rainwater, waste water or soil waste to a disposal system. Disposal is effected as follows:

Local Authority main sewer, the modern treatment and disposal.

Private cesspool, found in many older properties in rural areas and on occasions used today in districts where main sewers do not exist. It consists of a single large underground tank which needs to be emptied of the sediment content in order to prevent overflowing.

Private septic tank, constructed where main sewers are not available. It is preferable to a cesspool. Septic tanks are formed of two tanks, a settling tank and a filter tank, together with an overflow to dispose of the purified water. In these tanks sewage receives treatment in separation, sedimentation and oxidation followed by filtration. They require emptying occasionally.

Soakaways, for the disposal of rainwater only. A soakaway consists of a pit 1.0–1.2 m in diameter and 2.0 m deep which is filled with filter media, to allow rainwater to disperse into the ground strata. It should be situated away from the building to prevent water from affecting the foundations. Sewers, cesspools and septic tanks must each be watertight and sewage must not escape into the ground.

Local Authority sewers

Separate systems These provide for the foul sewer, which is for the disposal of waste water and soil wastes and is connected to and disposed of at sewage plants, and the storm sewer, for the disposal of rainwater into local rivers or watercourses.

Combined system This is an older type of system that exists in many districts where waste water, soil wastes and rainwater combine and connect for disposal into a single sewer where they are dealt with together at the sewage plant. Combined systems cause overwork at the treatment plant and are gradually being replaced by the separate system.

Pipes

Stoneware These may be salt glazed inside and out, or glazed inside and unglazed outside, or they may be unglazed inside and out. They are in 600 mm and 900 mm lengths. They are jointed by means of:

A tarred gaskin packing, sealed with a cement mortar finished bevelled joint.

Patent bitumen seal in two parts, the joint being completed with cement grout.

Flexible joints formed with a rubberized ring that provides a sealed joint. These are very useful in districts where ground movement may occur.

Stoneware pipes require continuous support, which is provided by concrete in the form of bed and haunch to pipes lower than 600 mm deep, or bed and surround to pipes of less than 600 mm deep.

Cast iron These are of cast iron or cast spun, and bitumen coated in lengths of 2.70 m or 3.60 m, which are jointed with caulked lead wool, or tarred gaskin and molten lead.

In areas where ground movement is expected, flexible joints are provided by a rubber ring that forms a sealed joint. Cast-iron pipes are used inside buildings, or in poor ground, or suspended above ground level. They require a limited amount of concrete support, and cover for protection.

Pitch fibre Another form of pipe used in certain areas, they are formed of bitumized fibres that provide rigid and durable pipes; joints are made with a standard taper coupler joint. Some older forms of this pipe were liable to decay, but modern ones are more durable.

Access to drainage

Access is provided by means of manholes or inspection chambers (*Figure 8.27*). They are positioned at changes of direction, changes of falls, or where branch connections are made on the main drain. They allow for easy access for inspection and means of rodding when clearing blockages. Manholes are required to be watertight in construction, including the walls and base. The concrete top and access covers are to be airtight. The cast cover and frame may have a single seal or a double seal; the actual seal should be filled with grease in order to maintain airtightness. Concrete benching requires steep sides that drain into the drain channel; branch pipes must be of a type to direct the discharge into the flow of the drain.

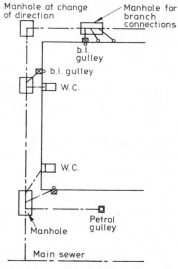

Figure 8.27

The drainage system is connected to the main sewer by means of a straight length of drainage that falls from the last manhole and connects the two levels. The actual connection to the main sewer is made with a saddle joint that must be watertight.

Defects and deterioration

Manholes   These may be found to be not watertight, leaking through walls, defective rendering or joints, or at the concrete base. If joints are filled tight and built to manhole bond then leakage is unlikely (*Figure 8.28*). Unsealed covers and frames may allow the escape of gases, and the cover may be broken or unsealed and in need of replacing or resealing. Concrete benching and channel pipes may be defective and in need of renewal; channel branch pipes must be intact and functioning correctly.

215

Pipes A drainage test may reveal leakages in the drain runs. This may be due to the following defects (*Figure 8.29*):

Broken collars or poor joints; these need to be replaced or rejointed.
Lack of concrete support; the defective length should be relaid and given adequate concrete support.

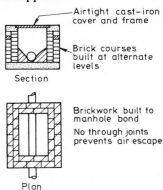

Airtight cast-iron cover and frame

Brick courses built at alternate levels

Section

Brickwork built to manhole bond

No through joints prevents air escape

Plan

Figure 8.28

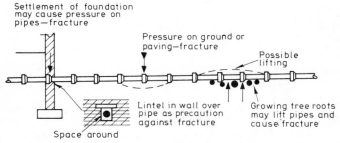

Settlement of foundation may cause pressure on pipes—fracture

Pressure on ground or paving—fracture

Possible lifting

Lintel in wall over pipe as precaution against fracture

Space around

Growing tree roots may lift pipes and cause fracture

Figure 8.29

Tree roots may cause pipe fractures.
Settlement may cause fracture in pipes passing through or under buildings.

Fittings Trapped gullies or back inlet gullies used for the collection of waste water, normally of stoneware material, may leak or have insufficient water seal. Defects may be due to:

Fractured collars or poor joints.
Support concrete may be insufficient, or have subsided and caused fracture of the pipe.

216

Traps or bends may have silted up, so causing stoppages and overflowing at the gully cover.

Concrete dishing around the gully may be fractured, unsound, or leak water; it should then be repaired or renewed.

Petrol gullies are fitted to catch petrol and grease or oil particles, and are situated in car wash areas. They contain a galvanized bucket to collect silt and impurities, and they must be in good working condition.

Testing

Drains may need to be tested at the time of laying the drainage system before the pipes are covered with earth, and also at an inspection in order to ascertain the condition of the system. The following tests and methods of operation should be used.

Water test   A stopper plug is fitted into the end of the drainage pipe at the lower manhole to form a seal, and the next manhole higher up is filled with water to the top. The waver level is observed over a period. If it is maintained then the length of pipes and manhole are watertight; if not, a leak exists. (See *Figure 8.30(a)*.)

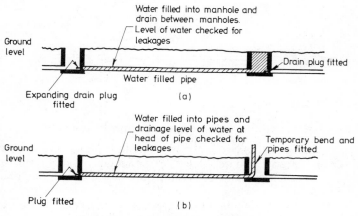

Figure 8.30   (a) Simple water test; (b) Water test

A temporary bend and a vertical pipe can be fitted (*Figure 8.30(b)*) in order that the length of pipes are tested and not the manhole, and the degree of leakage may be observed. Swift falling indicates a serious leak that may require the drain to be relaid; slight or slow falling indicates small leakages only, which can be repaired.

Smoke test (Figure 8.31) Although not such a searching test as the water test, the smoke test does locate the position of a leak better than the water test. Stopper plugs are fitted to each end of a drain length, smoke being pumped through a nozzle in one stopper and the pressure maintained; any leakages will be located by escaping smoke.

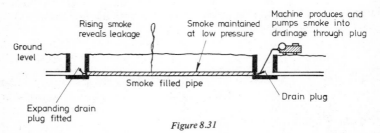

Figure 8.31

Air test (Figure 8.32) Stopper plugs are fitted at each end of a drain length and pressure is applied by air pumped through the nozzle inlet at the stopper; pressure is maintained and measured on a pressure gauge. Any loss of pressure indicates leakage in the pipes. This is a more searching test but will not indicate the actual position of a leak.

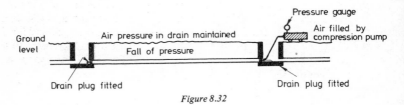

Figure 8.32

Testing of existing drains Existing drains may be tested by:

Simple inspection, carried out by flushing the toilet pans and observing the discharge. Flush out the gullies with a bucketful of water and observe the discharge; at the same time observe the flow through each manhole. A quick and adequate flow will indicate satisfactory conditions. Check on the conditions of the surface fittings; old cast iron and other aged gullies may indicate the age of the system, which may mean that further exacting tests should be carried out.

Smoke test. This is a simple test that can be carried out in order to establish the condition and locate any defects.

Water test. This is a simple test, in which the manhole is filled and observations are made on the level of water. A fall in level or rate of fall will indicate the degree of watertightness. Testing may be carried out on

218

a section between manholes, each dealt with separately, and then branches from manholes to fittings and then the ventilation can be tested normally by the smoke method. The section from the last manhole to the sewer can be tested by means of a special inflatable bag which is fitted to drain rods and pushed along the pipes towards the sewer, where it is inflated so that the test can be carried out.

Many properties may have no means of access to the underground drains, and if stoppages or fractures do occur it may then be necessary to excavate and break open the drain at suitable positions in order to clear the stoppage, or to locate leakages. A test can then be carried out, and a manhole afterwards constructed at this position.

Other properties may have a single manhole only, which allows limited testing, and others have several manholes and so provide satisfactory testing arrangements.

Testing of drainage may be needed outside the boundaries of the property and so will need the permission of other owners. It may also cause inconvenience to the occupiers of properties, and so must be kept to a minimum.

When the Local Authority main sewer is independently ventilated, an interceptor trap needs to be fitted. The trap is fitted at the last manhole, and prevents ventilation of the main sewer into the drainage system; it may also check the movement of sewer rats. The stopper must be correctly fitted, and the water seal maintained. The last manhole must be ventilated by a fresh air inlet unit, which is situated near to ground level and is fitted with a mica flap for the control of air inlet. The mica flap may be damaged and foul gases escape; it will then need to be renewed.

General considerations

Drainage systems need to be constructed in a first class and efficient manner, to be free of trouble during the life of the building; once they are buried underground they create problems if failure occurs, which will be difficult to detect.

Modern drainage is laid to regulation standards, and is tested before use, but many old existing systems may not be so efficient. It is therefore necessary that regular inspections and tests are carried out in order to maintain efficiency, and gullies, traps, manholes and other fittings are kept to a high standard of cleanliness. In carrying out remedial work it is important that the efficiency and smooth flowing of the system is maintained. This can be attained by using correct fittings and form of construction, and where necessary taking advantage of modern materials. It may be found necessary to renew the complete drainage system, which could prove economical during the remaining life of the building.

Bibliography

Building Research Establishment Digests, HMSO:

No. 15, 'Pipes and Fittings for Domestic Water Supply'
No. 32, 'Simplified Plumbing for Housing'
No. 80, 'Soil and Waste Water Pipe Systems for Housing'
No. 81, 'Hospital Sanitary Services, Design and Maintenance Problems'

CHAPTER 9

FLOOD DAMAGE

Building materials and structures deteriorate and decay in many conditions and situations, in most cases moisture being part of the cause. In the construction of buildings it is a fundamental principle to make provisions to prevent moisture from gaining access to the inner building from outside. Flooding causes a reversal of this situation, water gaining access by other means and being unable to get out again. Special action is therefore necessary.

Causes

Flooding may be due to:

A general rise in the level of a local river after heavy rains.
High tides at coastal or river areas, flooding by sea water.
Burst water mains or storage tanks, causing local flooding.
Water from fire fighting appliances following a building fire.

In all cases the rise of water floods into and around buildings, flooding basements, foundations and ground floor areas, causing saturated conditions by the immersion of structure and materials, followed by deterioration, decay and filthy conditions. Flooding may occur once during the life of a building, causing isolated damage, the effects of which would clear; in other cases it may occur more frequently, sometimes once or twice a year, in which case the effects may persist and deterioration may be continuous and difficult to check. In areas where flooding is probable, special precautions must be taken, such as:

The correct siting of the building, with suitable elevation of the ground level to one above possible flood level.

221

Choice of a suitable form of construction in order to minimize the effect of flood waters.

Use of suitable types of material that are less liable to deterioration.

The designer should therefore acquire a knowledge of past floods and their extent in the locality so that the above precautions can be taken to prevent excessive damage.

Effects

The general effect of flooding is mainly that of water penetration and saturation, which contributes towards deterioration and decay. But the water also brings along debris and silt which is left behind when the water subsides. This can cause a health risk, with unwanted deposits of mud and water filling crevices and depressions where it is trapped and unable to escape. Trapped water remains a problem, causing absorption and saturation, different materials absorbing moisture by varying amounts according to their porosity and length of immersion. Structural damage may be caused by severe pressure or buffeting by waves and floating debris. Long periods of immersion will cause surface deterioration of poor quality materials and corrosion of metals, particularly when sea water is involved.

Foundations

Types of ground soils differ in their reaction to the addition of water. Danger to the stability of the foundations can be created when the soil supporting them may be washed away by underwashing currents of water. Clays react in a positive manner but shrinkable clays may swell when wetted, so causing a lifting stress and possible cracking of the wall structure. The cracks may close again as the structure dries out and shrinks. Damage to foundations will require careful examination of the structure in order to ascertain its condition before remedial work is carried out.

Wall structures

The immersion and saturation of the walls by flood water do not normally create serious defects, but there are a few points to look for:

Damage by buffeting of water causing movement of wall and possibly a small collapse.

Surface damage by scouring and erosion; this is more likely to occur in soft quality materials.

Frost damage to saturated structures.

Damage by soluble salts—efflorescence, described on page 60.

Lightweight structures may expand when the moisture content rises and shrink when it lowers. This may cause cracking.

Cavity wall structures may be affected by deposits of mud and silt in the cavity; this may allow moisture penetration to bypass the damp-proof course and also allow moisture to bridge the cavity.

Wall finishes

Lime mortar tends to soften in saturated conditions, so mortar joints may suffer and surface erosion occur. Calcium sulphate plasters may soften and deteriorate, followed by expansion and a disturbed face when drying. Saturated plasters may be affected by frost action, causing surface spalling. Plasterboard and fibreboard absorb moisture rapidly, soften, warp and become mis-shapen by sagging and bellying.

Ground floor finishes

Solid ground floors normally remain structurally sound, although deterioration may occur if burnt colliery shale or chalk is used for the hard core bed; this causes expansion and cracking. Timber in boards or blocks may swell, buckle or lift, causing loss of adhesion and contact with its base. Penetrating moisture will cause deterioration of plastics tiles, floor coverings, timber tiles and screeds, allowing lifting and breaking up of the surface.

Timber

Wet timber is ripe for fungal decay, and the longer it remains saturated the greater the risk. Wet timber is more likely to be attacked by cellar fungus (*Conidiophora cerebella*), and immediate drying is therefore essential. Early inspection may reveal partial decay of long standing; new decay is not likely to occur immediately, but is possible some months later.

Timbers that are attached to, or embedded in damp walls, such as ground floor timbers, skirting boards, wall panelling, door and window frames, are vulnerable to dampness and decay and must be checked. Painted timbers may have been protected but unpainted ones will not have been, and painted surfaces that have deteriorated will absorb water. This will result in blistering and flaking of the paint film.

Metals

Metals are always liable to corrode in contact with water, a process accelerated with salt water, which may be sea water or salts found in and about certain industrial work or stores. Visible surfaces of metal can be cleaned but hidden metals tend to be left to deteriorate by corrosion.

External paved areas

Flood waters may affect ground soils beneath pavings, causing clays to swell and lift the paving, or they may wash away soils and hard core filling from beneath. This often causes the paving to break up, subside and collapse.

Drainage systems

Drainage systems could, in serious situations, be damaged by loss of support and eventual fracture, but more often pipes and fittings are filled with silt causing partial or complete blockage.

Cleaning and remedial work

Cleaning up

After the subsidence of flood waters it is an urgent necessity to drain away trapped water from within and about a building as soon as possible. The use of pumps will be of great assistance, and with holes drilled through walls and floors will help to clear the water. It will also be necessary to clear basements, service ducts and pits. The cavities in cavity walls should be cleared by drilling holes or removing bricks to form outlets.

Cleaning These operations should start as soon as possible. Debris, rubble and mud should be cleared away, making sure that silt is removed from damp-proof courses and air ventilators. Mud finds its way under boarded floors, which must be lifted to help remove it and also to provide drying air currents; it may be necessary to spray disinfectant around the affected area to produce healthy conditions. As mentioned on page 223, mud and silt collect in cavities, which should be inspected by removing an occasional brick. If mud is found in the cavity more bricks can be removed and the holes used to scrape and flush out the mud.

Drying out   After cleaning it is necessary to allow the structure to dry out completely before remedial work is begun. All affected structures must be fully ventilated to provide drying conditions; porous materials absorb large quantities of water during immersion and this takes many weeks or months to dry out. Soluble salts that form on the drying wall surface should be brushed off as they appear. Timber needs to be thoroughly dried as soon as possible. A moisture meter will indicate its true condition and it should be inspected until the moisture content is reduced to less than 20 per cent and then visually inspected six months later for signs of fungal growth.

Drying is helped by keeping doors and windows open and fires and heaters lit, the removal of floor covering, wallpaper and damaged wall plaster. Air ventilating draughts should be created around floor timbers, ventilating bricks cleaned out and holes cut for new ones. Drain pipes and gullies should be cleared out to allow for positive drainage, metal fittings will need to be washed, cleaned and dried, and then greased as a precaution against corrosion.

Remedial work

When the structure is adequately dried the following remedial work may be carried out.

Wall decorations   Defective plastering will need to be re-plastered where necessary; the use of porous plaster will allow partial evaporation. Any mould growths should be treated with fungicide antiseptic solution. The wallpapering should be delayed as long as possible.

Decayed timbers   Decayed timbers that are uncovered can be removed and replaced by sound timber that has been treated with a preservative. Plywoods are affected by saturation, the non-water-resistant adhesives being directly affected, by breakdown and loss of bond; this also applies to flush doors, and those that deteriorate will need to be replaced. Saturated timber will swell and warp and after drying will need to be re-fixed; opening doors and windows bind and will not open, but may, however, return to their normal fitting after drying out, so it is advisable to wait until the timber has dried before refitting.

Foundations Foundations that have been underwashed and the ground support affected will require inspecting to ascertain the actual ground conditions. Then they should be either removed or consolidated, then made good with mass concrete as described on page 42.

Concrete floors and pavings Where affected, these need to be reinstated after the swollen subsoils have returned to normal. Damaged areas should be removed, hard core bases consolidated and new concrete beds laid, which if necessary can be reinforced with fabric mesh. This will be followed by relaying the floor finish.

Drainage Drains will need to be cleaned, rodded and tested to make sure that they have not been fractured. If there is any doubt about a length of drainage the ground should be excavated at the point of the suspected damage and a visual inspection made; new lengths of pipe can then be laid where necessary.

Electrical installations Electrical installations in flooded or wet conditions must first be disconnected until tested by an electrician or Electricity Board Inspector. It will then be necessary to clear away mud deposits and drain water away, mopping up the remainder.

Water may be trapped in ducts and conduits and must be removed by disconnecting conduit boxes and connections to allow draining and drying. Connections and terminations can be exposed, cleaned and left to dry out, after which connections must be examined for surface tracking across the installation surfaces which may have occurred before the supply was disconnected. Components that retain moisture may have to be replaced. After cleaning and drying operations have been completed, the installation will need to be tested for earth continuity and installation resistance as required by the IEE regulations.

It is not always possible to clear damp conditions completely. Some installations may operate in damp atmospheres for some time following flooding, which may cause a breakdown due to tracking in moist films, and overheating at outlets. Heating may be detected by cracking, buzzing, sizzling or emission of smoke, in which case the main supply must be switched off immediately.

Corrosion of ferrous metal parts is always possible in damp conditions. This may affect the return path in steel conduit installations, poor contacts may result in overheating, and rust, being absorbent, attracts moisture and must be prevented. Electrical installations must be inspected and tested initially, then regularly at monthly intervals for some six months after flood damage has been rectified.

Section 2

Internal Environment

CHAPTER 10

HEATING

Ever since men have possessed homes of their own they have attempted to make the internal environment as comfortable as possible. It is mainly the thermal environment which affects bodily comfort and the scale upon which thermal comfort is based is shown below. It is known as the Bedford Scale and divides thermal comfort into seven zones:

(1) Much too cool
(2) Too cool
(3) Comfortably cool
(4) Comfortable and neither too cool nor too warm
(5) Comfortably warm
(6) Too warm
(7) Much too warm.

The factors which affect our bodily comfort when we are placed in a closed environment can be itemized and considered separately, as was done by Bedford. He produced the following requirements for a pleasant environment:

The air should be as cool as possible for comfort.

The surface temperatures, which are summarized by a quantity known as the mean radiant temperature, should be greater than the air temperature. As this is not usually possible the value of this mean radiant temperature should be as near as possible to the room's air temperature.

The air movement in the room should be variable but in colder seasons the mean air velocity should not be less than 170 mm/s and this minimum value should be greater in warmer seasons.

The relative humidity, which is a measure of how near to saturation by water vapour the air is, should be between 45 and 65 per cent and should never exceed 70 per cent. An extremely dry atmosphere, however, can be just as uncomfortable as a very humid one.

The air temperature should not rise excessively with the height above the floor and the occupants' heads must not be subjected to too much radiant heat.

In the UK and a large part of Western Europe, the actual environment for the major part of the year is too cold for comfort. In order to produce comfortable surroundings it is therefore necessary to have sources of heat to increase both air and surface temperatures. The way in which these sources of heat are usually categorized is either as 'direct heating' or as 'central heating'.

A direct heating system is usually based in a room and emits heat to that room only, while a central heating system is used to provide heat for a large number of rooms from a central source. Both types of heating can sometimes be modified to provide a supply of hot water in addition to heat.

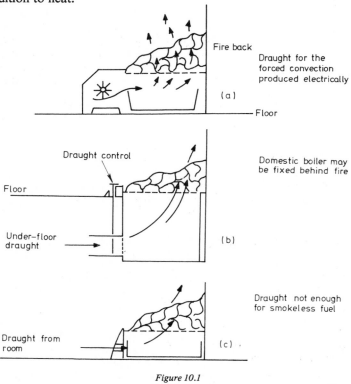

Figure 10.1

DIRECT HEATING

Solid fuel

Solid fuel was the original form of direct heating in the traditional open fire. However, it is now becoming less popular as a heating source (except to provide a focal point in a room) because it is extremely inefficient, at least 50 per cent of the energy produced going straight up the chimney to waste; and the older type of fire is not able to burn the type of fuel required in a smokeless zone.

A range of fires and stoves have been produced, however, which utilize smokeless fuel and these are usually operated in conjunction with a back boiler to provide hot water and a limited amount of central heating. The main way in which they vary from the older type of fire is the method by which they obtain a strong enough draught to enable the combustion of the smokeless fuel to take place. Sketches of several types of solid fuel heaters are shown in *Figure 10.1*.

Oil

Small, portable, oil (paraffin) heaters are sometimes used as a supplementary or standby source of heating. However, they emit a large amount of water vapour into a room's atmosphere, thereby increasing the relative humidity. A sketch of a typical type of oil heater is shown in *Figure 10.2(a)*).

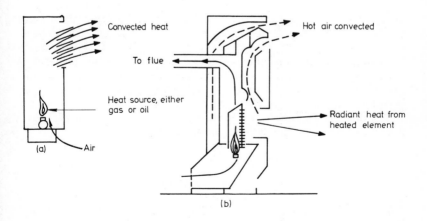

Figure 10.2 (a) Gas or oil flueless convector heater; (b) Radiant convector (with flue)

233

Gas

Gas fires are now produced which are capable of supplying enough heat to warm the room of a normal sized house, but they must be fitted with some form of external flue (*Figure 10.2(b)*)) and are therefore fixed items in the same way as a solid fuel fire or stove. They may be produced either to supply enough heat simply to warm the room, or to operate in conjunction with a back boiler to provide hot water and limited central heating.

Electricity

As a form of direct heating, fires with an electrical source of energy are the most versatile. There are many forms, as shown in *Figure 10.3*, which illustrates the common types of radiant, 'forced' convector and 'natural' convector heaters. In addition to these, a large amount of research is being directed towards the production of electric wallpapers and paints which would enable whole wall areas to provide the required radiant heat when connected to a source of electricity. Some housing developments recently have also incorporated the use of radiant ceilings, but this seems to contradict the thermal comfort requirement concerning air movement (page 231).

Another form of electrical direct heating which is sometimes confused with central heating is the 'off-peak' storage system. This may take the form of either block storage heaters or underfloor heating, both of which are shown in *Figure 10.4*. In this method the electricity is used during 'off-peak' periods to heat up a material with a high specific heat capacity. This heat is then allowed to escape gradually, thereby warming the room. The advantage of the system is that it obtains fuel at a much cheaper rate than is normal, but the main disadvantage is that if the surroundings become much colder during 'peak' hours the extra heat must be found from other sources.

The different fuels used for direct heating are shown in *Table 10.1*, with their relative advantages and disadvantages.

CENTRAL HEATING

Types of central heating are usually placed in one or other of the following two categories. One type uses water to transport the heat, the other uses ducted air.

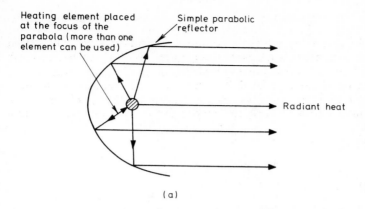

Heating element placed at the focus of the parabola (more than one element can be used)

Simple parabolic reflector

Radiant heat

(a)

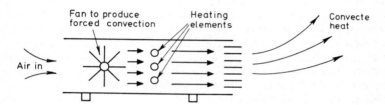

Fan to produce forced convection

Heating elements

Convecte heat

Air in

(May also be used for cooling if the elements are not switched on)

(b)

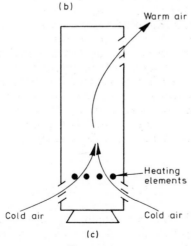

Warm air

Heating elements

Cold air

Cold air

(c)

Figure 10.3

Table 10.1 FUELS USED FOR DIRECT HEATING

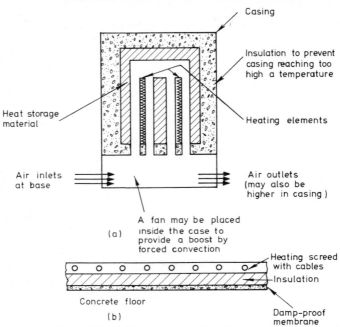

Figure 10.4 (a) Block storage; (b) Underfloor heating

Fuel	Approximate efficiency, %	Comments
Solid fuel	50–60	In open fires or stoves. Supplies hot water in addition to direct heat. Used mainly as focal points for living rooms
Oil	60–70	Portable oil heaters to supplement existing sources. Gives out a large amount of water vapour to surroundings. No fire required
Gas	60–75	Larger ones require flues. Can be designed to supply hot water if required
Electricity	100	Cleanest form. Portable or fixed; radiant heaters or convectors, also storage heaters either underfloor or block storage
Sunlight		Amount governed by window area, orientation and amount of sunlight available

Water transported systems

In the water transported type of system the water is heated by the use of a fuel, which may be either solid fuel, gas, oil or electricity. The type of fuel chosen depends on many factors such as the cost of installation, running costs, storage space available, size of delivery charges and the efficiency of the apparatus, etc., and some of the considerations are shown in *Table 10.2*.

Table 10.2 FUELS FOR CENTRAL HEATING

Fuel	Calorific value	Storage space needed	Comments
Solid fuel	10–25 GJ/m³	Yes	Inefficient, subject to delivery delays
Oil	35–45 GJ/m³	Yes	Stocked by pipe from tanker to tank, subject to delivery delays
Town gas	0.02 GJ/m³ (better for natural gas)	No	No delivery problems. Appliances require conversion from one form of gas to the other
Electricity	3.5 MJ/kW	No	As storage system, can not respond quickly to demand
Heat pump		No	Only fuel required is electricity to drive the pump. A reversible system, high efficiency

However, no matter which type of fuel is used, the remainder of the central heating system will follow a typical pattern. We will concentrate on the small bore system, which uses either 22 mm or 15 mm piping to carry the water. For larger installations a larger bore pipe is required and at the moment a 'micro' bore pipe system is being developed for domestic use. *Figure 10.5* shows several types of system and also a few of the faults which it may develop.

The water is made to flow round the system either by a combination of convection and gravity (*Figure 10.5(a)*) or by the use of a pump (*Figure 10.5(b)*). The gravity system has only limited application as a small supplier of background heating in the domestic situation, and it is the pumped system which forms the basis of most household central heating systems. When the water reaches the rooms where the heat is

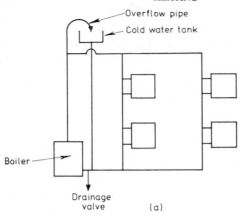

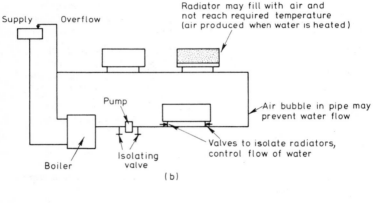

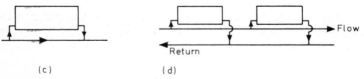

Figure 10.5 (a) Gravity feed system; (b) Simple ring system; (c) One-pipe system; (d) Two-pipe system

required it is made to give up its heat by heating metal surfaces (radiators or metal vanes in skirting) which then pass on the heat to the room by a combination of radiation and convection. If the natural means of heat dissipation are not efficient enough then a fan may be used to produce 'forced' convection currents. Different types of heat dissipators are shown in *Figure 10.6*.

238

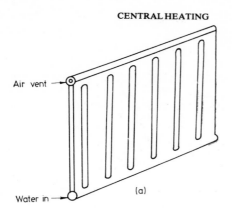

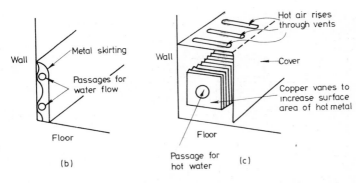

Figure 10.6   (a) Pressed steel radiator; (b) Radiant skirting; (c) Skirting convector

The boiler which produces the hot water for the central heating may also provide hot water for other uses if required, and a set-up for this type of system is shown in *Figure 10.7*.

Air transported systems

Oil, gas and electricity are also frequently used as source fuels for systems which use air to carry the heat. The air is heated by the boiler and then circulated through ducts to the rooms where it is required. For large scale installations this type of system can be incorporated into a ventilation plant which will control the temperature, humidity and cleanliness of the circulated air.

239

Heat pump

The heat pump is an alternative source of energy that can be used with either water or air systems, but due to its high installation costs and other difficulties it is not yet in general use in the UK. Its main advantages are its high efficiency and the fact that it can be used either for

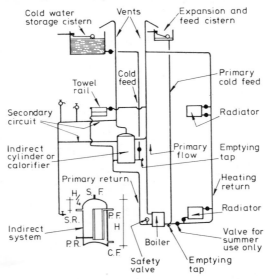

Figure 10.7   C.F. Cold feed; P.F. Primary flow; S.F. Secondary flow; P.R. Primary return; S.R. Secondary return

heating or for cooling. Further details of this system may be found in *Physical Aspects of Building Science*, Hutchinson, B. D., and Barton, J., Butterworths, 1970.

HEAT LOSS

Once the heat has been produced it begins to be lost to the atmosphere by several methods, most of which are illustrated in *Figure 10.8*. The ways in which heat is lost may also be summarized as follows:

Draughts and cold currents of air replacing the warm air in the room.
Conduction of heat through the building materials.
Radiation of heat from the building as a whole.
Convection of heat by the air in contact with the outside of the building.

When all these losses have been estimated and allowed for, enough extra heat must be supplied continually inside the building to enable a steady state to be achieved. The ways in which the heat is lost are considered below.

Draughts

Draughts may be reduced or eliminated by filling cracks and openings, and by the use of draught excluders around windows and doors.

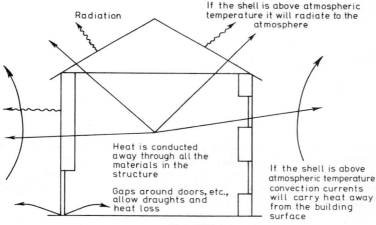

Radiation

If the shell is above atmospheric temperature it will radiate to the atmosphere

Heat is conducted away through all the materials in the structure

Gaps around doors, etc., allow draughts and heat loss

If the shell is above atmospheric temperature convection currents will carry heat away from the building surface

Figure 10.8

Theoretically it should be possible to remove all the draughts completely, but this is not desirable since, if all ventilation were removed, people inside the rooms would suffocate and combustion of materials would not be possible. Furthermore, the comfort requirements listed on page 231 specify minimum values for air velocities, the values of which will be reduced as draughts are reduced.

Conduction

All solid materials allow heat to pass through them to a certain extent. Some are good conductors, while those that are bad conductors are known as insulators. The ability of a material to conduct heat is known as its thermal conductivity or, in certain cases, its thermal conductance, and some common conductivities are shown in *Table 10.3*. As far as the

Table 10.3 THERMAL CONDUCTIVITIES

Material	Conductivity, $W/m°C$
Brickwork	0.7–1.4
Concrete	1.4
Aerated concrete	0.2
Plaster	0.5
Plasterboard	0.16
Timber	0.14
Fibreboard	0.06–0.07
Hardboard	0.14
Compressed strawboard	0.08–0.1
Wood-wool slabs	0.11
Expanded polystyrene	0.033
Foamed polyurethane	0.02–0.025
Glass wool blanket	0.32–0.4
Vermiculite	0.4–0.6
Glass	1.02
Air (stationary)	0.029

reduction of heat losses is concerned it is the thermal resistance of the material which interests the householder. Thermal resistance is a measure of the insulating property of the material; the greater the thermal resistance the better the insulation. The value of the thermal resistance for a material is found from the relationship

$$\frac{\text{Thermal}}{\text{resistance}} = \frac{\text{Thickness of}}{\text{material (metres)}} \times \frac{1}{\text{Thermal conductivity}}$$

If, as is usually the case, a structure consists of more than one type of material then the total thermal resistance of the compound structure is found by adding the individual resistances together according to the equation:

Total thermal resistance $= R_1 + R_2 + R_3 + R_4 \ldots$

where $R_1 =$ thermal resistance of the first material
$R_2 =$ thermal resistance of the second material
$R_3 =$ thermal resistance of the third material
$R_4 =$ thermal resistance of the fourth material, etc.

The calculation of the total resistance for a cavity wall and a single glazed window are shown in *Table 10.4(a)* and (*b*) and the quantity known as the *U* value for each structure is also found. This *U* value, or total thermal transmittance as it should be called, enables the heating engineer to calculate the rate at which heat is being lost through a structure. To do this he uses the equation:

Rate of loss of heat = U value × Cross-sectional area of the structure (square metres) × Temperature difference between the two sides of the structure (°C)

This total thermal transmittance (U value) is the reciprocal of the total thermal resistance:

Total thermal transmittance (U value) = 1/Total thermal resistance

It should be mentioned that nature provides two additional insulating layers on the inside and outside surfaces of any compound structure, due to the fact that a layer of stationary air is produced on the structure.

Table 10.4(a) CALCULATION OF THE TOTAL THERMAL RESISTANCE AND TOTAL THERMAL TRANSMITTANCE OF AN UNVENTILATED CAVITY WALL

Material	Conductivity, k	Resistivity, 1/k	Thickness, d, m	Resistance, d × (1/k)
External air	—	—	—	0.053
Brick	1.15	1/1.15	0.112	0.097
Cavity	—	—	—	0.176
Aerated concrete	0.2	1/0.2	0.100	0.500
Plaster	0.47	1/0.47	0.015	0.032
Internal air	—	—	—	0.123

Total thermal resistance = 0.9810 m² °C/W
Total thermal transmittance = 1/0.9810
= 1.0193 W/m² °C

Table 10.4(b) CALCULATION OF THE TOTAL THERMAL RESISTANCE AND TOTAL THERMAL TRANSMITTANCE OF A SINGLE GLAZED SYSTEM

Material	Conductivity, k	Resistivity, 1/k	Thickness, d, m	Resistance, d × (1/k)
External air	—	—	—	0.053
Glass	1.02	1/1.02	0.005	0.005
Internal air	—	—	—	0.123

Total thermal resistance = 0.181 m² °C/W
Total thermal transmittance = 1/0.181
= 5.525 W/m² °C

Table 10.5 STANDARD U VALUES

Table 10.5 gives standard U values for a selection of wall and roof constructions. The values can be adjusted to meet variations in construction by the following method:

(1) Calculate the reciprocal of the U value. This gives the total resistance of the construction including surfaces and air spaces.
(2) Deduct from the foregoing the resistance R of any layers that are to be omitted.
(3) Add the resistance of any layers there are to be added.
(4) Calculate the reciprocal of the figures resulting from (3) to obtain the new U value.

Part 1. Standard U values for external walls

Construction	U value, W/m²°C	Material		Notes
		Density, kg/m³	Conductivity k, W/m°C	
Brickwork				
(1) Solid wall, unplastered		Brick 1700	0.84	
105 mm	3.3			
220 mm	2.3			
335 mm	1.7			
(2) Solid wall, with 16 mm plaster (see notes) on inside face	(a) (b)	Plaster	0.50 (a)	(a) With dense plaster
105 mm	3.0 2.5		0.16 (b)	(b) With lightweight plaster
220 mm	2.1 1.9			
335 mm				
(3) Solid wall, with 10 mm plasterboard lining fixed to brickwork with plaster dabs		Plasterboard	0.16	
105 mm	2.8			
220 mm	2.0			
335 mm	1.6			
(4) Cavity wall (unventilated) with 16 mm plaster on inside face	(a) (b)	Brick (outer leaf)	0.84	(c) 220 mm outer leaf; 105 mm inner leaf
260 mm	1.5 1.3	Brick (inner leaf)	0.62	
375 mm (c)	1.2 1.1			

244

						With dense plaster
(5) Cavity wall (unventilated), with 105 mm brick outer leaf, 100 mm lightweight concrete block inner leaf and with 16 mm plaster on inside face	260 mm	0.96	Concrete block	600	0.19	
(6) As (5), but with 13 mm expanded polystyrene board in cavity		0.70	Expanded polystyrene		0.033	
Concrete						
(7) Cast	150 mm 200 mm	3.5 3.1	Concrete	2100	1.40	
(8) Cast, 150 mm thick, with 50 mm wood-wool slab permanent shuttering on inside face finished with 16 mm dense plaster		1.1	Wood-wool slab	450	0.09	
(9) As (8), but 200 mm thick		1.1				
(10) Pre-cast panels, 75 mm thick		4.3				
(11) As (10), but with 50 mm cavity and sandwich lining panels composed of 5 mm asbestos cement sheet, 25 mm expanded polystyrene and 10 mm plasterboard		0.80	Asbestos cement sheet	1500	0.36	
(12) Pre-cast sandwich panels comprising 75 mm dense concrete, 25 mm expanded polystyrene and 150 mm lightweight concrete		0.72	Concrete Lightweight concrete	2100 1200	1.4 0.38	

Table 10.5, *Part 1 (continued)*

Construction	U value, W/m²°C	Material Density, kg/m³	Material Conductivity k, W/m°C	Notes
Concrete (*continued*) (13) Pre-cast panels 38 mm on timber battens and framing with 10 mm plasterboard lining and 50 mm fibreglass insulation in cavity	0.62	Fibreglass Timber	0.035 0.14	Assumed 10 % area of fibreglass bridged by timber
Composite cladding panels (14) Comprising 25 mm expanded polystyrene between 5 mm asbestos cement sheets set in metal framing, 50 mm cavity, 100 mm lightweight concrete block inner wall, finished with 16 mm plaster rendering on inside face	0.81			Assumed 5 % area of expanded polystyrene bridged by metal framing
Tile hanging, on timber battens (15) Framing with 10 mm plasterboard lining, 50 mm fibreglass insulation in the cavity and building paper behind the battens	0.65	Clay tiles	0.84	Assumed 10 % area of fibreglass bridged by timber
Weatherboarding on timber (16) Framing with 10 mm plasterboard lining, 50 mm fibreglass insulation in the cavity and building paper behind the boarding	0.62	Weatherboarding	0.14	Assumed 10 % area of fibreglass bridged by timber

			No allowance has been made for effect of corrugations on heat loss
			0.36
		Asbestos cement sheeting	

Corrugated sheeting

(17) 5 mm thick asbestos cement	5.3
(18) As (17), but with cavity and aluminium foil-backed plasterboard lining	1.8
(19) Double-skin asbestos cement with 25 mm fibreglass insulation in between	1.1
(20) As (19), but with cavity and aluminium foil-backed plasterboard lining	0.78
(21) Aluminium	2.6
(22) As (21), but with cavity and aluminium foil-backed plasterboard lining	1.8
(23) Plastics covered steel	5.7
(24) As (23), but with cavity and aluminium foil-backed plasterboard lining	1.9

247

Table 10.5, *Part 2. Standard U values for roofs*

Construction	U value, W/m²°C	Material		Notes
		Density, kg/m³	Conductivity k, W/m°C	
Flat or pitched roofs				
(1) Asphalt 19 mm thick or felt/bitumen layers* on solid concrete 150 mm thick	3.4	Asphalt 1700 Concrete 2100	0.50 1.4	
(2) As (1), but with 50 mm lightweight concrete screed and 16 mm plaster ceiling	2.2	Lightweight concrete 1200 Dense plaster	0.42 0.50	
(3) As (2), but with screed laid to falls, average 100 mm thick	1.8			
(4) Asphalt 19 mm thick or felt/bitumen layers* on hollow tiles 150 mm thick	2.2	Hollow tile	R = 0.27	
(5) As (4), but with 50 mm lightweight concrete screed and 16 mm plaster ceiling	1.6			
(6) As (5), but with screed laid to falls, average 100 mm thick	1.4			
(7) Asphalt 19 mm thick or felt/bitumen layers* on 13 mm cement and sand screed, 50 mm wood-wool slabs on timber joists and aluminium foil-backed 10 mm plasterboard ceiling, sealed to prevent moisture penetration	0.90	Cement/sand 2100 Wood-wool slab 560 Plasterboard	1.28 0.10 0.16	

(8) As (7), but with 25 mm fibreglass insulation laid between joists	0.60	Fibreglass	0.035	
(9) Asphalt 19 mm thick or felt/bitumen layers* on 13 mm cement and sand screed on 50 mm metal edge reinforced wood-wool slabs on steel framing, with vapour barrier at inside	1.4			
(10) As (9), but with cavity and aluminium foil-backed 10 mm plasterboard ceiling below steel framing	0.90			Bridging effect of framing neglected. Assumed that aluminium foil acts as vapour barrier
(11) Asphalt 19 mm thick or felt/bitumen layer* on 13 mm fibre insulation board on hollow or cavity asbestos cement decking, with vapour barrier at inside	1.5	Fibreboard	0.050	
(12) As (11), but with 25 mm fibreglass insulation in cavity, with vapour barrier	0.73			
(13) Felt/bitumen layers on 25 mm expanded polystyrene on hollow or cavity asbestos decking, with vapour barrier	0.87	Expanded polystyrene	0.033	

* The difference between the thermal resistance values of 19 mm of asphalt and three layers of roofing felt set in bitumen is sufficiently small to be ignored.

Table 10.5, *Part 2 (continued)*

Construction	U value, W/m²°C	Material Density, kg/m³	Conductivity k, W/m°C	Notes
Flat or pitched roofs *(continued)*				
(14) Asphalt 19 mm thick or felt/bitumen layers* on 13 mm fibre insulation board on metal decking, with vapour barrier	2.2			
(15) Felt/bitumen layers on 25 mm expanded polystyrene on metal decking, with vapour barrier	1.2			
Pitched roofs, 35° slope				
(16) Tiles on battens, roofing felt and rafters, with roof space and aluminium foil-backed 10 mm plasterboard ceiling on joists	1.5	Tiles Roofing felt	0.84 0.19	
(17) As (16), but with boarding on rafters	1.3	Wood	0.14	
(18) As (17), but with 50 mm fibreglass insulation between joists	0.50			
(19) Corrugated asbestos cement sheeting	6.1	Asbestos cement sheeting	0.36	
(20) As (19), but with cavity and aluminium foil-backed 10 mm plasterboard lining	1.9			

		No allowance has been made for effect of corrugations on heat loss
(21) Corrugated double-skin asbestos cement sheeting with 25 mm fibreglass insulation between	1.1	
(22) As (21), but with cavity and aluminium foil-backed 10 mm plasterboard lining; ventilated air space	0.80	
(23) Corrugated aluminium sheeting	3.8	
(24) As (23), but with cavity and aluminium foil-backed 10 mm plasterboard lining	1.9	
(25) Corrugated plastics-covered steel sheeting	6.7	
(26) As (25), but with cavity and aluminium foil-backed 10 mm plasterboard lining; ventilated air space	2.0	

From *BRE Digest 108*, courtesy HMSO.

* The difference between the thermal resistance values of 19 mm of asphalt and three layers of roofing felt set in bitumen is sufficiently small to be ignored.

They are known as surface resistances. Because of this the previous equation for total resistance is modified to:

Total thermal resistance = Sum of the individual resistances for the materials + External surface resistance + Internal surface resistance

A further list of common U values is shown in *Table 10.5*.

Calculation of heat loss

Once the U values are known the rate at which heat is lost through a structure can be calculated. Consider the two calculations below, based on the U values calculated in *Table 10.4*.

Cavity wall. U value = 1.02 W/m² °C.
Assume the outside temperature $= -1°C$ and the internal temperature $= 23°C$. This gives a temperature difference of $23 - -1 = 24°C$.
Also assume the dimensions of the wall are 6 × 3.5 m, giving a cross-sectional area of 6 × 3.5 = 21 m².

$$\therefore \text{Rate of heat loss} = 1.02 \times 24 = 514.08 \text{ W}$$

Single glazed window. U value = 5.53 W/m² °C.
Assume the same temperature difference of 24°C and the dimensions of the window to be 2.5 × 2 m, giving a cross-sectional area of 5 m².

$$\therefore \text{Rate of heat loss} = 5.53 \times 24 \times 5 = 663.6 \text{ W}$$

This type of calculation may be extended to cover the heating requirements of a whole room by considering each surface in turn and summing the amounts obtained. Once the requirements can be found it is then a simple step to calculate the heat load of the whole house. One extra consideration must be brought in, however. As can be seen from the calculation below, changes of air and the heat needed to warm up the cold new air are allowed for in the final summation.

Consider the room shown in *Figure 10.9*, taking each surface in turn.

(1) *External wall surfaces.* Three of the walls are external walls, two of them with single glazed windows. The total area of the walls minus the area of the windows is required for this calculation.

Wall area (with U value = 1.7 W/m² °C)
= (7 × 2.6) + 2 (5 × 2.6) − (3 × 1.5) − (3 × 3)
= 18.2 + 26 − 4.5 − 9 = 30.7 m²

Outside temperature = 1°C
Inside temperature = 21°C
Difference = 20°C
Rate of loss of heat = 1.7 × 30.7 × 20 = 1024 W

(2) *Internal wall*

Area = 7 × 2.6 = 18.2 m² $\quad$ U value = 2.4 W/m² °C
Temperature difference = 21 − 17 = 4°C
Rate of heat loss = 2.4 × 18.2 × 4 = 174.72 W

(3) *Windows*

Area = (3 × 1.5) + (3 × 3) = 13.5 m²
U value = 5.4 W/m² °C
Temperature difference = 21 − 1 = 20°C
Rate of heat loss = 5.4 × 13.5 × 20 = 1458 W

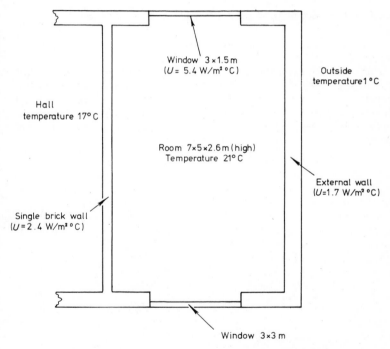

Window 3 × 1.5 m
(U = 5.4 W/m² °C)

Outside
temperature 1 °C

Hall
temperature 17° C

Room 7×5×2.6 m (high)
Temperature 21° C

External wall
(U=1.7 W/m² °C)

Single brick wall
(U = 2.4 W/m² °C)

Window 3×3 m

Wooden floor (U=2.0 W/m²° C)
Temperature underneath = 1°C

Ceiling (U=1.48 W/m²°C)
Temperature above =17°C

Specific heat of air = 1.3 k J/m³°C
Figure 10.9

(4) *Ceiling*

Area $= 7 \times 5 = 35$ m^2 U value $= 1.48$ W/m^2°C
Temperature difference $= 21 - 17 = 4$°C
Rate of heat loss $= 1.48 \times 35 \times 4 = 207.2$ W

(5) *Floor*

Area $= 7 \times 5 = 35$ m^2 U value $= 2.0$ W/m^2 °C
Temperature difference $= 20$°C
Rate of heat loss $= 2 \times 35 \times 20 = 1400$ W

(6) *Air changes*

Heat required $=$ Volume of air $\times$ Specific heat capacity $\times$ Rise in temperature $\times$ Number of changes per second

$= (7 \times 5 \times 2.6) \times) \times 0.36 \times 20 \times 2$
$= 1310.4$ (assuming two changes per hour)

Total heat requirements $= (1) + (2) + (3) + (4) + (5) + (6)$
$= 5570.36$
$= 5.6$ kW (say)

This calculation, although relatively simple, involves a large amount of time, especially if it has to be done for every room in the house, and shorter methods have been developed. One of these involves the use of a Mear's calculator (*Figure 10.10*). It is in effect a circular calculator which enables the total load to be calculated without any mathematical processes.

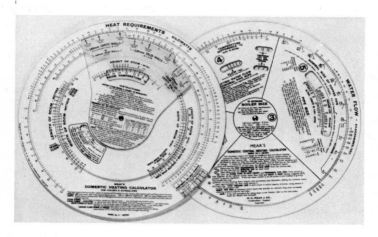

Figure 10.10   Mear's calculator

Reduction of heat loss

What if these heat losses are too great? The householder can do one of two things:

Reduce the temperature difference by settling for a lower internal temperature. As the whole process has been an attempt to increase internal temperatures, this is not a satisfactory solution.

Reduce the U values by the use of additional insulating materials.

The three parts of the structures which are easiest to treat are windows, walls, and roof space.

Windows

The most common way of reducing heat loss through window areas is by the use of double glazing instead of single glazing. This involves the use of two panes of glass separated by a gap of 6–18 mm, either in the form of a sealed system or as two separate sheets. The sealed system is the more efficient and less prone to condensation, but the unsealed system is cheaper and easier to install. Diagrams of these types of system are shown in *Figure 10.11* and the U value calculation for a double glazed system is shown in *Table 10.6*.

The new U value is 2.79 W/m² °C as compared to 5.53 W/m² °C for the single glazing and therefore approximately half the heat previously lost through the window has been saved. Apart from this saving of heat a double glazed system has other advantages which will be considered later.

Table 10.6 THERMAL RESISTANCE AND TRANSMITTANCE OF A DOUBLE GLAZED
WINDOW

Material	Conductivity, k	Resistivity, 1/k	Thickness d, m	Resistance, d × (1/k)
External air	—	—	—	0.053
Glass	1.02	1/1.02	0.005	0.005
Air	0.029	1/0.029	0.007	0.1724
Glass	1.02	1/1.02	0.005	0.005
Internal air	—	—	—	0.123

Total resistance = 0.3584 m² °C/W

Total thermal transmittance = 1/0.3584
$$= 2.79 \text{ W/m}^2 \text{ °C}$$

Actual double glazed systems would be more effective due to the use of thicker glass or even a wider air space. The same glass thickness has been used for comparison with *Table 10.4(b)*.

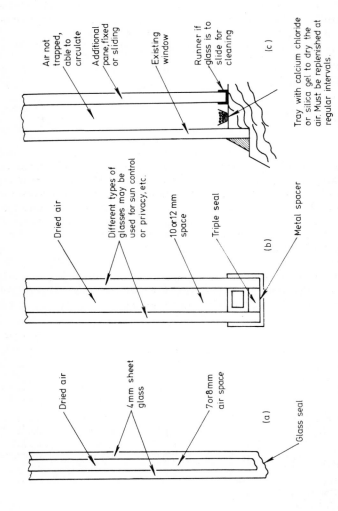

Dried air

4 mm sheet glass

7 or 8 mm air space

(a)

Glass seal

Dried air

Different types of glasses may be used for sun control or privacy, etc.

10 or 12 mm space

Triple seal

(b)

Metal spacer

Air not trapped, able to circulate

Additional pane, fixed or sliding

Existing window

Runner if glass is to slide for cleaning

(c)

Tray with calcium chloride or silica gel to dry the air. Must be replenished at regular intervals.

Figure 10.11   (a) Continuous piece of glass; (b) Two sheets of glass in sealed unit; (c) Non-sealed system

Walls

The two ways in which heat lost through walls can be reduced are either by fixing a thin layer of polystyrene to the inside surface of the wall or by filling the cavity with some insulating material. The two calculations involved are shown in *Table 10.7*.

Table 10.7(*a*) TOTAL THERMAL RESISTANCE AND TRANSMITTANCE OF AN UNVEN-
TILATED CAVITY WALL INSULATED WITH SHEET POLYSTYRENE

Material	Conductivity, k	Resistivity, 1/k	Thickness d, m	Resistance, d × (1/k)
External air	—	—	—	0.053
Brick	1.15	1/1.15	0.112	0.097
Cavity	—	—	—	0.176
Aerated concrete	0.2	1/0.2	0.100	0.500
Plaster	0.47	1/0.47	0.015	0.032
Polystyrene	0.03	1/0.03	0.002	0.067
Internal air	—	—	—	0.123

Total thermal resistance = 1.048 m² °C/W
Total thermal transmittance = 1/1.048
$$= 0.954 \text{ W/m}^2 \text{ °C}$$

Table 10.7(*b*) TOTAL THERMAL RESISTANCE AND TRANSMITTANCE OF A CAVITY WALL
WHEN THE CAVITY HAS BEEN FILLED WITH INSULATING MATERIAL

Material	Conductivity, k	Resistivity, 1/k	Thickness d, m	Resistance, d × (1/k)
External air	—	—	—	0.053
Brick	1.15	1/1.15	0.112	0.097
Cavity	0.01	1/0.01	0.05	5.000
Aerated concrete	0.02	1/0.2	0.100	0.500
Plaster	0.47	1/0.47	0.015	0.032
Internal air	—	—	—	0.123

Total thermal resistance = 5.805 m² °C/W
Total thermal transmittance = 1/5.805
$$= 0.1722 \text{ W/m}^2 \text{ °C}$$

The two values now obtained are 0.954 W/m² °C and 0.1722 W/m² °C. It can be seen that the second method gives the greater saving, reducing the heat loss to approximately one fifth of the previous value.

Roofs

From the values given in *Table 10.5* the U value for a roof space made up of tiles, felt, rafters and aluminium backed plaster board is 1.5 W/m² °C. If a layer of fibreglass quilt 50 mm thick is incorporated into the system the value becomes 0.5 W/m² °C, reducing the loss to one third of its previous value. The quilt is usually sold in 25 mm or 50 mm thicknesses, but there is one school of thought which suggests that a 100 mm thickness is the most effective to use.

The costs of these alternative methods are difficult to compare, depending as they do on labour charges, etc. However, for a four-bedroomed detached house it would probably cost between £20 and £50 for ceiling insulation, £80 and £150 for cavity insulation and £500 and £1000 for double glazing, depending on the type of system used.

The order in which the householder should adopt these methods depends on the money available, the relative areas of the walls, windows, and ceilings, and even whether the saving of fuel costs will justify the initial expense. For a complete treatment of these considerations, discount flow methods should be used and the final decision will depend on the individual.

SURFACE TEMPERATURES

In the Bedford recommendations on page 231 it was stated that the surface temperature should be in excess of the room air temperature. If the external air is colder than the internal air then this situation is almost impossible to achieve, but the degree of comfort will increase as the temperature of the surfaces increases. This quantity is measured as the mean radiant temperature and is defined as 'the surface temperature of a uniform enclosure which will give the same net radiation exchange as the actual surfaces and their associated temperatures'. In a room with unheated surfaces the mean radiant temperature is defined by the equation

Mean radiant temperature =

$$\Sigma (A_1 \theta_1 / A)$$

where A_1 and θ_1 = areas and temperatures of the individual surfaces
A = total surface area of the room
Σ is the mathematical abbreviation meaning sum all the individual quantities.

Measurement of mean radiant temperature

The mean radiant temperature may be estimated by the use of a globe thermometer (*Figure 10.12*). It consists of a hollow copper sphere coated black on the outside so that it will absorb as much thermal radiation as possible, with either a thermometer, thermocouple or some other temperature measuring device at the centre.

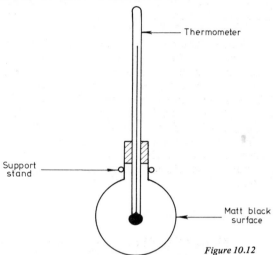

Figure 10.12

Improvement of surface temperature values

It is possible to calculate the surface temperature of the walls in a room from the equation:

Temperature difference between air and the surface = Rate of heat loss per unit area × Thermal resistance of internal stationary air

It is necessary to consider again the structures dealt with on page 243, where rates of heat loss were being calculated:

Unventilated cavity wall

Rate of heat loss = 514.08 W
assuming a temperature difference of 24°C
Rate of heat loss per unit area = 514.08
÷ 21 = 24.48 W/m²
Temperature difference to be found = 3.01°C i.e. 24.48 × 0.123
and surface temperature = 23 − 3.01
= 19.99°C

259

Unventilated cavity wall with layer of polystyrene

Rate of heat loss = 0.954 × 21 × 24 = 480.82 W
Rate of heat loss per unit area = 22.89 W/m²
Temperature difference to be found = 2.81°C
and surface temperature = 23 − 2.81
= 20.19 °C

Cavity wall with cavity filled with insulation

Rate of heat loss = 0.1722 × 21 × 24 = 86.79 W
Rate of heat loss per unit area = 4.13 W/m²
Temperature difference to be found = 0.50 °C
and surface temperature = 23− 0.50
= 22.50 °C

Similar calculations for the single and double glazed systems enable the following values to be obtained:

Single glazing

Surface temperature = 23 − 16.32 = 6.68 °C

Double glazing

Surface temperature = 23 − 8.23 = 14.77 °C

It should be apparent from these figures that the methods used to improve thermal insulation have also had the effect of increasing the internal surface temperatures and hence the thermal comfort.

AIR MOVEMENT

Minimum values have been suggested for the air velocities in a room under different conditions in order to produce a comfortable thermal environment. They can be obtained only by the use of ventilation which will, if excessive, produce the draughts which reduce air temperature. The householder must therefore produce a compromise situation in which he himself feels comfortable.

Measurement of air velocity

Air velocity is measured by means of either a Kata thermometer or a hot wire anemometer.

Kata thermometer

A Kata thermometer is an alcohol thermometer with a bulb 40 mm long and 18 mm in diameter. On the stem are graduations at 37.4°C and 40°C and the top of the stem is enlarged to allow for excessive heating and expansion (*Figure 10.13*). The surface of the bulb is silvered to

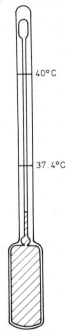

Figure 10.13

reduce thermal radiation effects to a minimum. To use the instrument the time is recorded for the alcohol to fall between the two graduations when it is suspended in the current of air, the velocity of which is being measured. The time found can then be related to the velocity of the air. Each instrument must be individually calibrated and has its own 'Kata factor' engraved on the stem.

Hot wire anemometer

The hot wire anemometer is simply a resistance wire energized by a constant voltage so that a current of approximately 0.5 A is produced. The temperature produced then depends on how much heat is being removed by the air movement and modern instruments are calibrated directly in metres per second. In most instruments the resistance wire is surrounded by a thin tube to prevent deposits of dust settling on the wire.

RELATIVE HUMIDITY

Relative humidity is defined as the ratio of the amount of water vapour in the air at room temperature to the amount of water vapour required to saturate the air at room temperature. For comfortable conditions the relative humidity should be between 45 and 65 per cent and should never exceed 70 per cent. If the air in the room is too dry (i.e. relative humidity less than 45 per cent) then extra water vapour can easily be added, either by placing a bowl of water in the room or by hanging a humidifier from the radiator. A humidifier is simply a water container which allows the water it holds to vaporise.

If the atmosphere is too damp then vapour must be removed by either:

Increasing the ventilation rates.
Extracting the water vapour at source by means of an extractor fan.
Drying the air during its circulation if a ducted air system is being used.

The subject of relative humidity need not be discussed further here, but it is closely involved with the modern problem of condensation, dealt with on page 263.

CONVECTION AND RADIATION FROM OUTSIDE THE BUILDING

For the sake of continuity of ideas and calculations, heat losses by convection and radiation from the outside of the building, referred to on page 241, have not yet been dealt with. In simple terms both types of heat loss will be related to the outside surface temperature of the building. These may be calculated in the same way as the internal surface temperatures (page 259). Considering the structures used in previous calculations, the equation to be used becomes:

Temperature difference between the external air and the surface = Rate of heat loss per unit area × Thermal resistance of the external stationary air

Unventilated cavity wall

$$\text{Temperature difference} = 24.48 \times 0.053°C$$
$$= 1.30°C$$

As the external temperature has been assumed to be $-1°C$ then the surface temperature $= +0.3°C$.

Similar calculations may be performed for the other systems, giving the following answers:

Unventilated cavity wall with a layer of polystyrene: surface temperature $= +0.21°C$.
Wall with insulation in the cavity: surface temperature $= -0.8°C$.
Single glazing: surface temperature $= 6.03°C$.
Double glazing: surface temperature $= 2.55°C$.

Again it should be apparent that the methods already introduced to improve the thermal insulation have also reduced convection and radiation heat losses by reducing the external surface temperature.

CONDENSATION

Relative humidity has already been considered (page 262). If the relative humidity of the air becomes 100 per cent then the air is said to be saturated with water vapour and condensation will occur on cold surfaces. The amount of water vapour that a given volume of air can hold varies with temperature, as shown in *Figure 10.14*. This means that warm air can hold much more water vapour than cold air and that if warm air not saturated with water vapour is cooled down, it will eventually reach a temperature when it is saturated. This temperature is

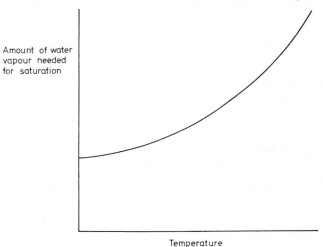

Temperature

Figure 10.14

known as the dew point temperature. The conditions necessary for condensation can therefore be summarized as follows.

Condensation will occur when warm air is cooled to a temperature known as its dew point temperature, either by contact with a cold surface or by passage into a cooler region. Each of these different phenomena should be considered separately. The first will primarily give rise to surface condensation, while the second may cause interstitial condensation if the colder region occurs inside the structure of the building components.

Surface condensation

The most common area for surface condensation to take place is on the inside surface of single glazed windows. Consider an extension of the calculation from pages 259 and 262 so that a graph of the temperature drop from inside the room to outside may be drawn for a single glazed window. This graph is shown in *Figure 10.15(a)*. If a relative humidity

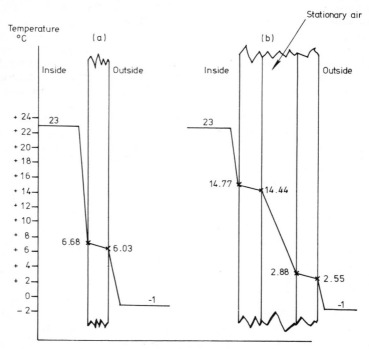

Figure 10.15   (a) Single glazed; (b) Double glazed

264

of 50 per cent is assumed inside the room then the amount of water vapour present in the air = 0.01 kg/m³. By consulting the relevant steam tables it can be shown that this amount of water vapour would saturate the air at 9.6°C. By looking at *Figure 10.15(a)* it can be seen that this temperature is reached before the window surface, and the actual surface of the glass is even colder than this. Condensation is therefore certain to appear on the window surface. (It should be noted that the value for relative humidity which has been chosen would be reasonable for a living room, but much larger values would be found in kitchens and bathrooms, etc.)

Consider now *Figure 10.15(b)*, which is for the double glazed unit. The critical temperature this time appears, not inside the room, but inside the air space of the double glazing. With a sealed unit the air from the room can not mix with the air in this space and condensation will not occur as the (trapped) air is always dried during the manufacturing process. With an unsealed system, however, the air from the room is able to enter the space and condensation may appear on the surfaces facing on to the air space. These surfaces are very difficult to wipe and if this problem is met it is usually solved by placing trays of drying agent, such as silica gel or calcium chloride, inside the space.

Prediction of condensation The graphs in *Figure 10.16* show the relationship (under conditions when condensation is just starting) between the four variables: relative humidity, thermal transmittance, internal temperature and external temperature. The graphs are in two parts and are then connected by the horizontal projection to produce the result. With the examples shown, condensation will occur with single glazing if the outside temperature falls to 2.5°C, but with a double glazed 'glastoglas' unit the outside temperature would have to fall to −5°C for condensation to appear.

Surface condensation on walls

With modern insulated structures it is unlikely that permanent condensation will appear on the surface of a house wall, but on the older type of wall which may have a U value greater than 1.7 or 1.8 W/m² °C then the problem may arise, as the surface temperatures will be much lower. The problem can be eased by increasing the surface temperature by the use of polystyrene on the wall surface or an insulated filling in the cavity. This solution will not prevent interstitial condensation and a vapour barrier must be used in this case to prevent the passage of moisture into the material.

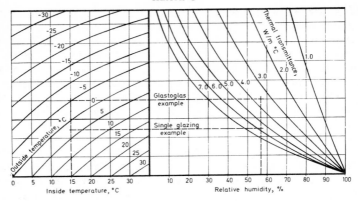

Figure 10.16   The graph shows the relationship (under conditions when condensation is just star-ting) between the four variables: relative humidity; thermal transmittance of the glazing; internal temperature; external temperature. The graphs are in two parts, each of which is used in the nor-mal way, then connected by horizontal projection to produce the result. The example shown in the SI graph is for a room with an inside temperature of 15°C and a humidity of 57 per cent. With Glastoglas double-glazed units (U value 3.52), condensation will not occur until the outside temperature falls to 5°C. Had the same room been single glazed (U value 5.68), condensation would occur when the outside temperature fell below 2.5°C. The graph may be used to determine any fourth variable when three are known.   (Courtesy Pilkington Bros.)

Interstitial condensation

Figure 10.17 shows graphically the temperature drop through the structure of a cavity wall. The temperature drop is shown by the solid line. Superimposed is a graph of the dew point temperature for the air as it passes through the porous structure, shown by a broken line. At any point on the graph where the actual temperature is lower than the dew point temperature, condensation can occur, which may cause damage to the structure.

In order to prevent this type of condensation it is necessary to line the wall with a vapour barrier which will prevent the passage of moist air to colder parts of the material (see *Figure 10.18*). *Table 10.8* gives the vapour resistivities of common materials and membranes. The greater the resistance or resistivity the more difficult it is for the vapour to pass through the material.

Causes of condensation

Condensation is a modern problem. It has been aggravated by the materials now used to conserve heat, the appliances used and the way in

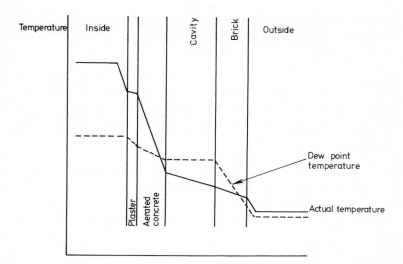

Figure 10.17 Condensation may occur where the broken line is above the continuous temperature line. (Details of how the position of the broken line is found are given in detail in B.R.E. Digest 110)

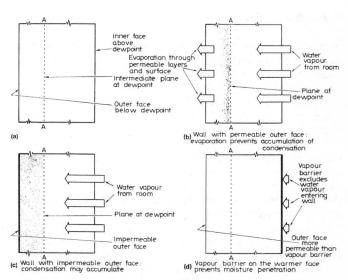

Figure 10.18 Temperature conditions in wall which may lead to interstitial condensation. (Courtesy HMSO)

267

which homes are used. In order for it to take place it is necessary for warm, moist air to be produced and to reach a cold surface or region.

Warm, moist air   Modern central heating systems and methods of thermal insulation enable much higher temperatures to be produced in rooms, and the air can then hold a relatively large amount of water vapour. The reduction of draughts and ventilation and the replacement of old open fires all prevent the introduction of colder, drier air from outside.

Table 10.8 TABLE OF VAPOUR RESISTANCES AND RESISTIVITIES
(from B.R.E. Digest No. 110)

(*a*) Vapour resistances (for membranes)

Membrane	Vapour resistance, MN s/g
Gloss paint film	7.5–40
0.06 mm polythene sheet	250
Aluminium foil	4000

(*b*) Vapour resistivities (for materials)

Material	Vapour resistivity, MN/g
Brick	25–100
Concrete	30–100
Timber	45–75
Fibreboard	15–60
Plasterboard	45–60
Strawboard	45–75
Wood-wool	15–40
Expanded polystyrene	100–600
Plywood	1500–6000

Modern appliances such as washing machines, dishwashers, driers, etc., are now all designed as pieces of furniture to fit into a modern kitchen and when in operation produce a large amount of water vapour. Previously they would have been outside in the 'wash house' so that the moisture could not get into the house, or the householder would not have been able to afford them anyway.

Some gas and oil fuel appliances do not have external flues and discharge moisture into the atmosphere.

Cold surfaces These have already been described but there is one habit of modern living that encourages condensation—the intermittent use of houses. This happens when all the occupants of a house are out for most of the day and, as the heating is usually off during this period, the house and all the surfaces inside it become cold. When the occupants return home, most activity takes place in either the bathroom or the kitchen and large amounts of water vapour are produced. If this water vapour then comes into contact with a cold surface condensation will be formed.

Other cold surfaces which produce condensation on them are cold water and service pipes, the temperature of the water in which is regularly 2 or 3°C, much below the temperature of the air in the room.

Prevention

For condensation to take place three conditions must exist at the same time:

(1) Warm, moist air must be produced so that the water vapour is available.

(2) A cold surface or a cold area must exist which will cause saturation to take place.

(3) Contact must take place between these two conditions.

If any of these conditions are removed then it will be more difficult for condensation to take place. The accumulation of warm, moist air may be prevented by increasing the ventilation rates, thereby introducing

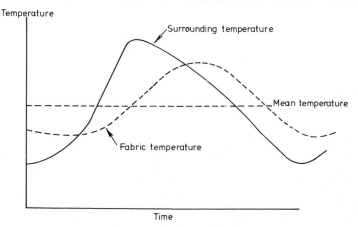

Figure 10.19

cooler, drier air, or by extracting the moisture as it is being produced by the use of extraction fans. Cold surfaces may have their temperatures raised, as has already been discussed in the section on thermal insulation (page 259). The warm, moist air must be isolated and kept away from the cold surfaces by keeping kitchen and bathroom doors closed. This will reduce the circulation and limit condensation.

Atmospheric conditions

If a period of cold weather is followed by a warm, damp spell then the fabric of a heavy structure which has not been completely heated does not warm up immediately, but a time lag ensues as shown in *Figure 10.19*. When the warm, moist incoming air comes into contact with the cold surface, condensation will form as previously described, but as the walls warm up the condensation will evaporate and the moisture disappear. A light construction will warm up more quickly and is therefore less likely to suffer from this type of condensation.

Anti-condensation paints

These work on the principle that condensed water can be absorbed and held on an absorbent surface until the conditions change and allow it to dry out. This can only be effective, however, if the drying periods are long enough relative to the condensation periods to ensure that complete saturation of the absorbent material does not occur.

CHAPTER 11

NOISE

NOISE POLLUTION

One of the newest threats to the environment, both inside and outside the home, is noise, or noise pollution as it is now frequently called. What has caused this problem to increase so rapidly in recent years? There are two main reasons:

There have been large increases in both road and air traffic noise due to new engine development, larger planes and lorries, new motorways, larger airports, etc.

Alongside this, the changes in building techniques and materials have tended to utilize lightweight components with dry and frequently poorly sealed joints.

These two factors have separately and jointly increased the level of sound that manages to penetrate into the home, thus causing discomfort. Recommendations and regulations have been formulated in an attempt to control and reduce the existing noise levels. Some of these attempts are described below.

Motor vehicle noise

In 1963 the Committee on the Problem of Noise suggested the following maximum sound levels of new vehicles:

Motor cycles	90dBA
All other vehicles	85dBA

This recommendation was emphasized in 1968 when legislation stated that all vehicles registered since 1931 must comply with the following maximum levels:

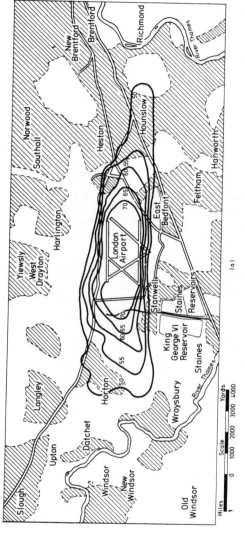

Figure 11.1 (a) Approximate noise and number index 1961

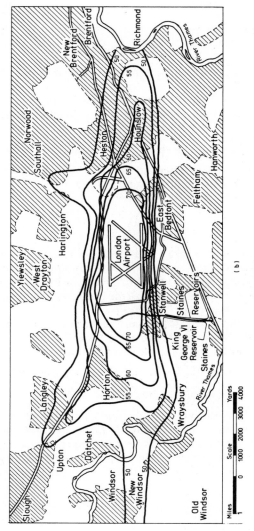

Figure 11.1   (b) Estimated noise and number index 1970. (Courtesy HMSO)

273

	dBA
Motor cycles less than 50 cm^3	80
Other motor cycles	90
Passenger cars	87
Light goods vehicles	88
Heavy goods vehicles	92

All new vehicles were (in 1970) made to conform to maxima 3 dBA less than those quoted above.

Recent work at B.R.E. has lead to the suggestion of a mathematical quantity known as the Traffic Noise Index (TNI) which is defined by the equation:

$$\text{TNI} = 4(10\% \text{ noise level}) - 3(90\% \text{ noise level}) - 30$$

Further details of this method may be found in B.R.E. publications and in *Acoustics* by B. D. Smith, Longmans, 1971.

Air traffic noise

The production of larger aircraft and the use of longer runways have meant that many more people are now affected by air traffic noise and it is not unusual to see noise contour diagrams in local and national newspapers in an attempt to emphasize the problem. Two typical noise contour diagrams are shown in *Figure 11.1*.

A numerical value for air traffic noise is known as the Noise and Number Index (NNI) which was derived to show the effect of the noise on the population at large. It is found from the equation:

$$\text{NNI} = \text{Average peak noise level} + 15 \log_{10} N - 80$$

where $N =$ the number of aircraft heard.

The relationship between NNI and the annoyance rating for a set of experiments carried out at Farnborough is shown in *Figure 11.2*.

Public pressure about noise levels near large airports has in several cases resulted in the limitation of night flights and the banning of aircraft with certain noise levels for some hours during the day and night.

Industrial noise

The criteria for dealing with industrial noise are dealt with in British Standard BS 4142, *Method of rating industrial noise affecting mixed residential and industrial areas*, 1967, to which the reader is referred.

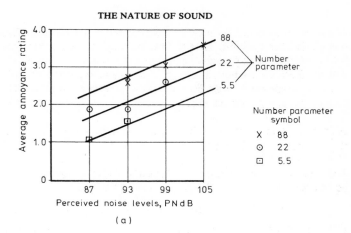

(a)

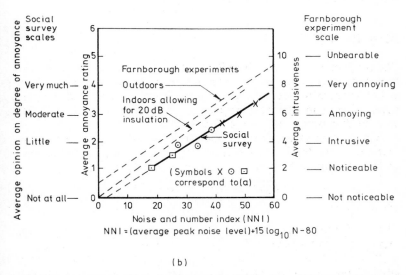

$$NNI = (\text{average peak noise level}) + 15 \log_{10} N - 80$$

(b)

Figure 11.2   (a) Relation between average annoyance and perceived noise levels; (b) Relations between annoyance rating and noise and number index obtained from social survey and Farnborough experiments.   (Courtesy HMSO)

The nature of sound

Sound is a pressure wave produced by a vibrating source and is carried through the medium separating the source from the observer in the form of a transverse wave. When it reaches the ear it sets the eardrum in

275

vibration, and this vibration is transmitted to the brain where it is recognized as a sound. Due to this method of recognition there are lower limits of sound levels (or pressures) below which nothing is heard and an upper limit when the observer experiences pain. The actual value of these limits varies with the individual and with the frequency of the sound, but typical values are:

	dB
Lower level	40
Upper level	140

These rough values do not take account of the frequency dependence, but a more accurate relationship is shown in *Figure 11.3*.

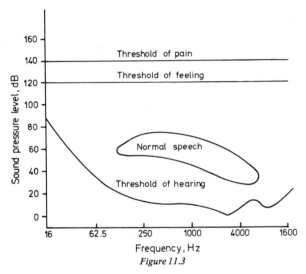

Figure 11.3

At noise levels below the pain threshold prolonged exposure to the sound will cause loss of hearing and sometimes permanent deafness. It is not surprising, therefore, that people should seek a quiet, peaceful, home environment. The problem of keeping noise out of the environment is known as sound insulation and is best considered, as shown below, by investigating what noise causes the annoyance, where it comes from, and then how it can be reduced as much as possible.

SOUND INSULATION

The main types of noise and their methods of transmission are listed below, and illustrated in *Figure 11.4*. The classification is not definite but simplifies the problem to be considered.

(1) Sound produced from outside the building.
(2) Sound produced from another room inside the building.
(3) Impact noise.
(4) Structure-borne plant noise.

Sound from outside the building

As can be seen from *Figure 11.4*, the sound from outside may be carried either through the ground or through the air. The sound transmitted through the ground is the lesser problem and need not be considered further here. It is the airborne sound which is significant.

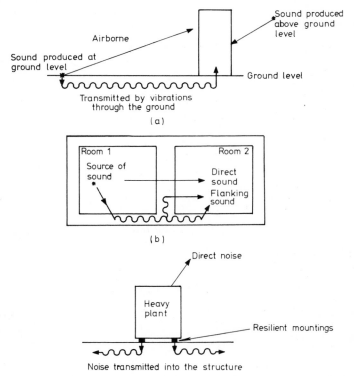

Figure 11.4 (a) Transmission of sound from outside of building; (b) Transmission of sound from inside building; (c) Plant noise

The three main principles to be considered in the reduction of this sound are:

The inverse square law. This states that the intensity of a point source of sound is inversely proportional to the square of the distance from the source. The further away from the source the observer is, the quieter his environment.

The mass/unit area law. This states that the insulating properties of an obstruction depend on the mass/unit area of the obstruction. The more solid the obstruction, the better is the sound reduction. This relationship is shown in *Figure 11.5.*

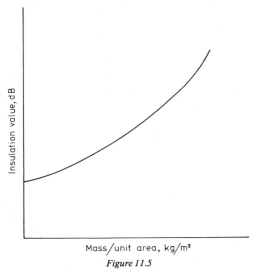

Figure 11.5

Sound will always find the weakest link (acoustically speaking) in any obstruction and pass through this.

Reduction of sound from outside buildings

Airborne sound from outside the building may be produced either at ground level or from above ground level. Noise produced at ground level can be reduced as follows:

By moving the source of the sound as far away from the observer as possible. This is obviously impracticable in most situations.

By the use of some obstacle placed between the sound and the observer. For the optimum effect the mass/unit area of the obstruction should be as large as possible. This is not always feasible and in some cases bushes and trees placed between the source and the observer will produce some reduction in noise level even if it is only marginal. If trees are to be used they must be of a leafy variety and thick right down to ground level.

Filling all cracks round doors and windows with a good mastic. In most cases this will produce an immediate improvement in the indoor noise level.

Windows are not very good sound insulators. In order to reduce the interior sound either the glazed area facing the sound should be reduced or alternatively a double glazed system should be used. This is sometimes known as a double window due to the spacing between the panes and the fact that both panes usually open independently. A typical double glazed system and its insulation values compared to a single system are shown in *Figures 11.6(a)* and (*b*). Recent work at B.R.S. has resulted in the production of an automatic double glazed window which closes when the sound level reaches a certain value and opens again when the sound level drops to a reasonable value.

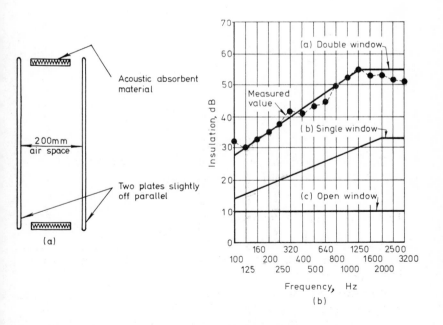

Figure 11.6   (Courtesy HMSO)

279

Table 11.1 INSULATION VALUES

Construction	Sound insulating grading	
	Airborne	Impact
Concrete floors		
Concrete floor (reinforced concrete slab or concrete and hollow pot slab) weighing not less than 220 kg/m², with hard floor finish	Grade II	4 dB worse than Grade II
Concrete floor with floor finish of wood boards or 6 mm linoleum or cork tiles	Grade II	Grade II
Concrete floor with floor finish of thick cork tiles or of rubber on sponge rubber underlay	Grade II	Probably Grade I
Concrete floor with floating concrete screed and any surface finish	Grade I	Grade I
Concrete floor with floating wood raft	Grade I	Grade I
Concrete floor with suspended ceiling and hard floor finish	Probably Grade I	2 dB worse than Grade II
Concrete floor with suspended ceiling and wood board floor finish	Probably Grade I	Grade II
Concrete floor with suspended ceiling and floor finish of thick cork tiles or rubber on sponge-rubber underlay	Probably Grade I	Grade I
Concrete floor with 50 mm lightweight concrete screed and hard floor finish	Probably Grade I	4 dB worse than Grade II
Concrete floor with 50 mm lightweight concrete screed and floor finish of thick cork tiles or of rubber on sponge-rubber underlay	Probably Grade I	Probably Grade I
Concrete floor weighing not less than 365 kg/m² (reinforced concrete slab 150–175 mm thick) with hard floor finish	Grade I	4 dB worse than Grade II
Concrete floor weighing not less than 365 kg/m² with floor finish of thick cork tiles or of rubber on sponge rubber underlay	Grade I	Grade I
Wood joist floors		
Plain joist/floor with plasterboard and single-coat plaster ceiling (no pugging)		
Thin walls	8 dB worse than Grade II	8 dB worse than Grade II
Thick walls	4 dB worse than Grade II	5 dB worse than Grade II
As above		

Construction	Sound insulating grading	
	Airborne	Impact
Plain joist floor with plasterboard and single-coat plaster ceiling and 15 kg/m² pugging on ceiling		
Thin walls	4dB worse than Grade II	6 dB worse than Grade II
As above *Thick walls*	Possibly Grade II	Possibly Grade II
Plain joist floor with heavy lath-and-plaster ceiling (no pugging) *Thin walls*	Probably 4 dB worse than Grade II	Probably 6 dB worse than Grade II
As above *Thick walls*	Grade II	Grade II
Plain joist floor with lath-and-plaster ceiling and 85 kg/m² pugging on ceiling		
Thin walls	Grade II	Grade II
As above *Thick walls*	Grade II or possibly I	Grade II
Floating floor and plasterboard and single-coat plaster ceiling (no pugging)		
Thin walls	4 dB worse than Grade II	3 dB worse than Grade II
As above *Thick walls*	Possibly Grade II	Possibly Grade II
Floating floor with single-coat plaster plasterboard ceiling and 15 kg/m² pugging on ceiling		
Thin walls	2 dB worse than Grade II	2 dB worse than Grade II
As above *Thick walls*	Grade II or possibly I	Grade II or possibly I
Floating floor with heavy lath-and-plaster ceiling (no pugging)		
Thin walls	2 dB worse than Grade II	Grade II
As above *Thick walls*	Grade II or I	Grade I
Floating floor with lath-and-plaster ceiling and 15 kg/m² pugging on ceiling		
Thin walls	Possibly Grade II	Grade II
As above *Thick walls*	Grade II or I	Grade I
Floating floor with lath-and-plaster ceiling and 85 kg/m² pugging on ceiling		
Thin walls	Probably Grade I	Probably Grade I
As above *Thick walls*	Grade I	Grade I

From *B.R.S. digests*, courtesy HMSO.

One problem which improved insulation may produce is a lack of the necessary ventilation rates in a room, and a balance has to be produced between these two considerations.

Further details on the problem of sound insulation may be found in *B.R.E. Digests 102* and *103*, and some typical insulation values are given in *Table 11.1*, taken from the relevant digests. These values are listed as the various grades, and the decibel reduction of each grade is shown in *Figure 11.7*, which also shows the grading curves for impact sound insulation, dealt with below.

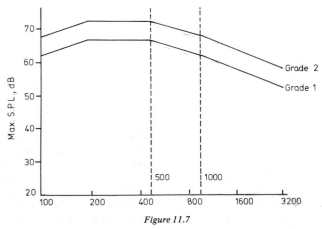

Figure 11.7

Sound from another room

As shown in *Figure 11.4*, there are two types of sound from another room, direct sound and sound travelling by what is known as flanking transmission. Direct airborne sound can be reduced in the following ways:

By commonsense use of the rules already given for airborne sound, as far as they can be applied.

By further use of commonsense in the placing of rooms. Wherever possible quiet rooms should be situated together and not near noisy rooms.

Figure 11.8 shows three types of floor with satisfactory insulating properties and also the method of 'pugging' which is used to increase the insulation value of existing floors.

The use of acoustic doors in place of the normal, lighter door. A section through an acoustic door is shown in *Figure 11.9*.

The building of floor-to-ceiling cupboards against the wall through which the sound is being transmitted may also produce a reduction in noise level.

The flanking transmission must be reduced by the use of resilient pads to break up the continuity of the structure. The principle of this is shown in *Figures 11.10* and *11.13*.

One other problem that may be found with sound produced elsewhere in the building is that caused by low frequency sound. This problem is illustrated in *Figure 11.11*.

Impact noise

Impact noise, as its name suggests, is caused by impacts such as footsteps, movements of furniture, the slamming of doors and windows, etc. It is reduced by absorbing the impact energy at source, and by preventing the impact from taking place. Damped door closers to prevent doors closing rapidly, foam padding on door frames and windows to absorb the impact and the use of carpets with resilient or foam underlay are some of the methods that may be used. In actual construction a floating floor incorporating a blanket of fibreglass or another absorbent material should be used to absorb the sound energy at the point of impact (*Figure 11.8*).

Structure-borne plant noise

Most structure-borne plant noise is produced by vibrations of a piece of plant machinery. From this point of view the ground must be considered as part of the structure and vibrations from the machinery in one building may cause noise in an adjacent structure. Machinery which produces this type of vibration must be isolated from the structure by use of resilient pads or spring mountings, which will absorb the unwanted energy (*Figure 11.12*).

Ventilation plant may also transmit noise through a building, as the noise can travel long distances through ducts with very little reduction in intensity unless special precautions are taken. It is usual to line the inside of the ducts with an absorbent material and also to introduce obstructions into the ducts to split up the sound.

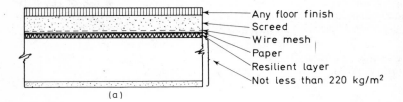

(a) Concrete floor with floating screed. (Courtesy HMSO)

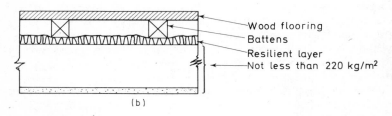

(b) Concrete floor with floating wood raft. (Courtesy HMSO)

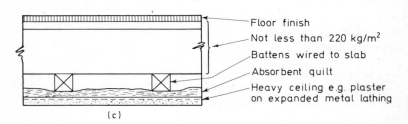

(c) Concrete floor with suspended ceiling. (Courtesy HMSO)

Figure 11.8

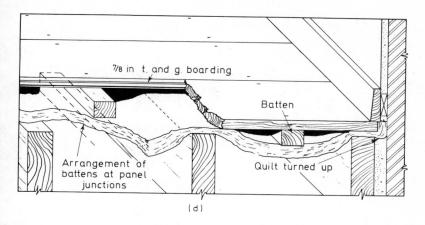

(d) *Section of a floating floor on joists.* *(From* Acoustics, Noise and Buildings, *H. R. Humphries and P. H. Parkin, Faber and Faber, 1969)*

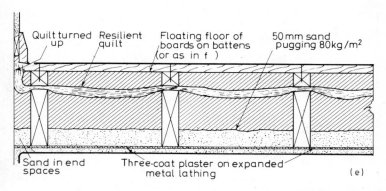

(e) *Insulated wood-joist floor, with heavy pugging.* *(Courtesy HMSO)*

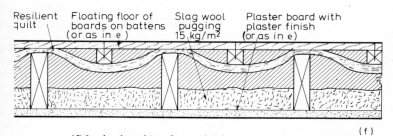

(f) *Insulated wood-joist floor, with light pugging.* *(Courtesy HMSO)*

Figure 11.8

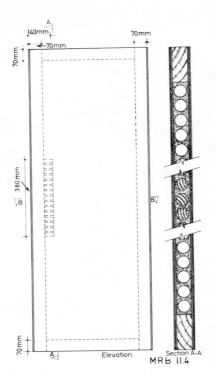

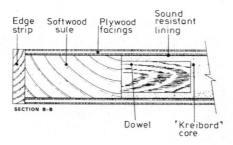

Figure 11.9   An acoustic door.   (Courtesy F. Hill and Sons Ltd.)

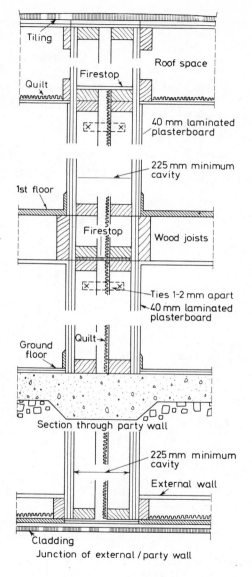

Tiling

Quilt

Firestop

Roof space

40 mm laminated plasterboard

225 mm minimum cavity

1st floor

Firestop

Wood joists

Ties 1-2 mm apart

40 mm laminated plasterboard

Ground floor

Quilt

Section through party wall

225 mm minimum cavity

External wall

Cladding

Junction of external / party wall

Figure 11.10   (Courtesy HMSO)

287

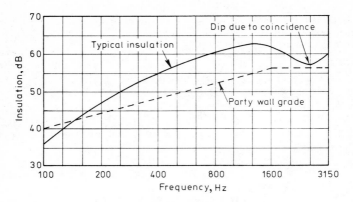

Figure 11.11   (Courtesy HMSO)

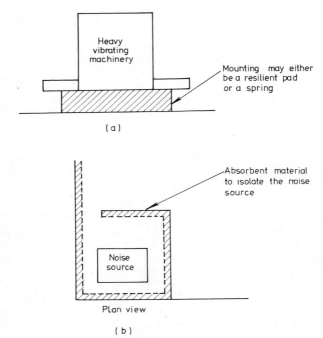

Figure 11.12

ROOM ACOUSTICS

Once the noise from outside a room has been controlled it is necessary to consider what happens to sounds which are produced in the room itself. The sound that a person actually hears is a mixture of two sounds: the direct sound is that which comes directly from the source to the listener, and the reverberant sound is that sound which has suffered multiple reflections from the walls of the room but has not yet become inaudible. A good balance between these two sounds is necessary for pleasant conversation to take place. Too much reverberant sound may obscure the direct sound, making listening difficult, and too little reverberant sound will make the direct sound seem 'dead'.

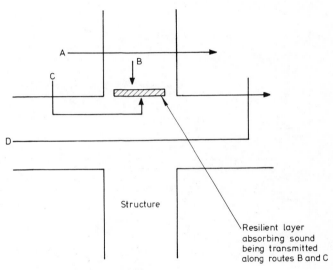

A

B

C

D

Structure

Resilient layer
absorbing sound
being transmitted
along routes B and C

Figure 11.13

In order to obtain a good balance, some form of absorbent material must be used on the walls. However, the efficiency of absorbent materials is dependent on the frequency of the incident sound and therefore the absorbent chosen must be able to deal with the sound being considered. Several typical absorbent systems are shown in *Figure 11.14*, and *Table 11.2* gives some typical values of absorbent coefficients of materials.

A mathematical measurement of this reverberant sound is given by the reverberation time (R.T.), i.e. the time taken for the intensity of a sound to drop by 60 dB. It may also be found from Sabin's formula, which gives

$$R.T. = 0.16 \, V/A$$

Table 11.2 TABLE OF ABSORPTION COEFFICIENTS

Type of surface	Frequency, Hz					
	125	250	500	1000	2000	4000
COMMON BUILDING MATERIAL						
Brickwork, plain or painted	0.05	0.04	0.02	0.04	0.05	0.05
Clinker (breeze) concrete unplastered	0.2	0.3	0.6	0.6	0.5	0.5
Concrete, constructional or granolithic	0.02	0.02	0.02	0.04	0.5	0.5
Cork tiles (thin), wood blocks, linoleum or rubber flooring on solid floor (or wall)	0.02	0.04	0.05	0.05	0.1	0.05
Cork tiles 25 mm thick on solid backing	0.05	0.1	0.2	0.55	0.6	0.55
Fibreboard (normal soft) 12 mm thick—solid backing	—	0.1	0.15	0.25	0.3	0.3
Fibreboard (normal soft) 12 mm thick—25 mm airspace	—	0.3	0.3	0.3	0.3	0.3
Floor tiles (hard) or composition floor	—	0.03	0.03	0.03	0.5	0.5
Glass; windows glazed with up to 4 mm glass	—	0.3	0.3	0.1	0.05	0.05
Plaster, on solid backing	0.03	0.03	0.02	0.03	0.04	0.05
Plaster, on joists or studs including plasterboard	0.3	0.15	0.1	0.05	0.04	0.05
Plaster, plasterboard ceiling with large airspace	0.2	0.2	0.1	0.1	0.04	—

COMMON ABSORBENT MATERIALS

Material						
Carpet, thin, over thin felt on concrete floor	0.1	0.15	0.25	0.3	0.3	0.3
Carpet, on wood-board floor	0.2	0.25	0.3	0.3	0.3	0.3
Carpet, thick pile over thick felt on concrete floor	0.07	0.25	0.5	0.5	0.6	0.65
Curtain, medium or similar fabric against solid backing	0.05	0.1	0.15	0.2	0.25	0.3
Curtain, ditto but hung in folds	0.05	—	0.35	—	0.5	—
Curtain, (dividing), double, canvas	0.03	0.04	0.1	0.15	0.2	0.15
Felt, hair, 25 mm thick with perforated membrane (i.e. muslin) against solid backing	0.1	—	0.7	—	0.8	—
Felt, with no covering or very porous (scrim or open-weave fabric) or open metal mesh covering	0.15	0.35	0.7	0.85	0.9	0.9
Felt, with 5% perforated hard-board covering	0.1	0.35	0.85	0.85	0.35	0.15
Felt, with 10% perforated or 20% slotted hardboard covering	0.15	0.3	0.75	0.85	0.75	0.4
Polystyrene (expanded) board 25 mm thick, spaced 50 mm from solid backing	0.1	0.25	0.55	0.2	0.1	0.15
Polyurethane flexible foam 50 mm thick on solid backing	0.25	0.5	0.85	0.95	0.9	0.9
Wood-wool slabs 25 mm thick mounted solidly, unplastered	0.1	—	0.4	—	0.6	—
Ditto, mounted 25 mm from solid backing	0.15	—	0.6	—	0.6	—
Ditto, plastered and with mineral wool in cavity	0.5	—	0.2	—	0.1	—

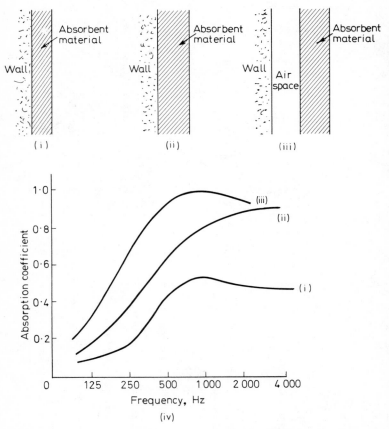

Figure 11.14(a)   Low frequency absorbers, (i) Plywood panel over an air space, (ii) same panel with the air space filled with a porous material, (iii) panel constructed from roofing felt, (iv) absorption characteristics of the three types of panel shown in (i), (ii) and (iii)

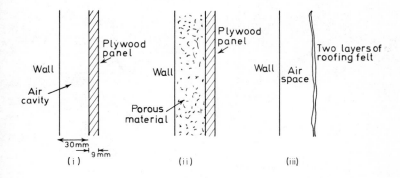

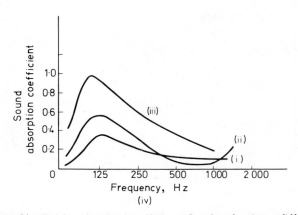

Figure 11.14(b)   High frequency absorbers, (i) 18 mm of wood-wool against a solid backing, (ii) 25 mm rock wool against a solid backing, (iii) 25 mm rock wool with an air space, (iv) absorption characteristics of the three materials shown in (i), (ii) and (iii)

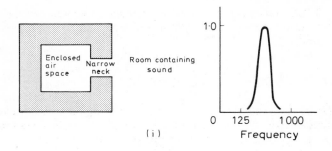

(i)

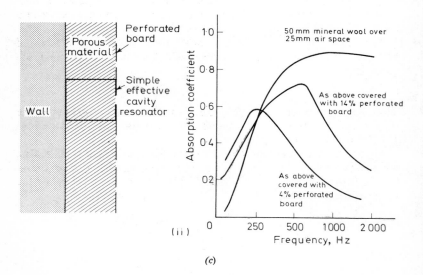

(ii)

(c)

Figure 11.14(c)   Medium frequency absorbers, (i) Typical Helmholtz resonator, with absorptivity curve, (ii) perforated board forming a series of cavity resonators

where V = volume of the room in metres

$A = \Sigma aa$, which represents the total absorption of all the surfaces in the room.

The B.R.E. have produced recommended reverberation times for various sized rooms and *B.R.E. Digest 82* is devoted to 'Improving room acoustics'.

THE DECIBEL SCALE

As mentioned above, a sound wave is in fact a pressure wave in a material such as the air, and the decibel scale which measures sound intensity is a logarithmic ratio which relates two pressures:

$$\text{Sound pressure level dB} = 20 \log (P_1/P_0)$$

This is obviously not an absolute scale but a comparative one. However, if P_0 is taken to represent the hearing threshold pressure at a given frequency an 'almost absolute' scale is produced.

The sound intensity is proportional to the square of the sound pressure, and this means that the dB scale can be used to compare two sound intensities:

$$\text{Decibel difference} = 10 \log (I_1/I_0)$$

This means, if we relate it to reverberation time, that a drop in intensity of 60 dB means that the sound intensity has been reduced to 1/1 000 000 of its original value.

There are three different dB scales: the dBA, dBB and dBC scales, which all correspond to a different weight response. The most commonly used is the dBA scale, and the difference between them is beyond the scope of this book.

CHAPTER 12

LIGHTING

ILLUMINATION LEVELS

Different tasks require different levels of illumination. Some typical requirements, taken from the code of the Illumination Engineering Society, are given in *Table 12.1*. As can be seen, at least three widely differing values may be required in a living room: 100 lx for general illumination, 200 lx for general reading, and 600 lx for sewing, drawing

Table 12.1 RECOMMENDED ILLUMINATION VALUES IN DOMESTIC AND OTHER SITUATIONS

		lx
Living rooms	General	100
	Reading (casual)	200
	Prolonged reading	400
	Sewing	600
Bedrooms	General	50
	Bed head	200
Kitchens	General	200
	Food preparation	400
General building areas		
Corridors		100
Lifts		200
Enquiry desks		400
Medical consulting rooms		40
Rest rooms		50
Cloakrooms		100
Fine precision work rooms		2000

From Illumination Engineering Society code

or other intricate work. It should be obvious that it is not possible for a single light source to provide all the different illuminations required. The days when a single, central, pendant fitting was considered adequate for a domestic living room are past. Several different fittings are usually provided in a single room, each one designed for a specific purpose.

In order to understand how these illumination levels may be achieved it is necessary to understand the units of measurement and also the various factors upon which the illumination depends.

Units and definitions

The three types of unit which are involved relate to the three processes by which the illumination is produced: the power or intensity of the source, the flow of light from the source to the surface, and the illumination produced on the surface.

Candela (cd). The candela is the unit of luminous intensity in the SI system. It is basically used for point sources and in this case one candela is equivalent to 4π lumen (see *Figure 12.1*).

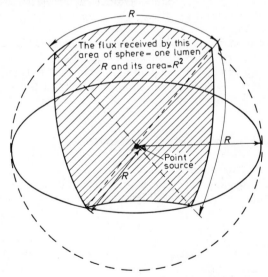

Figure 12.1   If the total light emitted by one candela is equal to the light received by the inner surface area of the sphere and the light received by one unit area is equal to one lumen, then if its area equals R^2 and the surface area of the sphere equals $4\pi R^2$

$$1 \; cd = 4\pi R^2$$
but $$1 \; lm = R^2$$
$$\therefore 1 \; cd = 4\pi \; lumen$$

297

Luminance. Luminance is the term which expresses the intensity of the light emitted per unit area of the surface. It is usually measured in candelas per square metre.

Luminous flux (ϕ). Luminous flux is a measurement of the light emitted by a source or received by a surface irrespective of the direction, and is measured in lumens (lm).

Illumination. Illumination relates to the amount of luminous flux falling per unit area on to a surface. It is measured in lux (lx), when one lux is equivalent to one lumen per square metre.

The above are the basic definitions of the quantities which will be referred to from time to time in this chapter.

Influencing factors

Power of the source

If all other conditions remain equal then obviously the more powerful the source the greater the number of lumens available and therefore the greater the illumination produced. For a filament lamp the luminous efficiency (i.e. the number of lumens available for each watt of the electrical power supplied) is 12.6 lm/W approximately. This means that a 100 W filament lamp can supply 1260 lm, a 40 W filament lamp 50.4 lm, and a 1500 W filament lamp 2520 lm. The luminous efficiency of a fluorescent tube varies with the colour of the light to be produced, but several values are shown in *Table 12.2*.

Distance of illuminated surface from source

Again, it is obvious that in most cases as the distance from the source increases then the illumination will decrease. The way in which this decrease takes place, however, depends on the type of source being considered.

Point source (filament lamp) For a point source the illumination follows what is known as an inverse square law. This gives the relationship:

$$E = I \cos \theta / d^2$$

where E = illumination in lux

I = intensity of the source, in the relevant direction, in candelas

Table 12.2 LIGHT OUTPUT OF FLUORESCENT TUBES

The lumen outputs quoted are measured at 25°C in accordance with British Standard BS 1853, *Tubular fluorescent lamps for general lighting service*, 1967.

Lighting design lumens

	8 ft	8 ft Super 8	6 ft Super 6	5 ft Super 5	5 ft Super 5	5 ft Super 5	4 ft	3 ft 1½ in	3 ft 1 in	2 ft	2 ft	18 in 1½ in	18 in 1 in
	125 W	85 W	85 W	80 W	65 W	50 W	40 W	30 W	30 W	40 W	20 W	15 W	15 W
White	8400	6600	6300	4900	4500	3100	2600	1750	1950	1750	1100	720	730
Warm white	8200	6400	5550	4800	4400	3100	2600	1700	1900	1700	1100	720	730
Daylight	7900	6000	5500	4600	4200	2900	2500	1650	1850	1650	1050	690	710
Natural	6200	4800	4000	3500	3100	2300	2000	1300	1400	1150	750	530	530
Deluxe warm white	6100	4700	—	3400	3000	—	1950	1250	1350	1100	750	500	—
Kolor-rite	5600	4400	3850	3300	2900	2200	1800	—	1300	1100	750	—	—
Northlight/colour matching	5300	4100	3600	3100	2700	—	1700	1100	1250	1100	700	470	480
Deluxe natural	4600	3600	3150	2600	2400	1800	1500	950	1050	900	570	380	380
Artificial daylight	3400	2600	—	2000	1850	—	1100	—	—	—	450	—	—

Courtesy British Lighting Industries Ltd.

299

$\theta =$ angle away from a direction perpendicular to the direction of the light through which the surface has been turned

$d =$ distance between the source and the surface in metres.

This relationship is shown diagrammatically in *Figure 12.2*.

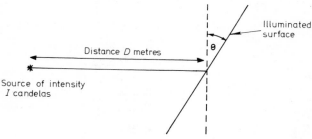

Figure 12.2

This law only holds if direct light alone is considered, i.e. if reflected light from any surface is ignored. Consider the set-up shown in *Figure 12.3*, in which a spotlight of intensity 20 000 cd along the centre of the beam is directed on to the surface. In this case

$$E = I \cos \theta / d^2$$

In the formula $I = 20\,000$ cd, $\cos \theta = \frac{3}{5}$, $d = 5$, $\therefore d^2 = 25$.

$$\therefore E = (20\,000 \times 3)/(5 \times 25) = 780 \text{ lx}$$

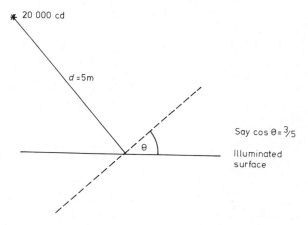

Figure 12.3

300

Line source (fluorescent tube) In this case it is not an inverse square relationship that needs to be considered. The illumination is now inversely proportional to the distance away from the source. This gives the relationship:

$$E = N \cos \theta / 2\pi d$$

where N = output of the line source in lumens per metre length
d = distance in metres
θ = the same angle as when considering a point source (page 298).

Plane source (luminous ceiling) If the reflections and absorptions of the walls are neglected then the illumination under an infinitely large plane source will be unaffected by the distance of the surface away from the plane source.

Shape and size of fittings

Different fittings direct the light produced inside them in different directions. Spotlights are meant to concentrate light while other types of fittings diffuse the light in different ways. Several different types with their typical classifications (in simple terms) are shown in *Figure 12.4*.

Room surfaces

Different surfaces reflect and absorb different amounts of light. A light coloured surface reflects much more than a dark coloured surface. This means that a room in which the surfaces are finished in light colours will have a higher illumination than one painted in darker, duller colours. This factor is allowed for in the determination of the utilization factor which is described below.

Size of room

The larger a room the more fittings are needed to illuminate it to the required value. The shape of the room is also important, however. A tall room with a small plan area requires different fittings to a low room with a large plan area. The shape of the room is allowed for in the room index, which is also a factor considered when the utilization factor is being found. The room index is given by the equation

$$K = LW/H_m(L + W)$$

where K = room index
   L = length of the room in metres
   W = width of the room in metres
   H_m = mounting height of the fittings in metres.

The direct ratio and the B.Z. Classification

If the direct ratio of the amount of light from a fitting that falls directly on the surface to the total amount of light produced by the source is plotted against the room index then a British Zonal curve is obtained. Ten of these curves are used as a basis for the British Zonal Classification, shown in *Figure 12.5*. The B.Z. number of the fitting denotes the classification of that fitting in terms of the direct light that can be expected to fall on the working surface as described in Illumination Engineering Society (I.E.S.) *Technical Report No. 2*

Utilization factor

The utilization factor is a measure of the useful light available from any source in specified surroundings. It takes account of the room finishes,

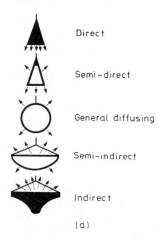

Figure 12.4   Types of fitting: (a) Simplest classification; (b) A more complex classification

Description of fitting, and typical downward light output ratio, %	Typical outline	Basic downward L.O.R., %	Ceiling	70			50			30		
			Walls	50	30	10	50	30	10	50	30	10
			Room index									
(M) Aluminium industrial reflector (72–76)		70	0.6	.39	.36	.33	.39	.36	.33	.39	.35	.33
			0.8	.48	.43	.40	.46	.43	.40	.46	.43	.40
(T) High-bay reflector, aluminium (72) or enamel (66)			1.0	.52	.49	.45	.52	.48	.45	.52	.48	.45
			1.25	.56	.53	.50	.56	.53	.49	.56	.52	.49
			1.5	.60	.57	.54	.59	.57	.53	.59	.55	.53
			2.0	.65	.62	.59	.63	.60	.58	.63	.59	.57
			2.5	.67	.64	.62	.65	.62	.61	.65	.62	.60
			3.0	.69	.66	.64	.67	.64	.63	.67	.64	.62
			4.0	.71	.68	.67	.69	.67	.65	.69	.66	.64
			5.0	.72	.70	.69	.71	.69	.67	.71	.67	.66
(T) Near-spherical diffuser, open beneath (50)		50	0.6	.28	.22	.18	.25	.20	.17	.22	.18	.16
			0.8	.39	.30	.26	.33	.28	.23	.27	.25	.22
			1.0	.43	.36	.32	.38	.34	.29	.31	.29	.26
			1.25	.48	.41	.37	.42	.38	.33	.34	.32	.29
			1.5	.52	.46	.41	.46	.41	.37	.37	.35	.32
			2.0	.58	.52	.47	.50	.46	.41	.42	.39	.36
			2.5	.62	.56	.52	.54	.50	.47	.45	.42	.40
			3.0	.65	.60	.56	.57	.53	.50	.48	.45	.43
			4.0	.68	.64	.61	.60	.56	.54	.51	.48	.46
			5.0	.71	.68	.65	.62	.59	.57	.53	.50	.48

Reflection factor, %

Figure 12.4(b)

Table 12.3 HOW TO OBTAIN A VALUE FOR A UTILIZATION FACTOR

VCZ 100 cylinder range attachment

Reflection factors				Room index									
Floor	Ceiling	Wall	H_s/H_m ratio	.6	.8	1.0	1.25	1.5	2.0	2.5	3.0	4.0	5.0
		50%	0	.15	.18	.21	.23	.25	.27	.28	.30	.31	.32
			0.3	.14	.17	.20	.22	.24	.26	.28	.29	.30	.32
			1.0	.13	.16	.19	.21	.23	.25	.27	.28	.30	.31
	75%	30%	0	.12	.16	.18	.21	.22	.25	.26	.28	.29	.31
			0.3	.12	.15	.17	.20	.21	.24	.26	.27	.29	.30
			1.0	.11	.14	.16	.19	.20	.23	.24	.26	.28	.29
		10%	0	.11	.14	.16	.19	.20	.23	.25	.26	.28	.29
			0.3	.10	.13	.15	.18	.19	.22	.24	.25	.27	.29
			1.0	.10	.13	.15	.17	.19	.21	.23	.24	.26	.28

10%	50%	50%	0	.14	.17	.20	.22	.23	.25	.27	.28	.29	.30
			0.3	.14	.17	.19	.21	.23	.25	.26	.27	.29	.30
			1.0	.13	.16	.18	.20	.22	.24	.26	.27	.28	.29
		30%	0	.12	.15	.17	.20	.21	.23	.25	.26	.28	.29
			0.3	.11	.14	.17	.19	.21	.23	.24	.26	.27	.29
			1.0	.11	.14	.16	.18	.20	.22	.24	.25	.27	.28
		10%	0	.10	.13	.16	.18	.20	.22	.24	.25	.27	.28
			0.3	.10	.13	.15	.17	.19	.21	.23	.24	.26	.27
			1.0	.10	.13	.15	.17	.18	.21	.22	.24	.26	.27
	30%	30%	0	.11	.15	.17	.19	.20	.22	.24	.25	.27	.28
			0.3	.11	.14	.16	.19	.20	.22	.24	.25	.26	.27
			1.0	.11	.14	.16	.18	.20	.22	.23	.25	.26	.27
		10%	0	.10	.13	.15	.17	.19	.21	.23	.24	.26	.27
			0.3	.10	.13	.15	.17	.18	.21	.22	.24	.25	.26
			1.0	.10	.13	.15	.17	.17	.20	.22	.23	.25	.26
All	0%	0%		.09	.12	.14	.16	.17	.19	.21	.22	.24	.25
		B.Z. Classification		5	5	5	5	5	5	5	5	5	5

Courtesy British Lighting Industries Ltd.

the size of the room and the British Zonal system, as well as the height of the fittings and the spacing between them. *Table 12.3* shows how to obtain the utilization factor for a particular fitting.

From *Table 12.3* assume the following quantities:

Floor reflection 10%   Ceiling reflection 75%   Wall reflection 30%
Spacing height/mounting height = 1.0
Room index of 1.25 or B.Z. classification 5
This gives a U.F. = 0.19

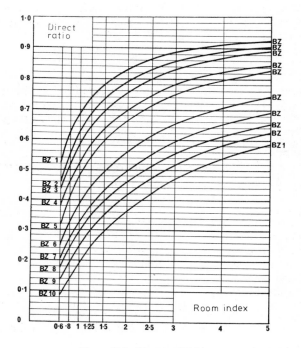

Figure 12.5   (Courtesy I.E.S.)

Maintenance factor

The maintenance factor allows for the fact that fittings become dirty and do not emit as much light as they could. It is taken in the I.E.S. *Technical Report No. 9* as the ratio of the illumination provided by an installation in its average condition of dirtiness, to the illumination from the same fitting when clean. Typical values are between 0.6 and 0.8.

Actual output from the source

Once the utilization factor and the maintenance factor are known the actual output of the fitting can be calculated:

Actual Output = Theoretical output
× Utilization factor × Maintenance factor

For example, a 150 W fitting with a luminous efficiency of 12.6 lm/W, a utilization factor of 0.5, and a maintenance factor of 0.8 would be expected to emit $150 \times 12.6 \times 0.5 \times 0.8 = 756$ lm. This gives rise to the simplest method of illumination calculations known as the total lumen method.

Total lumen method   In the total lumen method the number of lumens required for the illumination are compared to the total number of lumens available from each fitting and the number of fittings needed calculated from the relationship:

No. of fittings =
Total number of lumens required/Lumens available from each fitting

Consider the following simple calculation:

Illumination required	= 250 lx
Area to be illuminated	= 18 m × 8 m
Fitting wattage	= 200 W
Luminous efficiency	= 12.6
Utilization factor	= 0.5
Maintenance factor	= 0.8

Total amount of flux required = $250 \times 18 \times 8$ lm
Lumens available from each fitting = $200 \times 12.6 \times 0.5 \times 0.8$ lm

No. of fittings required =
$(250 \times 18 \times 8/200 \times 12.6 \times 0.5 \times 0.8) = 35.7$, say 36

Alternative ways of finding out these requirements are the use of a nomogram (*Figure 12.6*) or an illumination calculator (*Figure 12.7*).

Minimum mounting heights

In addition to the factors given above there are other important

Graphical solutions by means of nomograms are often sufficiently accurate for the purpose, and their use is justified by the speed and ease with which the answers are obtained.

Procedure to determine room index:

(1) Join values for width and length of room to cut the oblique scale.

(2) Take room height above the working plane and mark the resultant value on the nomogram height scale.

(3) Join the points found in (1) and (2) and note the value in the k_r scale. This is the room index.

Determining the number and power of fittings, using the lumen method of calculation:

(1) Establish the room index.

(2) With the room index, look up the utilization factor for the type of fitting to be used. Mark the u.f. on Scale 8.

(3) Mark the room length on Scale 1 and room width on Scale 2. Draw a line through these points to cut Scale 3.

(4) From this point on Scale 3 draw a line through the required illumination on Scale 4 to cut Scale 5.

(5) From this point on Scale 5 draw a line through the mark on Scale 8 to cut Scale 9. This gives a total light flux to be provided by all the lamps.

(6) A line drawn from the point on Scale 9 through an appropriate point (number of fittings) on Scale 10 will cut Scale 11 at the number of lamp lumens required per fitting. Alternatively, if the lumen output of lamps per fitting is known, a line between the point on Scale 9 and the appropriate point on Scale 11 will cut Scale 10 at the number of fittings required.

(7) The last two columns on the right give an approximate indication of suitable lamp combinations per fitting to give the light output required.

Note. When using this nomogram in conjunction with *Table 12.3* first enter, on Scale 8, the u.f. obtained from the table. If the downward light output ratio of the fitting to be used is the same as the basic d.l.o.r. given in the table, ignore Scales 6 and 7.

If the d.l.o.r. of the fitting to be used differs significantly from that listed in *Table 12.3*, enter the figures given in the table on Scale 7. Draw a line from this point on Scale 7 through the u.f. (from the table) on Scale 8 and produce to cut Scale 6. The intersection on Scale 6 then gives the utilance of the fitting. From the utilance on Scale 6 draw a line through the actual downward light output ratio of the fitting to be used on Scale 7. The intersection of this line with Scale 8 gives the corrected utilization factor which is then used to complete the calculation.

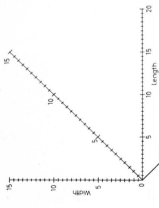

Figure 12.6 (Part 1)

308

When using this nomogram in conjunction with I.E.S. *Technical Report No. 2*, first enter the downward light output ratio on Scale 7 and the lower flux utilance on Scale 6. Joint these two points, and the intersection of this line with Scale 8 gives the downward coefficient. Next enter the upward light output ratio on Scale 7 and the upper flux utilance on Scale 6. Join these two points to cut Scale 8 in the upward coefficient. Add together both upward and downward coefficients (this cannot be done on the nomogram) to give the utilization factor and mark on Scale 8. This mark is then used to complete the calculation.

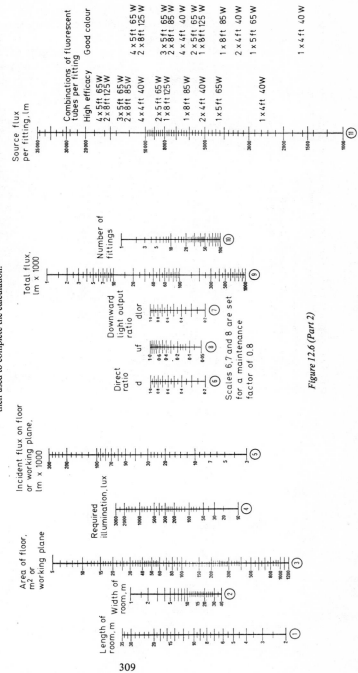

Figure 12.6 (Part 2)

considerations to be taken into account, one of which is the minimum mounting height.

There are recommended minimum mounting heights for all types of fittings. These are so that the fitting will not be mounted too low, thus causing distraction and glare. Some recommended heights are shown in *Table 12.4*.

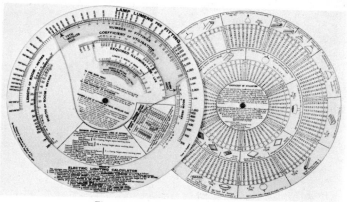

Figure 12.7   Illumination calculations

Glare

There are two forms of glare, discomfort glare and disability glare. In general the eye is able to adapt itself very quickly to differences in brightness which extend over a range of more than a million to one. But

Table 12.4 MINIMUM MOUNTING HEIGHTS

Wattage and type of lamp			Minimum mounting height, m
Incandescent	Mercury	Corrected mercury	
150	—	—	3
200	80	80	3.5
300	125	125	4
500	250	250	4.5
750	—	400	5
1000	400	700	6
1500	700	—	7.5
—	1000	1000	8.5

From *Interior Lighting Design*, courtesy Lighting Industry Federation.

above a certain value the eye finds it difficult and uncomfortable to see. Disability glare makes it too difficult to carry out any task, while discomfort glare just makes it uncomfortable to do so. Glare may be caused either by light which comes directly from the source (i.e. direct glare) or by light which is reflected from other surfaces (i.e. indirect glare). A relationship between the adaptation of the eye and glare is shown in *Figure 12.8*. The amount of glare in certain cases is known as the glare

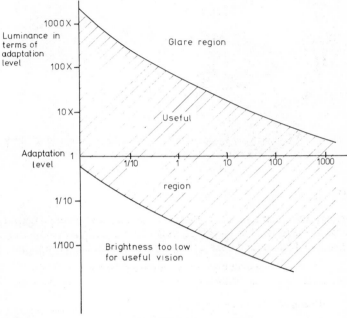

Figure 12.8

index, which is given by the formula below, and typical limiting glare values are shown in *Table 12.5*. A glare index calculator is shown in *Figure 12.9*.

$$\text{Glare index} = 10 \log [\text{constant} \times \Sigma(B_s{}^{1.6}\omega^{0.8}/B_b) \times 1/p^{1.6}]$$

where B_s = brightness of the source
B_b = brightness of the background
ω = solid angle subtended by the source
p represents a position relative to the direction in which the eye is looking.

311

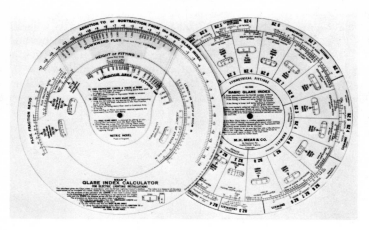

Figure 12.9   A glare index calculator

Figure 12.10 shows how glare of the direct type may be reduced by the use of louvres and also how reflected glare may occur.

Colour appearance of surfaces

The appearance of surfaces depends to a large extent on the colour of the light in which the surface is seen. Normal white light is a mixture of the seven coloured lights making up the visible spectrum. Different light sources, however, have the constituent colours present in different proportions. If these proportions vary from source to source then the

Table 12.5 LIMITING GLARE INDEX TABLE

Situation	Limiting glare index
Circulation areas	22
Kitchens	22
Food stores	25
Hospital wards	13
Pharmacies	19
Classrooms	16
Laboratories	19
Art galleries	10
General offices	19
Indoor car parks	28

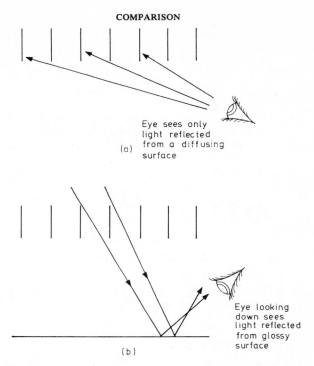

(a) Eye sees only light reflected from a diffusing surface

(b) Eye looking down sees light reflected from glossy surface

Figure 12.10   (a) The use of louvres to reduce glare; (b) Reflected glare

appearance of the surface being viewed will vary. *Figure 12.11* shows the spectral (or colour) make-up of various sources of light. If these compositions are compared it will be seen why, if different lights are used, surfaces will have different appearances. This is why it is preferable to inspect cloth or other goods in daylight rather than inside a shop lit by fluorescent lighting.

COMPARISON OF FILAMENT LAMPS AND FLUORESCENT TUBES

Filament lamps and fluorescent tubes work on a quite different basis and there are several differences both in cost and methods of fixing.

Light production

A filament lamp is a hot source which produces light when the filament becomes hot enough. A fluorescent tube produces light both by ionic

313

discharge and phosphar excitement. Both methods of operation are shown in *Figure 12.12*.

Connection

A filament lamp simply needs to be connected to a supply of electricity a.c. or d.c. at any voltage for which the lamp is designed. A fluorescent tube, however, needs a form of current limiting device, and some form

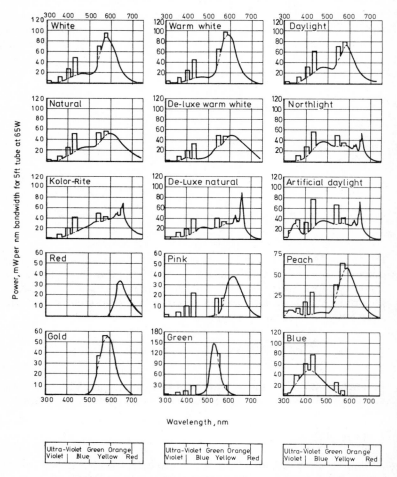

Figure 12.11   (Courtesy British Lighting Industries Ltd.)

314

of starting control gear. This is usually designed to limit the current without consuming too much energy. Two typical circuits are shown in *Figure 12.13*.

Costs

Consider again the luminous efficiency of the filament lamp and the fluorescent tube. The filament lamp has an efficiency of 12.6 lm/W, which means that for every watt of electricity used 12.6 lm are produced. The fluorescent tube, on the other hand, can produce 40–80 lm for each watt used. The running costs of fluorescent tubes will therefore be less than the running costs of filament lamps. However, this

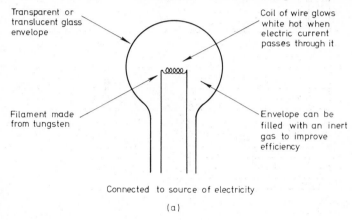

Connected to source of electricity

(a)

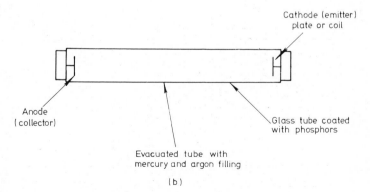

(b)

Figure 12.12 (a) Filament lamp; (b) Fluorescent tube

315

is not the only consideration, as the original expense of installation and also the cleaning costs must be considered. A fluorescent scheme costs more on installation due to the control gear that must be fitted, though in most cases its higher efficiency compensates for this extra cost. In general, therefore, a filament lamp system is cheaper to install and more expensive to run.

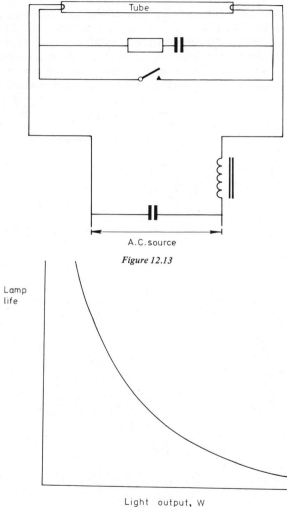

Figure 12.13

Figure 12.14

Expected life

British Standard BS 161, *240 V tungsten filament general service electric lamps*, 1968, suggests that 1000 h is the best compromise for a filament lamp, so that when all costs have been taken into account, the maximum amount of light per penny is being obtained. It is possible to produce filament lamps with a longer life, but as the life increases the light output falls. A graph showing this relationship is shown in *Figure 12.14.*

A fluorescent tube, on the other hand, has an extremely long life but its output decreases gradually with time. A stage will therefore be reached when it is desirable to replace the lamp before it fails, or else use some form of supplementary lighting. The replacement period, in order to obtain the maximum amount of light per penny, can be calculated if all the relevant costs are used. This lumen output/time relationship is shown in *Figure 12.15.*

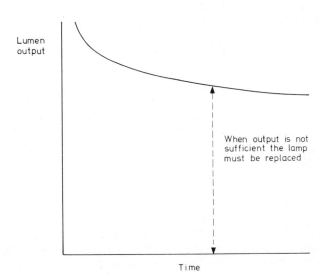

Figure 12.15

DAYLIGHTING

So far, only artificial lighting has been considered. In most environments, however, some of the illumination will be provided by daylight. The amount of daylight at a point in a room is measured by what is known as the daylight factor.

317

Daylight factor

The daylight factor is defined as the ratio of the illumination at a point on a given plane within an internal environment due to the light received directly and indirectly from a sky of known or assumed luminance distribution, to that on a horizontal plane due to an unobstructed hemisphere of this sky, assuming that direct sunlight is excluded from both illuminations. *Table 12.6* gives recommended values for daylight factors in various types of room.

Table 12.6 RECOMMENDED DAYLIGHT FACTORS

Situation	Daylight factor, %
Entrance hall	1
General offices	2
Typing rooms	4
Drawing offices	2
Libraries	1
Classrooms	2
Art rooms	4
Hospital wards	1
Living rooms	Not less than 1% over 8 m² to half the depth of the room from the window
Bedrooms	Not less than ½% over 6 m² to half the depth of the room from the window
Kitchens	Not less than 2% over half of floor area

Makeup of daylighting

As suggested in the above definitions, the daylighting in a room may be due to either direct light or indirect light, and this is shown in *Figure 12.16*. The amount of direct lighting will depend on:

The area of glazing.
The type of glass and thickness used.
Whether or not there is an unobstructed sky outside the glazed area.

The amount of indirect lighting depends mainly on the finishes to the room for the internally reflected component and on the surfaces of the external buildings for the externally reflected component.

Measurement of daylight factor

In practice the daylight factor in an actual environment can be measured either by the use of a daylight factor meter or by the use of a daylight photometer. Details of the use of the instruments can be found in the relevant textbooks and B.R.E. digests. In the planning stage the

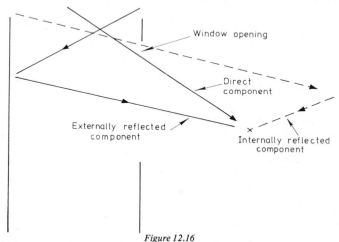

Window opening

Direct component

Externally reflected component

Internally reflected component

Figure 12.16

daylight factor, or a close approximation to it known as the sky factor, is found by the use of a B.R.E. daylight protractor. This is also described in the relevant B.R.E. digests.

Fall off of daylighting

The fall off of the daylighting in a room is shown in *Figure 12.17* as a drop through a section of a room (*Figure 12.17(a)*) and as a contour (daylight contour) map of the room (*Figure 12.17(b)*). It can be seen that as the distance from the window increases, the illumination and daylight factor in the room decreases. There is a simple way of converting the two values. A typical value for outside illumination is 5000 lx. A daylight factor of 1 per cent would mean that the internal illumination is 1 per cent of the external illumination and therefore equal to 50 lx. In some rooms the illumination level due to external illumination will be too low for visual tasks to be performed. In this case it is necessary to install artificial lighting which needs to be operative for the whole time. This is known as a permanent supplementary artificial lighting of interiors, which is one system of integrated daylight and artificial light.

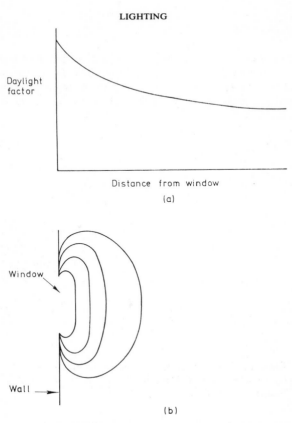

Figure 12.17   *'Fall off' of the daylighting value in a room: (a) Through a section; (b) As a contour diagram on a plan of the room*

SAFETY

It should be obvious that in the internal environment positions of danger or places where accidents are likely to happen should be adequately illuminated. Dark positions on stairs, etc., should be avoided. It can be seen that adequate lighting is necessary both for a pleasant environment and a safe one.

Section 3
Administrative Aspects

CHAPTER 13

REPORT WRITING

A very necessary part of the surveyor's work is writing reports. Whether he merely looks, makes a study or carries out a detailed inspection, it will be necessary to prepare the information gathered into a written report, so that it may be passed on to the client.

Report writing is a specialized form of communication written with the client in mind, so that he can form a clear picture of what has been concluded. It can be considered under the following headings:

Collection of information
Arrangement of information
Presentation of information.

Collection of information

When making the survey collect all relevant information, using explanatory notes, sketches and photographs wherever possible.

Ensure that all facts are accurate; never assume anything.

Remember that it is always better to collect too much information than too little.

Prepare a check list before making the survey in order to ensure that nothing is forgotten.

Arrangement of information

The arrangement of the report should adopt the following principles:

Introduce the report in a concise manner, stating the terms of reference, methods used and the manner of presentation of the report.

Collect all the information under a logical sequence of main divisions.

Sub-divide the information within these main divisions under sub-headings.

Make any necessary conclusions and recommendations, referring to facts where appropriate. Always keep facts and conclusions separate.

Summarize the main points of the report in a concise manner in order to assist the reader in deciding whether or not it is advisable to study the main body of the report.

Presentation of information

When writing the report the following points should be borne in mind:

The reader. What does he want to know and what does he already know? Has he a technical or non-technical background?

The information. Any facts should be accurate, and written in as concise a manner as possible. Long words and long-winded sentences should be avoided wherever possible. Visual aids in the form of sketches, diagrams, charts and photographs often convey information more successfully than the written word.

The subsequent report should be informative and easy to read. Always remember that the person reading the report will have a lot more things to do than just read reports and does not want to have to wade through a lot of irrelevant information to find a few conclusions.

Survey reports

Types

There are several types of reports that may be used in connection with building surveys. They are:

General reports of the construction or condition of property.

Structural reports which give information as to the main structural condition.

Decorative reports, as to the condition of general decorative finishes and preservation.

Sanitary reports concerning the living and health conditions of properties.

Division of reports

Reports are usually classified as follows:

Under trade headings, e.g. bricklayer, carpenter. This is applicable if the report also contains a specification or schedule of works, as will be seen below.

Under elements of structure, e.g. walls, floors. This is commonly used when the report is a description of the state of the structure.

General, structural and decorative reports

The requirements of general, structural and decorative reports are all very similar. The following outline procedure should be adopted.

Initial inspection

The actual inspection of property fabric is the first stage of the report. It is then that the property should be inspected closely and all relevant notes, sketches, measurements and photographs taken. Remember that if sufficient information is not obtained it will mean an incomplete report or a second site visit.

General details

The first task is to obtain a general impression of the site, when the following items should be noted:

Type of structure, materials used and general state of repair of the structure.

Position of buildings, presence of trees and other growths.

Relationship between actual ground level and finished floor levels.

Assessment of type of ground.

Detailed information

During the detailed inspection the following considerations should be made regarding each element:

The condition of the structure, observing any deterioration or defects. Note the presence and extent of any faults or failures which may cause trouble or concern.

The cause of the defect. Find out the reasons for the defects, be they of a structural or material nature. This will have to be ascertained during the inspection.

Remedial work. Based on the previous information it is then possible to decide upon the necessary remedial work.

Nature of remedial work. The requirements of the remedial action will need to be specified, and how it will be done, with any possible consequences.

Maintenance, e.g. painting, will be necessary as soon as the remedial work is completed.

Example of general type of survey report

The following example shows the layout of a typical report with some typical findings.

Report on 210 Blackbrook Avenue, Meadowfields, Leics., for Mr A. Black, 20 Thorne Road, Bushlands

This report is concerned with the nature and condition of the structure. It then goes on to recommend the necessary remedial work.

1. *General details*
   1.1 The house is one of a pair of semi-detached houses situated in an open residential area.
   1.2 It is a brick structure faced externally with red facing bricks, having a pitched and slated roof, hipped at the ends with projecting eaves.
   1.3 The windows are timber casement type, the front entrance is glazed and set in a recessed porch.
   1.4 The ground floor is of solid construction and the upper floor of suspended timber construction.

2. *Results of inspection*
   2.1 Roof
       2.1.1 The roof is covered with blue welsh slates, the hips and ridge being finished with blue angular tiles. The general condition is satisfactory except for some loose ridge tiles.
       2.1.2 The eaves are formed by a deep cast iron half-round gutter, secured on brackets to a softwood fascia with projecting soffit. The general condition is satisfactory except for two decayed lengths.
       2.1.3 The two cast iron rainwater downpipes are badly jointed and the fixings to the wall are insecure.
       2.1.4 Parapet walls
       2.1.5 Chimney stacks
   2.2 External walls
       2.2.1 Structure and materials
       2.2.2 Finishes
       2.2.3 Foundations
       2.2.4 Doors and windows

2.3 Floors
    2.3.1 Ground floor
        2.3.1.1 Base to ground floor
        2.3.1.2 Floor finish
    2.3.2 Upper floor
        2.3.2.1 Construction—noting possible decay
        2.3.2.2 Floor finish
2.4 Internal finishes
    2.4.1 Internal walls and ceilings
    2.4.2 Internal doors
    2.4.3 Skirting boards and architraves
2.5 Staircase
2.6 Sanitary fittings
    2.6.1 Bathroom fittings
    2.6.2 Kitchen fittings
    2.6.3 W.C. fittings
2.7 Wastes and drainage
2.8 Services
    2.8.1 Gas
    2.8.2 Electric
    2.8.3 Water
    2.8.4 Drainage
2.9 External works
    2.9.1 External buildings
    2.9.2 Pavings
    2.9.3 Fences and gates

3. *Remedial work*
3.1 Roof
    3.1.1 Reset loose ridge tiles and point with gauged mortar.
    3.1.2 Replace two decayed lengths of deep cast iron half-round gutter.
    3.1.3 Rejoint two cast iron rainwater downpipes and fix securely to wall.
    3.1.4 Remedial work to parapet walls
    3.1.5 Remedial work to chimney stacks
3.2 External walls
List any remedial work under the same headings as those under Section 2.
3.3 Floors
As 3.1 and 3.2
Continue the remedial work under the appropriate headings as outlined.

4. *General comments*
    4.1 Remarks on general condition of property
    4.2 Remedial work involved
    4.3 Future remedial work that may be required

Signed:

Sanitary reports

Sanitary reports, although compiled in a similar way to other types of report, differ appreciably in content, in as much as they are concerned with the habitable conditions of the buildings, considering such things as:

Conditions of dampness and cleanliness and freedom from disease.
Adequate conditions of ventilation and fresh air supply.
Adequate drainage, sanitation and water supply.
Suitable safe storage of food and safety of the occupants.

Legislation affecting sanitary reports

Public Health Act   The main piece of legislation affecting sanitary conditions is the Public Health Act, which is implemented by Building Inspectors or Public Health Inspectors. The main considerations of this Act are health and safety.

Other acts   Other acts affecting the conditions and occupation of property are:

The Housing Act 1957, which sets out requirements for minimum standards of properties for habitable occupation.

The Food and Drug Act 1955, which is concerned with the condition of property where foods are prepared, stored and sold.

The Offices, Shops and Railway Premises Act 1963, which controls the occupation and use of these properties.

Legal requirements

The main requirements of the Public Health Act are as follows.

Dampness   Dampness may be due to ground water rising through the foundations, ground floor or structural walls, or moisture from external weather conditions penetrating the structural walls. Condensation may result. This can be remedied by the inclusion of effective damp-proof courses in walls, damp-proof membranes under structural ground floors or various treatments to external walls.

Dampness can also be caused by inefficient roof coverings and roof drainage. It is essential, therefore, that any deteriorating roof coverings or rainwater goods are repaired immediately in order to prevent damp conditions.

Condensation   Structural damp, atmospheric conditions or excess steam from cooking or washing processes can cause condensation. The excess moisture will need to be cleared and this can be done by:

Providing suitable temperatures that will absorb the moisture.
Suitable insulation of cold impervious surfaces, to help reduce surface condensation.
Improving the ventilation by natural or mechanical means.

Natural light   The area of natural light available to each habitable or occupational room should be a minimum of one tenth of the actual floor area.

Sanitation   An adequate number of w.c.s are required, depending on the type of building. All waste water and soil pipes should be maintained in an airtight and watertight condition, properly trapped and connected to the drainage system.

Drainage systems   These should be self-cleansing in operation, well ventilated and free from any leakage. Manholes should be well constructed, having adequate facilities for cleansing and inspection.

Storage, preparation and cooking of foods   Areas intended for such activities require adequate ventilation, a sink with hot water and means for the disposal of waste water. Cleanliness is of prime importance, so that surfaces of walls, ceilings and floors should be easy to clean.

Safety   Unsafe conditions should be noted and remedial action taken. They may take the form of:

Unsafe structures, e.g. walls, gables, parapets or chimney stacks.
Loose tiles or slates.

Uneven or decayed timber floors.

Staircases being either decayed, too steep or having inadequate hand-rails and guard rails.

Poorly drained or uneven steps and footpaths.

Grants

As an incentive to the improvement of building standards, the Housing Compulsory Improvements Act requires properties to be of a minimum standard, and financial assistance is offered for this purpose. The basic amenities include an internal water closet, fixed bath, wash hand basin, kitchen, sink (all fitted with hot and cold water), together with a food store.

CHAPTER 14

SPECIFICATIONS

Specifications are written instructions describing specific items of work. A specification can be used as a legal document when a contract without a Bill of Quantities is required, as a means of providing instructions for the work content of particular operations, or as information additional to prepared drawings. It is necessary, therefore, that a specification can be read and fully understood by architect, contractor, foreman or craftsmen.

Contractors and craftsmen will normally do what is required and use the materials requested provided they are given sufficient information. If information is lacking then they have no guidelines and often do what they consider ought to be done, which can often lead to a claim for extra payment.

The writing of specifications for remedial and small works poses certain problems which need special consideration. Specifications are prepared from information produced on the actual site and any drawings that may be available. A good knowledge of construction is required, together with good powers of observation and an appreciation of what is involved.

Requirements of a specification

The instructions contained in the specification should include the following information:

What is required? This should refer to the materials to be used and the form of construction.

How is it done? This should refer to the method of working.

Where is it done? This should state where the work is to be done.

These instructions should be clear and informative and written in a logical manner. The style of presentation should be direct, thus enabling a clear understanding of what is required. Each instruction should be the subject of a separate sentence and wherever possible the sentence should start with a verb, e.g.

Materials shall be . . .

Excavate trench for . . .

Lay concrete 100 mm thick . . .

Build half-brick wall . . .

Contents

The contents come under four main headings of Preliminaries, Materials, Workmanship, and Description of Work. Preliminaries are kept separate and put at the beginning of the specification. Materials, workmanship and description of work may be dealt with individually, or more often they are dealt with collectively under items of work.

Preliminaries These are instructions and information of a nature applicable to the general organization and administration of the contract. They are made for the specific purpose of providing common agreement and a clear basis for the proper carrying out of the contract work. Reference should be made to such items as the contract, methods of payment, insurance, materials, site access, protection, safety regulations, site clearing, etc., where appropriate.

Materials These should be fully described, so that the materials that are required will in fact be supplied. Descriptions should include the manufacturer's reference, the size or weight, shape or colour, and a safeguard against the use of defective materials.

Workmanship These descriptions should indicate what preparations are required, type of mixings, fixings and finishes, and give a clear picture of the class or standard of workmanship to be expected. This provides a basis for the supervision of the work when it is being done.

Description of work This should include a full description of the actual items of remedial or constructional work to be done, including all details necessary to complete the particular item.

The example on pages 333–338 shows the contents of a typical specification for alteration and maintenance work.

Presentation

The work to be done will normally be set out in separate items, each being described under individual sub-headings, e.g.

Form new door opening . . .

These detailed descriptions would have been prepared from the surveyor's notes taken on site, e.g. a note from the surveyor's report entitled 'Take out window frame and replace with new door opening' would be extended to produce a more detailed description of the work to be done, as follows:

Remove existing window frame complete and clear away to tip.
Prop up and provide the necessary support to the wall structure.
Enlarge new opening to 1.350 m wide and 2.050 m high.
Trim and build brick jambs in facing bricks to match existing brickwork.
Cut out for and build in 225 × 150 mm deep precast reinforced concrete lintel, reinforced with No. 3 12 mm mild steel bars.
Make good brickwork above new lintel.

Items of repair should also be written out in detail, e.g. an item should not be written 'Repair door' but

Remove door, prepare and re-frame complete, renew two bottom panels and new bottom rail, each to match existing.
Reglue and wedge up.
Clean off and prepare for painting.
Refix and rehang on and including new pair of 75 mm cast butt hinges.

In both instances the requirements have been indicated precisely. By using these guidelines the specification is made useful to all who may read it and as such becomes a worthwhile document.

Examples of specification for alterations and maintenance work

Preliminaries and general conditions

Contract   The work referred to in this specification consists of carrying out alterations and remedial work at No. 24 Southbound Road, Northdown.

Employer The employer referred to in this Contract shall be known as B. Smith Esq., and his Architect as A. B. Design, A.R.I.B.A., and the whole of the work referred to in this specification is to be executed to his satisfaction.

Specification The specification is intended to cover the whole of the work required, but the Contractor is to allow for the proper completion of the work, and to include for all work implied by the drawings, whether mentioned in this specification or not.

Site The Contractor is advised to visit the site and acquaint himself of the conditions affecting the execution of the work.

Notes and regulations Give all notices and pay all fees as may be required to the Local and other Authorities. The whole of the work shall be executed in accordance with the Building Regulations and planning requirements.

Materials All materials to be the best of their kind and to conform to the requirements of the British Standards and descriptions, all to the satisfaction of the Architect.

Workmanship The whole of the work shall be carried out with good quality workmanship to the satisfaction of the Architect.

Extent The Contractor shall include for all labour and materials, supervision, plant tools, scaffolding and any other equipment necessary for the carrying out of the total work content. Allow for all necessary propping, shoring and supporting timbers as may be required in carrying out the work content.

Insurance The Contractor shall insure and allow for the cost of all insurances, and keep insured for the duration of the Contract until completion, for insurances in the National Insurance Act, Employer's liabilities, third party risks, injury to persons and property, and fire risks, including that of all sub-contractors.

Rubbish Clean down and cart away all rubbish from time to time, and on completion leave site clean and tidy. Clean down all floors, pavings, windows in and out, eaves, gutters, gullies, drains, and downpipes, leave all clean and tidy, and perfect for occupation on completion.

General specification

(1) Prepare and construct foundations for external walls and extensions

Excavate   Excavate for new foundations to the depths and widths shown on drawings, take necessary precautions to support sides of excavations, consolidate trench bottoms.

Concrete   Mix concrete to a 1:3:6 mix of cement, sand and gravel, lay in trench to 225 mm thickness, level and consolidate.

Brickwork   Build 225 mm thick brick walls to foundation composed of local hardburnt common bricks, built in gauged mortar 1:1:6 mix up to ground level, and with two courses of Staffordshire blue wire cut bricks as external splash course above ground level. Lay Astos bituminous felt damp-proof course 225 mm wide in continuous lengths on brick wall 150 mm above ground level. Backfill excavated earth and consolidate, carting away all surplus excavated earth to tip.

(2) Take down existing external wall to low building at rear and rebuild

Preparation   Shore up and make safe the concrete flat roof to outbuildings, take down defective brick wall to ground level, clean all sound bricks for reuse.

Rebuilding   Rebuild 225 mm thick brick wall with all good and sound bricks, in gauged mortar 1:1:6 mix of cement, lime and sand, off existing foundation walls, making out with new facing bricks to match existing, pointing with flush joints to both sides, wedge and pin top course up to concrete roof with fine concrete and mortar—laying Astos felt as damp-proof course, 150 mm above ground level.

Clearancy   Remove shoring and make good as required, clearing away all rubbish on completion.

(3) Rebuild top courses of brickwork to chimney stack, take off and reset chimney pots, repointing remainder of stack—refix lead flashings

Rebuild   Erect suitable scaffolding to chimney stack and remove on completion, remove chimney pots and clean, take down top eight courses brickwork, clean good sound bricks and rebuild to original height, make out with new pressed bricks in gauged mortar—1:1:6 mix—reset chimney pots and one new 450 mm high red pot, flaunch around with fine concrete to sloping sides.

Pointing   Rake out all remaining joints 10 mm deep, well squared out and washed, repoint with a weather struck joint in cement mortar.

Flashings   Clean down roof and eaves gutters, clean out all firegrates, leaving in sound and clean condition, clear away all rubbish on completion to tip.

(4) Roof repairs—strip and retiling of roof complete

Roof   Erect scaffolding as required, remove on completion, making good to brickwork as required. Strip off roof tiles to whole of roof areas, including ridge and hip tiles, all soft wood battens and clean down all rafters.

Tiling   Lay untearable slating felt over rafters with 150 mm overlaps, well lapped at hips and into eaves gutter, fixed with 20 mm flathead galvanized nails to rafters, fix new 20 × 30 mm softwood battens to 100 mm gauge secured to rafters with 50 mm wire nails, fix plain faced tiles to battens nailed every fifth course with 20 mm galvanized slate nails—with extra tile eaves course, include for all cuttings as required.

Ridge   Bed and point 250 mm diameter half-round ridge tiles and hip tiles to suit pitch of roof, include and fix galvanized hip iron, well secured to hip rafter.

Flashings   Provide and fix 9 kg lead soakers to each course at side of chimney stack, 9 kg lead stepped flashing cut and fixed to brick joints and pointed. All well bedded to brickwork. Clean out all eaves gutters on completion, clear away all rubbish, leave site clean and tidy.

(5) Repairs to faulty eaves gutter—cracked lengths, leaking joints, rainwater pipes stopped up and leaking

Rainwater gutters   Take down four lengths half-round eaves gutter, clean, remove all rust, refix three lengths on new wrought iron fascia brackets, two to each length jointed with red lead putty and 25 mm counter sunk gutter bolts, together with one new length 125 mm deep half-round gutter, all fixed to correct falls and painted two coats flat paint and one coat gloss paint in and out.

Rainwater pipes   Take down three lengths rainwater pipe, unstop and well clean out inside and wire brush outside, refix two lengths and one new length 75 mm diameter cast iron rainwater pipe, jointed in red lead putty, secured to brick wall with two strong 75 mm wrought iron pipe nails, paint two coats flat paint, one coat gloss paint.

Ground Floor—Internal

(6) Front room. Remove defective floor timbers attacked with dry rot—lay site concrete—add additional air bricks—lay new boarded floor—softwood joists—provide suitable damp-proof courses

Take up ground floor boarding and joists, all affected with dry rot, remove and burn on site. Clear out all dirt and rubble from under floor area, sterilize all brickwork with blow lamp and spray with Cuprinol well worked into all joints. Cut holes through 250 mm cavity for and fix 225 × 150 mm blue square holed air bricks (four in number), holes through wall lined with slate, clean out each existing air brick to allow free air flow. Build half-brick honeycomb walls along two outer walls, with blue brick course on top to required heights. Fix 50 × 100 mm softwood floor joists, all pre-treated with Cuprinol, at 400 mm centres all correctly spaced. Lay 25 × 125 mm tongues and grooved floorboards on softwood joist, each board well secured with No. 2 60 mm floor nails to each joist, tightly cramped and cleaned off on completion. Lay 100 mm thick bed site concrete 1:3:6 mix upon 100 mm hard core bed to areas under floor, levelled and spade finished.

First Floor

Front
bedroom

Cut out all floorboards affected with beetle attack—to front bedroom floor (approx. area 3.60 × 1.50 mm) together with three floor joists also affected, remove and burn on site. Remove part plaster ceiling below and clear away. Prepare three new 50 × 200 mm softwood floor joists pre-treated with Cuprinol woodworm killer and fix into position, treat other joists with same solution. Lay new 25 × 125 mm softwood tongued and grooved floorboards, secured with No. 2 60 mm floor nails to each joist, nails punched and boards cleaned off. Fix 10 mm plasterboards to soffit floor joists with 40 mm galvanized nails at 250 mm centres. Joints scrimmed, skimming boards with Thistle board finish plaster, make neat joint with existing ceiling plaster,

337

prepare and apply two coats emulsion to ceiling with one additional coat to new plaster.

(7) Repairs to defective wall plaster to ground floor room together with decoration

Wall plaster — Hack off all defective wall plaster to external walls to height of 1.20 m above floor level and cart away from site. Well brush down walls, hack joints to form a key, well douse brick walls with water, replaster with a render coat of one part Browning plaster to three parts plastering sand, finish with a setting coat of neat finishing plaster all finished neat and level, neatly finished level to existing wall plaster.

Wall decoration — Strip off all paper from plaster walls, wash down and neatly cut out all cracks, fill with hard wall plaster, prepare all walls with a coat of Polycell cellulose adhesive, prepare and hang wallpaper, prime cost (p.c.) sum 75 p per piece, to prepared walls with Polycell wallpaper adhesive, all neatly trimmed with good fitting joints.

(8) Repair casement window

Casement window — Take off side hung casement light, prepare and make new 50 mm casement to sizes to fit frame, fit and hang on, include 75 mm steel butt hinges, prepare and glaze with clear sheet glass, bedded and pointed with linseed oil putty. Fit new 250 mm Japaned casement stay and Japaned Cockspur casement fastener. Prepare, knot prime and paint two undercoats and one coat gloss paint to match existing frame.

(9) Skirting board

Skirting board — Remove 3 m length skirting board, clean wall of all decayed plugs and loose wall plaster, plug wall for and fix new length 25 × 150 mm chamfered skirting board, well nailed to plugs and fitted to existing skirting at each end. Apply two coats to back and two undercoats, one gloss coat paint to front of board. Make good wall plaster as required.

CHAPTER 15

SCHEDULES OF DILAPIDATIONS

Inspections of properties may reveal dilapidation in the form of general maintenance work, small or large defects or structural alterations. The information required to carry out this work can be collected together and presented in the form of a schedule.

Types of schedule

Schedules can take various forms, as follows:

A simple setting out of work giving details of work content and materials.

A more detailed description of work content and materials, including dimensions.

A comprehensive schedule, setting out description of work, dimensions, unit costs and extensions for pricing purposes.

Use of schedules

The prepared schedule can be used in a variety of ways:

A prepared schedule conveying the requirements of the necessary remedial work.

A prepared schedule with dimensions to allow for an approximate value of the work to be calculated for the client's benefit.

A prepared schedule with unit values which can then be used as a basis for obtaining tenders from contractors.

A prepared schedule of completed remedial work together with final measurements. This can then be priced using previously agreed rates for payment purposes.

Contents of schedule

Depending on its use a schedule should contain any or all of the following pieces of information.

Description of work

As with specifications, the details of the work should be written in a clear and concise manner and set out under main and sub-headings, e.g.

Internal finishes.
Dining room.
Timber floor.

These descriptions should include the following aspects of work as appropriate:

(1) Removal of the deteriorated materials or structure and its disposal.
(2) Cleaning out and preparation of the existing structure ready for the remedial work.
(3) The remedial work in terms of content, materials and workmanship.
(4) Protection of the new and existing work.
(5) Cleaning up and clearing away on completion.

Dimensions of Work

The work should be measured in accordance with the Standard Method of Measurement of Building Works:

In cubic metres, e.g. excavate foundations 10 m³.
In square metres, stating the thickness, e.g. brickwork 112 mm thick, 30 m².
In linear metres, stating the thickness and width, e.g. 50 × 100 mm softwood timber fixed to wall, 10 m.
In numbered items, e.g. fix mortice lock, No. 1.

Cost

Cost can be calculated by using unit costs, which consist of the following items:

Material cost, i.e. cost of the actual material.
Labour cost, i.e. cost of the labour required to do the work.
Plant cost, i.e. cost of any items of plant required.
Overheads and profit, i.e. cost of the administration of the work.

A typical synthesis of a unit cost would be as follows:

Item. *Prepare and fix 50 × 100 mm softwood timber*

Materials: 50 × 100 × 1 m long softwood	15p
4 screws	3p
Labour: 1 carpenter 10 min at 50p per hour	8p
Plant: machining	3p
	29p
Add 20 per cent overheads and profit	6p
	35p

∴ Unit cost = 35p per metre length.

These unit costs can then be applied to the appropriate items in the schedule, thus allowing a total cost of the whole work to be built up.

Preparation of the schedule

The schedule can be prepared either from accurate notes taken on site, together with any relevant sketches, or by entering the details of operations and dimensions directly whilst making the site visit.

All these principles are illustrated in the following example (page 342).

Example of Schedule of Dilapidations

Property—No. 303 Dark Lane, Whitemores   *Owner*—Mr Tom Brown   *Date*—Jan. 1969

Reference	Descriptions	Dimensions	Quantity	Unit	£	£
Front elevation						
(1)	*Repairs in connection with settlement in brick base of front wall—by underpinning and all connected base*					
	1. Excavate for new foundation, including cutting off concrete to existing foundation as required	5 × 1 × 2 m deep	10 m³	£0.80	8.00	
	2. Mix and deposit concrete 1:3:6 mix to foundations in short lengths to underpinning	5 × 1 × 0.5 m deep	2.5 m³	£6.50	16.25	
	3. 22.8 cm brickwork in short lengths to underpinning in common bricks in gauged mortar 1:1:6 mix	5 × 1 m deep	5 m²	£4.50	22.50	
	4. Concrete backfilling behind brickwork 1:12 mix	5 × 0.3 × 1 m deep	1.5 m³	£5.50	10.25	
	5. Allow all support to excavation and wall structure as required	item	item	£20.00	20.00	
	6. Blue brick damp-proof course—two courses deep	5 m	5 m	£0.80	4.00	
	7. Allow for making good internal wall plaster	5 × 1 m high	5 m²	£0.50	2.50	
	8. Refix length 25 × 150 mm softwood skirting board	5 m	5 m	£0.20	1.00	
	9. Clear up and cart away all rubbish to tip	item	item	£4.50	4.50	89.00
(2)	*Repairs to wall pointing*					
	10. Rake out joints of brickwork 12 mm deep, clean out and repointing with gauged mortar 1:1:6 mix, with flush joint	8 × 4 m high	32 m²	£0.75	24.00	24.00

(3) *Repairs to front roof*

11. Strip off slates in various areas of roof—renailing and refix sound slates, with new slates as required	3 × 2 m	6 m²	£1.30	7.80	
12. Take off and reset half-round ridge tiles, include bedding and pointing in cement mortar	5 m	5 m	£0.75	3.75	11.55

(4) *Eaves gutter*

13. Clean out eaves gutter, remake joint with red lead putty	5 m	5 m	£1.10	5.50	
14. Prepare and paint 125 mm gutter—two coats paint outside, two coats bitumen inside	5 m	5 m	£0.30	1.50	7.00

(5) *Repairs to chimney stack—take down and rebuild*

15. Remove chimney pots, clean ready for reuse	No. 2	Two No.
16. Take down brickwork to roof level, clean bricks for reuse	item	item
17. Rebuild stack, using old bricks in gauged mortar 1:1:6 mix, and making good with new facing	2.40 × 1.35 m	4 m²
18. Parge and core flues and reset chimney pots, flaunching around in cement mortar	No. 2	Two No.
19. Build two course blue bricks around pots	2.40 m × 150 mm	3.24 m²
20. Refix lead flashings around base of stack	item	item
21. Allow repair of broken slates	No. 20	Twenty No.
22. Provide scaffolding, and take down on completion	item	item
23. Clean down and clear away all rubbish	item	item

Reference	Descriptions	Dimensions	Quantity	Unit	£	£
(6)	*Repairs to kitchen casement window*					
24.	Remove two brick courses cill—clean and rebuild after repairs completed	2 m long	2 m			
25.	Prepare new 75 × 175 mm hardwood cill and fix to frame, include removing decayed cill	2 m	2 m			
26.	Remove opening casement light, prepare and fix new bottom rails 50 × 100 mm softwood	No. 1	One No.			
27.	Fit and hang opening casement on and include pair 75 mm cast butt hinges	No. 1	One No.			
28.	Cut out broken glass, prepare and reglaze with 3 mm clear sheet glass	600 × 900 mm	0.54 m²			
29.	Rub down paintwork—prepare and paint two undercoats, one gloss coat paint, to window frame externally	2 × 1 m	2 m²			
30.	Refix window board	2 m	2 m			
31.	Make good wall plastering internally	2 × 0.60 m	1.20 m			
32.	Clean down and clear away all rubbish	item	item			

Internal

(7)	*Dining room*					
	Ceiling					
33.	Hack off area loose and damaged plaster, cut for and fix 10 mm plasterboard nailed to joists with 38 mm galvanized flathead nails, and finish with Thistle board plaster	1.5 × 2 m	3 m²			

34. Scrape and wash down ceiling, make good all cracks and defects—prepare for and paper ceiling	4 × 3 m	12 m²

Walls

35. Hack off wall plaster under bay window, provide key, prepare and plaster with two coats gypsum plaster	3 × 0.6 m	1.5 m²
36. Strip off wallpaper, clean down, hang paper p.c. £1 roll	14 × 3 m	42 m²

Floor

37. Cut out defective floorboards and softwood joists, treat with preservative and lay new 50 × 150 mm softwood joists and 25 mm tongued and grooved floorboards	3 × 1.2 m	3.6 m²
38. Clean out all air bricks and vent holes	item	item
Prepare and fix 225 × 150 mm blue air bricks in one brick wall	No. 3	Three No.

Decoration

39. Wash down all paintwork and apply one undercoat and one gloss coat paint to skirting boards 150 mm wide	6 m	6 m
40. Wash down walls and ceiling, prepare and apply two coats emulsion paint	16 × 3 m	48 m²

Door

41. Remove door, prepare and hang on pair 75 mm steel butt hinges	No. 1	One No.
Provide and fix mortise lock and lever handles p.c. £1.25	No. 1	One No.

Reference	Descriptions	Dimensions	Quantity	Unit	£	£
(8)	*Bathroom*					
	W.C.					
	42. Take out defective w.c. pan—provide and fix new white pedestal basin—make good connection to cast iron soil pipe, and to flush pipe with rubber core joint to basin, fix new plastic seat	No. 1	One No.			
	W.H.B.					
	43. Take out wash hand basin—provide and fix new 550 × 400 mm Twyfords basin on new cast iron brackets, provide and fix new 30 mm copper trap and	No. 1	One No.			
	waste pipe 1.5 m long	No. 1	One No.			
	Fit new Easyclean taps and connect to pipes	No. 2	Two No.			
	44. Allow p.c. sum £12 for sanitary fittings	item	item			

CHAPTER 16

MANAGEMENT OF MAINTENANCE WORK

The management of maintenance work can be considered from two points of view. First, the client has to organize his maintenance workload, and second, this work has then to be executed by direct labour, contract labour or a combination of both.

Organization of maintenance workload

The organization of a maintenance workload can vary, on the one hand, from a policy of neglect until faults start to appear, to an integrated policy of planned maintenance. The first policy results in irregular financial commitments for the client, thus posing him cash flow problems, and an irregular workload for the maintenance contractor which means an inefficient utilization of his resources. As it benefits neither client nor contractor it is obviously a short-sighted policy and should not be recommended. These shortcomings can be overcome by the use of planned maintenance.

Planned maintenance

Planned maintenance can be defined as 'The necessary work organized and carried out with forethought, control and records' and can be further subdivided into corrective and preventive maintenance.

Corrective maintenance is 'The work undertaken to restore an installation to an accepted standard'. This system relies on an accurate estimate of the lives of the various components of the building so that they can be replaced at the relevant times.

Preventive maintenance is 'The work directed to the prevention of failure of an installation'. This system relies on a planned inspection of the building in the hope that flaws or potential flaws will be spotted in time and dealt with accordingly. The frequency of these inspections depends on an estimate of the life of various parts of the structure. Any form of planned maintenance policy usually combines certain aspects of both of these forms of maintenance.

Financial aspects

Considerations of maintenance costs should be taken first of all at the design stage, when a technique known as 'costs in use' can be used. Once the property has been designed and erected, maintenance costs can be controlled by the use of budgetary control techniques.

Costs in use　When comparing alternative methods of construction, materials or services it is important to consider future maintenance and operating costs as well as capital costs, thus arriving at a more realistic comparison. For example:

COSTS OF INSTALLING A SERVICE UNIT

	Method 1	Method 2
	£	£
Capital cost of unit	2000	2500
Annual maintenance	250	150
Operating cost	1000	400
	3250	3050

In the above example, by comparing capital costs alone it would appear that Method 1 is the cheapest method, whereas by applying the principles of costs in use, Method 2 is found to be more economical.

Budgetary control　This technique is necessary when financial resources are limited, as is often the case with maintenance work. The first essential of budgetary control is an accurate estimate of maintenance costs for a given period, usually two to five years. This can be obtained from a feedback of past costs, which can then be made the basis of a budget of capital available for the maintenance programme.

For example:

First year	£
Remedial work to building	120
Replacement of joinery units	60
Modernize services	110
External painting	150
Internal decoration	60
Allowances for emergencies	75
Contingencies	50
	625

Second year	
Small remedial work	60
Replacement of services	30
Internal decoration	75
Allowances for emergencies	75
Contingencies	40
	280

A budget of £650 for the first year, followed by an annual budget of £300 should cover the likely maintenance costs for the property.

Establishing a maintenance policy

Bearing all the above considerations in mind it is then possible to establish a maintenance policy based upon a planned maintenance programme, as follows:

(1) Establish a standard required for maintaining suitable conditions of the property. This will be governed by the financial resources of the owner and the maintenance requirements of the property.

(2) Decide upon the cycle of maintenance. This varies according to the needs of the property and is usually a five-year period, although in certain circumstances a three-year cycle is used.

(3) Decide the means by which general maintenance work, major renewals and emergency repairs are to be carried out. The alternatives are direct labour, contract labour or a combination of both, and will be discussed later in the chapter.

(4) Determine some method of control and administration of the maintenance work.

These basic requirements have to be modified slightly, depending on whether the property concerned is new or existing. In the case of new buildings the structure is sound and the materials new, and a regular maintenance policy can be operated immediately. With existing buildings, however, it is necessary to bring the property to the required standard by carrying out remedial and renewal work before implementing a planned maintenance policy. The object of such a policy is to provide a constant flow of maintenance work, thus enabling the client to forecast his maintenance expenditure realistically.

Preparation of maintenance programme

In order to achieve the aim of a constant flow of work a maintenance programme is devised to operate in most cases over a five-year period. It is normal to carry out all foreseeable remedial work and decorating in order to achieve the required standard in the first year, which entails high maintenance costs. In the remaining four years expenses should be small, as the only work necessary will be emergency work and annual servicing. After five years the cycle recommences, with a year of heavy workload and redecorating and therefore a year of high maintenance costs.

It is also advisable to carry out any necessary alterations and improvements to the property during this first year of the cycle, as this concentrates all the major work and therefore major inconvenience to the client into as short a time span as possible.

If the client owns more than one property a master programme should be prepared, staggering the maintenance cycles for each property (*Figure 16.1*), thus enabling him to utilize his finances at a constant rate.

The same principle can be applied to a large single property by dividing it into floors, rooms or areas, and dealing with the workload on a rota basis over the five-year period. The repairs and decorations can be completed for a particular area or floor in a sequence related to its use and accommodation.

Administration of maintenance programme

One of the main requirements of planned maintenance programmes is the keeping of comprehensive and accurate records. Each property should have a property manual or log book containing all the relevant information in terms of plans, structural design, materials used, details of services, decorative schemes and specialist items, and should be kept up to date if any alteration, additional or renewal work is carried out. The R.I.B.A. have produced a maintenance manual and it would be

Property	No. Bldgs.	1960	61	62	63	64	65	66	67	68	69	1970	71	72	73	74	75
No.20/30 Bell Lane Longcliffe	6																
No. 2/4 Ring Close Longcliffe	2												Property for next programme				
No.25/31 Bull Lane Marton	4																
No. 5 Trout Street Laketon	1																
No. 6/8 Pasture Lane Meadowfield	2																
No. 15/21 Cork Street Ashby	4												Property for next programme				
No. 2/4 Brown Lane Ashby	2																
No. 4/10 Bullhead Street Ringway	4																
No. 12 Broad Road Longton	1																
No. 5/9 Silver Street Longton	3																
No. 12 King Street Leicester	1												Property for next programme				

Beginning of new financial year abstract properties to be included on the next year annual maintenance programme

Barchart and squares to be coloured.

Red: Major maintenance   Grey: Minor maintenance

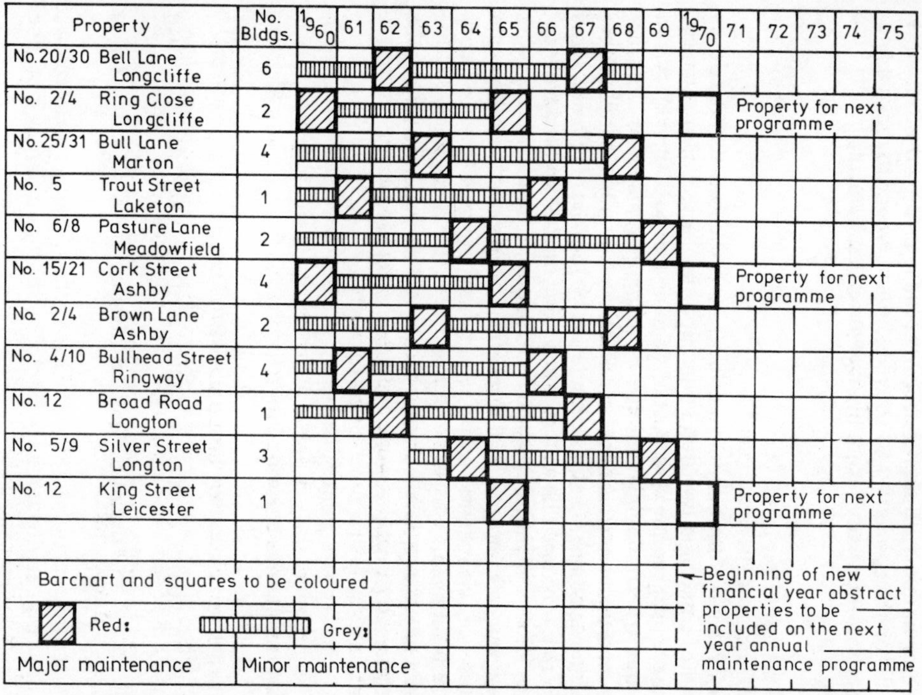

Figure 16.1 Master maintenance plan for Abee Property Co. Ltd., 21 Downtown Street, Upton.
A typical master plan for a number of properties, showing programme to date, and those outlined being those for next year's programme

advisable to base such a property manual on this. Records should be kept of all surveyors' inspection reports, specifications, work record cards, decorative schemes and details of fittings.

This information will provide a comprehensive record of all work carried out on the property and so enable the surveyor to make an accurate assessment of any future maintenance requirements.

Planned cleaning

Effective cleaning of the building fabric assists preservation and reduces maintenance work, and is therefore an important aspect of any general maintenance programme. The cost of cleaning can be budgeted for and carried out by employing suitable cleaning personnel or contract cleaners on a planned cleaning basis. Such a programme should cover all aspects of cleaning, both externally and internally. Different areas have different uses and this will have a bearing on the type and frequency of the cleaning. Bearing these considerations in mind, a rota of work can be organized to ensure that all parts of the property are kept in a good state of cleanliness and the amount of maintenance work necessary is reduced.

By adopting the principles outlined above, management should be able to organize its maintenance workload effectively.

Executing maintenance work

Maintenance work may be carried out as follows:

By a maintenance contractor doing contract work as and when required.

By direct labour organizations, always on hand to carry out a programme of work.

By using direct labour organizations for general routine maintenance work, and using maintenance contractors to carry out larger jobs, and hence even out the work flow.

Maintenance contractors

Maintenance contractors tend to be small, with very few resources, and it is not uncommon to find the principals performing the functions of estimator, planner and supervisor all at once. The nature of the work is such that supervision is difficult, as plans have to be made to carry out

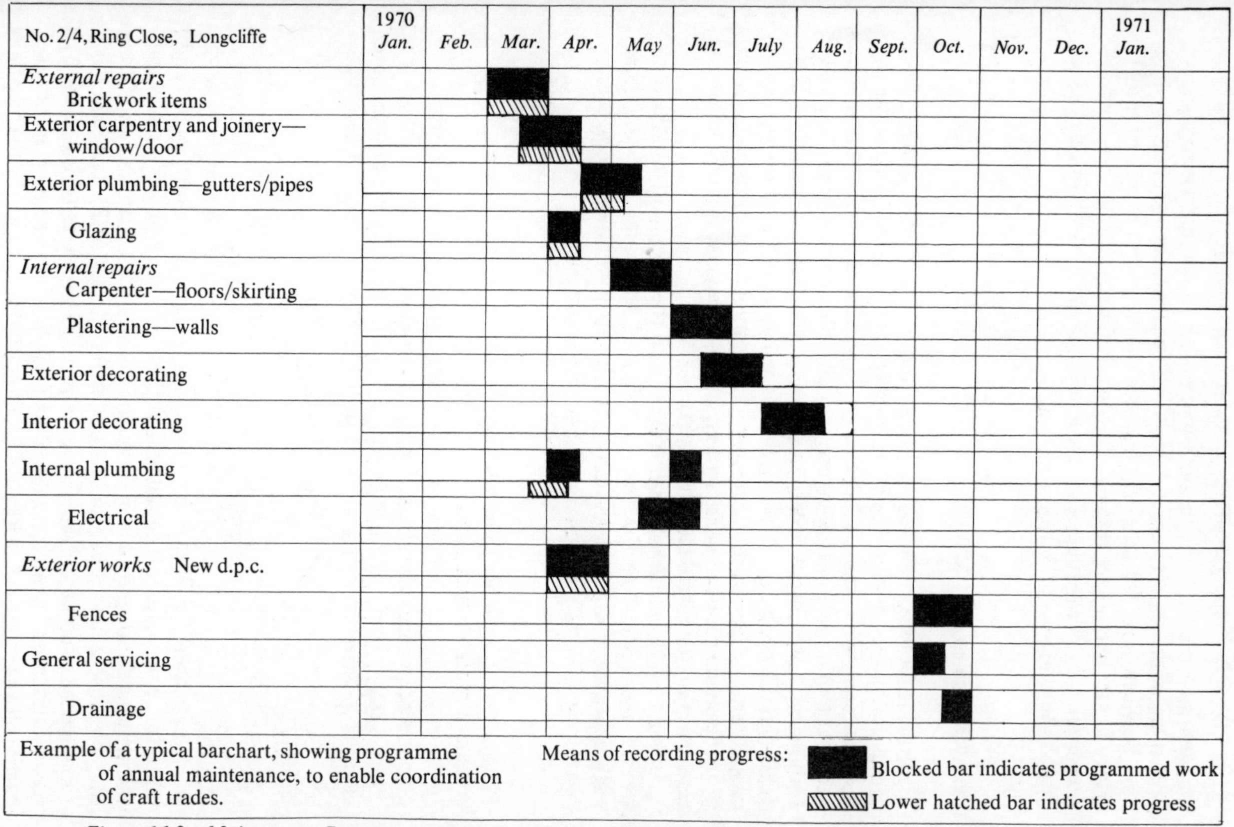

No. 2/4, Ring Close, Longcliffe

	1970 Jan.	Feb.	Mar.	Apr.	May	Jun.	July	Aug.	Sept.	Oct.	Nov.	Dec.	1971 Jan.

External repairs
  Brickwork items
Exterior carpentry and joinery—window/door
Exterior plumbing—gutters/pipes
Glazing
Internal repairs
  Carpenter—floors/skirting
Plastering—walls
Exterior decorating
Interior decorating
Internal plumbing
Electrical
Exterior works New d.p.c.
Fences
General servicing
Drainage

Means of recording progress: ■ Blocked bar indicates programmed work
   ▨ Lower hatched bar indicates progress

Example of a typical barchart, showing programme of annual maintenance, to enable coordination of craft trades.

Figure 16.2 Maintenance Programme and Progress Chart, 1970, for Abee Property Co. Ltd., 21 Downtown St., Upton

353

maintenance contracts with built-in provisions for emergency work, very often of an urgent nature. This often necessitates a lot of travelling time between jobs for labour, and also the need for travelling supervisory staff, who therefore have problems maintaining standards of workmanship. The result is that the smaller firms tend not to be as effective as they might be.

Direct labour organizations

A direct labour organization is normally under the control of a professionally qualified surveyor whose job it is to determine the maintenance work that is necessary, supervise the work, obtain the necessary materials and measure and cost the work once it has been completed. The composition of the labour force under his control will be determined by the type and volume of work required to maintain the property at the desired standard, but in the majority of cases will consist of tradesmen from the main trades, e.g. bricklayers, joiners, painters, etc., and the necessary cleaning staff.

In view of the fact that the organization of the workload and the control of work itself is the responsibility of the same person, these organizations lend themselves very easily to a planned maintenance policy.

Planning and control of maintenance work

In the case of both maintenance contractor and direct labour organization the basic problem in executing the work is to ensure that all the various trades and materials are on site at the correct time and that the client is inconvenienced as little as possible. The only way of achieving this is to ensure that the work is properly planned beforehand and strictly controlled during its execution.

The planning of the work requires a thorough knowledge of what is required in order to determine the correct sequence of activities and a realistic estimate of the durations of these activities. A programme of work can then be drawn up giving all details of labour, plant and material requirements, the dates that they will be required on site and the length of time that they are required on site. All this information can then be presented in the form of a bar chart (*Figure 16.2*). The bar chart can then be used as a basis for recording the progress of the work by recording actual work against planned work. This system relies on accurate measurement of work whilst it is in progress and will be the responsibility of the surveyor or travelling supervisor.

Benefits of planned maintenance

It can be seen, therefore, that by adopting a planned maintenance policy the client is able to budget his finances in a realistic manner, thus obviating the need for the occasional large maintenance bill at regular intervals.

The contractor also benefits, in as much as he is then in a position to allocate his resources knowing the client's requirements over a five-year period. In fact it would be possible for the contractor to enter into a contract with the client based on a planned maintenance programme. A contractor with several such contracts has then a constant flow of work for his labour force and can therefore plan his work accordingly.

INDEX